SUN & MOON
SIGNS

SUN & MOON SIGNS

AN ASTROLOGICAL GUIDE TO LOVE, CAREER & DESTINY

MARISA ST. CLAIR

SMITHMARK

© 1999 Brown Packaging Books Ltd

This edition published in 1999 by SMITHMARK Publishers, a division of U.S. Media Holdings, Inc.
115 West 18th Street
New York, New York 10011

SMITHMARK books are available for bulk purchase for sales promotion and premium use. For details, write or call the manager of special sales,
SMITHMARK Publishers
115 West 18th Street
New York, New York 10011
(212) 519-1300

ISBN 0-7651-1667-7

Library of Congress Cataloging-in-Publication Data

St Clair, Marisa.
    Sun & moon signs : an astrological guide to love, career, and
destiny / Marisa St Clair.
        p. cm.
    Includes index.
    ISBN 0-7651-1667-7
    1. Astrology.   I. Title. II. Title: Sun and moon signs.
BF1708. 1. S68   1999
133.5' 31--dc21
                                                        99-1326
                                                          CIP

Sun & Moon Signs
was conceived and produced by
Amber Books Ltd
18 Bradley's Close
74–77 White Lion Street
London N1 9PF

Editor: Brian Burns
Design: wda
Picture research: Samantha Nunn

Printed in Singapore

10 9 8 7 6 5 4 3 2 1

CONTENTS

SUN AND MOON SIGNS

Introduction

Every man, woman and child is born with a distinct and different destiny. There are no exceptions. Everyone, no matter how humble, has cosmic significance and a part to play in the life of the universe. This is innate and inescapable, and goes beyond the tiny boundaries of nation, creed and color.

As we live out our lives on planet Earth, we are, however unknowingly, acting in a greater drama and reacting to impulses that come from distant astronomical bodies, stars and planets millions of light-years away. Sceptics pour scorn on the idea that far-distant Saturn, for example, can have any effect on our lives, as the ancient art and science of astrology teaches. But the fact is that we are sparks of energy inhabiting bodies made of the same stuff as the stars, responding like tiny radios to the distant messages they send to Earth.

Each infant carries within it a double blueprint for life: its genetic programing and the pattern of character that comes from the astrological "clock" that was set in motion at the moment of birth. No one knows the full extent of genetic influence, although it seems to be astonishingly far-reaching, but the power of the horoscope has been well known to the wisest men and women for many, many centuries.

Our Sun and Moon Signs provide essential inside information about our destinies. They reveal the secrets of who we really are and why we are here – laying out before us our potential, the sort of joys and achievements our character-istics may bring about, and warn us of problems to be overcome through the triumph of free will.

Read *Sun and Moon Signs* with an open mind and discover who you really are.

Marisa St. Clair
LONDON 1999

6

Finding Your Sun Sign

Aries	March 21 – April 20
Taurus	April 21 – May 21
Gemini	May 22 – June 21
Cancer	June 22 – July 22
Leo	July 23 – August 23
Virgo	August 24 – September 22
Libra	September 23 – October 23
Scorpio	October 24 – November 22
Sagittarius	November 23 – December 21
Capricorn	December 22 – January 20
Aquarius	January 21 – February 18
Pisces	February 19 – March 20

THE ELEMENTS

Up to the beginning of the Age of Enlightenment – the modern scientific era – in the eighteenth century, it was commonly believed that everything, including human beings, was made up of the four elements: Earth, Air, Fire and Water. These were thought of as the building blocks of life, and each astrological sign had a predominance of one or another. Each element created its common characteristics, although too much of any one element can produce an unbalanced personality.

EARTH SIGNS

Those signs ruled by Earth are Taurus, Virgo and Capricorn. Each manifests the element in different ways. However, in all cases, Earth makes those born under these signs tend to be more practical, sensible and stable than most. They are better "grounded" or, to put it in another way, they keep their feet on the ground. Whereas others may rush off on madcap schemes or sit around and day-dream, those born under Earth Signs roll up their sleeves and quietly get on with the job. For example, Arians may be the great explorers and adventurers of the zodiac, but it is Taureans who follow behind, set up camp for them and arrange for provisions to be sent ahead up river. Taureans are "the salt of the earth," the plodders who may strike the more dynamic and extroverted signs of

the zodiac as being uninspired, but who are invaluable and upright members of society.

Virgos, always organized, tidy and efficient, are the analysts and notekeepers who keep track of records, accounts and archives so that society knows its history. They are the ones who ensure that the great exploits of the Arian adventurers are known to posterity. Capricorns always have an eye to the future, planning ahead for a rainy day from their lofty mountain peaks like the Goat that symbolizes their sign. And if they are occasionally dour and pessimistic – thanks to the influence of their ruling planet, Saturn, which nevertheless encourages them to be disciplined and careful – then they succeed all the more in keeping the wilder excesses of the Fire and Air Signs under control.

WATER SIGNS

The Water Signs are Cancer, Scorpio and Pisces. They are emotional, intuitive and often psychic, strongly in touch with the hidden, mysterious side of life and with the ebb and flow of unseen energies. Like the ocean tides, they have surges of inspiration and bursts of euphoria, or they can be plunged into gloom and introspection. Cancers are emotionally tied to their homes and families; like their sign, the Crab, they jealously guard their own particular little rock pool, hiding their softest feelings under a hard shell.

Scorpios are the occultists and profound thinkers of the zodiac, very sexy and magnetic, but sometimes too intense. They are the still waters that run deep – very, very deep.

Pisceans' emotions can lie undisturbed for long periods, then suddenly rise to the surface. They can be fast and elusive – sometimes slippery customers – and change direction for no apparent reason, often against their own best interests. But, like the other two Water signs, they operate almost entirely through their feelings, which can be very positive when set against the dour practicality of a Capricorn or the most reliable investment banker of a Taurean. They give depth to the adventures of the Arian and the madcap schemes of the Gemini, and reveal some of the mysteries of the Universe, which is never a bad thing.

AIR SIGNS

The Air Signs are Gemini, Libra and Aquarius. These inspirational, communicative signs of the zodiac can talk alot of "hot air," and their ability to cause a "wind of change" to run through society is a mixed blessing.

This tendency is viewed with horror by the Earth signs, to whom all change is fraught with danger. Often the Air Signs are blown this way and that by sudden enthusiasms and conflicting, contradictory opinions; but they can throw new light on apparently intractable problems. It is their influence that helps sweep away outmoded ways of doing things, bringing in all manner of brave new worlds. Geminis talk and act fast, and live life at a furious pace, often doing several things at once – one of which is forever talking on the telephone. Libras are more cool and collected, the arbiters and diplomats of the zodiac; but they can be great ditherers, prone to sudden reversals of opinion.

Aquarians, the idealists and New Agers of the zodiac, can move swiftly if their crusading zeal is fully engaged and their motivation is razor-sharp.If they feel something is best for mankind, they will go for it, dropping everything else – including all thoughts of personal comfort or gain. However, they can also be irritatingly nebulous and "air-headed," often lost in their dreams of creating a brave new world while failing to make their mark on this one .

FIRE SIGNS

The Fire Signs are Aries, Leo and Sagittarius. Consumed with passion – which all too often takes the form of self-love and burning ambition – these are the natural stars of the zodiac. They are fired up with motivation, and sparks really fly when they get going. It is difficult to keep a Fire Sign doing things at a measured pace (steady old Taureans can sometimes do it, though) because their enthusiasms soon spread like wildfire, catching the imaginations of more and more people. Fire Signs are the leaders – especially Leo, King of the Jungle, the most regal and imperial of all the signs of the zodiac.

They do, nevertheless, have great warmth and charisma, and light the way for others to follow. Arians can burn with a cold flame or with the raging fires of revolution. Either way, their passion is based on a childlike – even childish – desire to get their own way, without any thought for the future or the feelings of others. But they are willing to go where others fear to tread, and without them human progress would always be a great deal slower and more difficult.

Sagittarians are the great enthusiasts of the zodiac, sparky and constantly generating ever more energy. Like the centaur-archer and the horse-man of their sign, Sagittarians can rush into things, galloping at the gate that is never going to magically open at the last minute, or shooting very wide of the mark. But they will pick themselves up and start again, without complaining and forever encouraging more timid souls, while keeping their own eyes on new horizons.

BALANCE

B alance is essential where the elements are concerned. Each of them may provide us with what is necessary for life – drinking water, food, air to breathe and warmth – but once out of control, they are highly dangerous. When the Earth is unbalanced, for example, earthquakes rip cities apart, killing thousands and making millions homeless in just a few terrifying seconds. Landslides and avalanches also come out of nowhere to flatten human settlements like paper. Presently, we are suffering from our failure to understand that the Earth needs respect. By tearing down the rainforests, we have created almost unimaginable problems through the accumulation of greenhouse gases. At the same time, destruction of natural habitats is threatening the world's wildlife at a horrifying pace.

Fire is both Man's best friend and most terrifying enemy. Without fire, early groups of humans would never have survived. But once out of control, fire destroys everything in its path and has no respect for people. Bushfires regularly create rings of terror around some of the world's most prestigious residential areas – Malibu Beach and the South of France, for example – sometimes taking the lives of rich and poor alike. Fear of fire is ingrained in us. The police advise people who are being attacked to shout "fire!" in order to get help becausepeople are most likely to respond to that cry.

Air is essential for life, allowing us to breathe and draw the sun's rays into our bodies. Fresh air is a balm to the soul, too, and can do wonders for the burned-out c ity dweller or someone

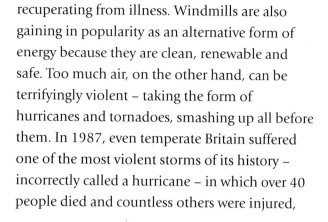

recuperating from illness. Windmills are also gaining in popularity as an alternative form of energy because they are clean, renewable and safe. Too much air, on the other hand, can be terrifyingly violent – taking the form of hurricanes and tornadoes, smashing up all before them. In 1987, even temperate Britain suffered one of the most violent storms of its history – incorrectly called a hurricane – in which over 40 people died and countless others were injured,

made homeless or in some way traumatized. Those who live in the United States' "hurricane zone" or "tornado alley" know how helpless even the most sophisticated and advanced of us can be against the full force of Nature.

Water, too, is life. We can do without food – if we have to – for weeks, but without water we will die in days. We drink it – in increasing quantities as bottled mineral water – bathe in it, swim in it and sail on it. But most of all, we are water: over

70 percent of our bodies is water, which is why we constantly need to replenish. Even mild dehydration can lead to a host of unsuspected problems, such as headaches and lack of concentration. But if water rages out of control, we can be swept away into oblivion – a threat that is increasingly likely as the oceans and seas rise due to global warming. At least once before in Mankind's history, large areas of the inhabited Earth were destroyed by a great flood; an event recorded in the myths of cultures all around the world. Noah, who built the Ark to escape the flood, is the best-known protagonist in such stories. In addition, the lost continents of Atlantis and Mu were believed to have come to an abrupt end in some kind of massive flood, perhaps caused by a massive volcanic eruption.

When two elements – Fire and Earth – come together in the form of volcanic eruptions, major cataclysms result. In turn, the other two elements are affected. Volcanic ash pollutes the air for months, even years, causing meteorological disturbances. Molten lava gushing into water results in plumes of hissing steam and undrinkable, unnavigable water.

It is no wonder that the ancients tried to placate the gods of the elements with sacrifices. In Hawaii, some locals still worship the goddess Pele, who lives in volcanoes, in order to avert her wrath.

We may go about our daily lives without much thought for the symbolism of the four elements, but the unconscious mind deals in such imagery; and dreams often speak to us, symbolically, of our relationship with Earth, Air, Fire and Water.

DREAMS

I n dreams, Earth tends to symbolize the need to keep our feet on the ground, tackle practical matters and get in touch with our true natures.

Flying and soaring dreams represent the element of Air, as do those involving storms and wind. Flying is often a very positive image and can relate to being an ambitious and successful "high flyer," or at least the desire to be one.

Flying dreams can also refer to deep – often hidden – desires to explore the Higher Mind, to get to know the mysteries of spirituality and the esoteric. Storms and wind symbolize a fear of uncontrolled passion, emotional upheaval or of being swept away by some over-whelming force.

Fire in dreams also refers to passion, although it may be of an intense and short-lived nature. It can be initiatory, a "baptism of fire" that relates to a difficult rite of passage that you are, or will be, facing in order to be cleansed in preparation for greater things. Fire also symbolizes the quick wits and sharp intellect of clever, bright people.

Water almost always signifies emotion or the secrets of the unconscious mind. Deep water is the depth of feeling or the place where your true self may be found – deep down. Raging water, as in tidal waves, means great passion or emotional upheaval, which can sweep you away. Rain can mean tears.

MAGIC

In magic and all kinds of esoteric lore, the elements are important, each being ruled by an archangel (see The Angelic Hierarchy). Each is also assigned to a point of the compass. The ruler of Fire is Michael, assigned to the South; Raphael rules Air and the East; Gabriel rules Water and the West; and Uriel rules the Earth and exercises dominion over the North.

In that most modern of "magical" systems, the Sino–Japanese art of *feng shui*, (which, although ancient in the Orient is new to the West) the elements must be balanced within each building to maximize harmony and luck. A simple way of doing this is to light candles (being very careful never to leave them unattended) to symbolize the element of Fire. Use scented joss sticks and/or door chimes for Air. A discreet scattering of salt around the corners of the rooms symbolizes the Earth and is believed to keep evil influences away. Indoor fountains, fish tanks or even a few puffs of water from a plant sprayer will bring the element of Water into balance.

COLORS OF THE ZODIAC

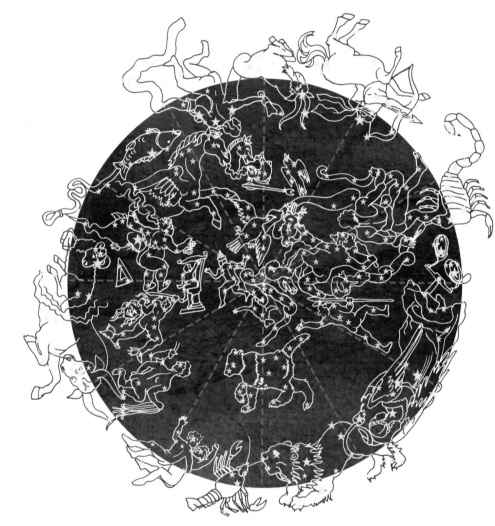

Traditionally, each sign of the zodiac has its own color, which is believed to be "lucky" or magically empowered for those born under that particular sign. In general, the colors are associated with the ruling planets and are symbolic of their attributes. Many people find that they feel most comfortable when wearing their sign's colors and often choose them without knowing the astrological background.

Aries

Ruling planet: Mars.

Color: Shades of red, usually the most vivid. Red is the color of energy, revolution, aggression, war and raw sexuality. Wearing red gives energy and promotes a sense of optimism and motivation, although some may find it too abrasive and combative.

Taurus

Ruling planet: Venus.

Color: Green – shades of the verdant Earth and the spirit of nature. Green is calming and meditative, and can be used to help balance the energies of mind, body and spirit. Too much green, however, can cause lethargy. It was once associated with witchcraft (because it symbolizes the cult of fertility and nature).

Gemini

Ruling planet: Mercury.

Color: Yellow or gold. This is the color of speedy communication and of healing. It is energetic without being confrontational (like red) and is also the color of optimism and of "sunny" temperaments. Too much yellow, however, can discourage realistic long-term planning.

Cancer

Ruling planet: the Moon.

Colors: Pale blue and silver. These aid the flow of intuition, constructive and revelatory dreaming, and put Cancers in touch with their secret, psychic selves. However, these colors can lead to unrestrained and inappropriate daydreaming. Cancers must remember that the chores have to be done sometime!

Leo

Ruling planet: The Sun.

Colors: Gold, yellowy-orange and sometimes red. These are the colors of ambition and extroverts, of bold Leos who seek the limelight. More timid people can benefit from wearing them, but naturally strong personalities may need to tone them down.

Virgo

Ruling planet: Mercury.

Colors: Rich brown and russet reds. These colors anchor the individual to the Earth, balancing the Mercurian potential for "flightiness." Many people find brown depressing, however, so it should be used in light touches and with some care.

Libra

Ruling planet: Venus.

Colors: Royal blue and rose-pink, the colors of love, care and emotional stability. Pink, in particular, encourages affection and romanticism.

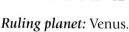

Scorpio

Ruling planet: Pluto.

Colors: Black and red. Dramatic, uncompromising and sexy, these are "dangerous" colors, especially when used together. They are the colors of mistresses rather than of wives. Wear them only if you mean it.

    ◇ 20

Sagittarius

Ruling planet: Jupiter.

Colors: Dark blue and purple. Expansive, luxury-loving and gregarious Jupiter also has a regal streak – hence the royal color purple. Although it is a difficult color to wear, it can, nevertheless, bestow dignity.

Capricorn

Ruling planet: Saturn.

Colors: Dark brown, black and gray. Introspective and wintry, those born under the sign of the Goat need to escape from, rather than use, their sign's traditional colors – or at least cheer themselves up with brighter, more positive and outgoing colors such as pink, yellow or red.

Aquarius

Ruling planet: Uranus.

This sign is unique in the zodiac for traditionally having all the colors of the rainbow – sometimes all at the same time.

Pisces

Ruling planet: Neptune.

Colors: Sea-green and mauve. Evocative of the ocean, seaweed and myths about mermaids, these greens encourage the ebb and flow of emotion, but should be worn sparingly. Pisceans need to get their feet on the ground occasionally.

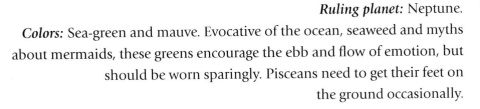

THE ANGELIC HIERARCHY

According to ancient tradition, each planet is governed by one of the great archangels, who are also rulers of certain aspects of human life. The following pages list the planets and signs they rule, their areas of influence and their special day of the week.

The Archangel Michael

Michael

Archangel of the Sun. Governs Leo. Rules human destiny,
ambition, monetary gain, careers and motivation.
Day: Sunday.

Raphael

Archangel of Mercury. Governs Gemini and Virgo.
Rules writing and all forms of communication and
learning, as well as healing.
Day: Wednesday.

Anael

Archangel of Venus. Governs Taurus and Libra.
Rules matters of the heart, romance, art and music.
Day: Friday.

Gabriel

Archangel of the Moon. Governs Cancer. Rules femininity,
intuition and all matters psychic.
Day: Monday.

Samuel

Archangel of Mars. Governs Aries.
Rules assertiveness, bestows courage
and protects against danger from violence or fire.
Day: Tuesday.

Sachiel

Archangel of Jupiter. Governs Sagittarius.
Rules financial gain, windfalls and material luck.
Day: Thursday.

The Archangel Raphael

The Archangel Gabriel

Cassiel

Archangel of Saturn. Governs Capricorn. Rules property,
land and legacies, and also matters concerning the elderly,
the Eastern belief of ultimate justice through rebirth, karma,
and the fate of humanity.
Day: Saturday.

Uriel

Archangel of Uranus. Governs Aquarius.
Rules magic, astrology, mysticism and sudden change.
Day: Uriel is not associated with any particular day.

Azrael

Archangel of Pluto. Governs Scorpio.
Rules death and rebirth, the mysteries of the afterlife and karma,
and buried treasure.
Day: Azrael is not associated with any particular day.

THE GREAT YEARS

The Great Mother

Most people are aware that we are about to enter the Age of Aquarius, but what of the preceeding ages? What influence has each Age – or Great Year – had on the development of the human race? Each Great Year is approximately 2500 years long – the length of time it takes for the Sun to travel backwards through each sign of the zodiac. The influence of any Great Year can be felt up to 500 years beforehand and as many after, so it is an oversimplification to state, categorically, that the Age of Aquarius will begin in the year 2000. Its influence has been very strong for some time. Traditionally, each Great Year may also be influenced by its polar sign, that is, its opposite sign in the "wheel" of the zodiac. The dates used on the following pages are approximate.

THE AGE OF LEO

10000-8000 B.C.

This is as far back in time as our knowledge of human civilization goes. Although Man existed for thousands of years before this time, it was only around the eleventh century BC that people left permanent examples of their art and craft behind them for posterity. The beautiful and marvelously lifelike cave paintings found at Lascaux, in the south of France, and at Altamira, in Spain, reveal the high standards of primitive art and demonstrate the creative fire of Leo.

This was a highly significant time for the Earth: the last great Ice Age was ending and survivors emerged into a warmer, more welcoming world. Perhaps, for this reason, in many areas the Sun became the focus of worship that often involved blood sacrifice. As far as we can determine, for the people of the Age of Leo, the daily rising of the Sun was a miracle that had to be sustained by supplication and appeasement. The memory of the Ice Age must have created great global anxiety about the death of the Sun.

By modern standards, of course, life was extremely hard and precarious. The earliest humans led a nomadic life, hunting animals, gathering food and, later, living in caves. However, with the emergence of farming and civilization around

6000–4000B.C., dwellers of cities were no longer universally concerned with finding food. This meant that some were free to explore more spiritual and philosophical pursuits – a reflection of the polar sign of Aquarius.

Recently, some writers have suggested that the Age of Leo began at a specific dateline, and that the Great Sphinx at Giza in Egypt – generally accepted as being built around 2250B.C. – is much older, being originally the likeness of a giant lion positioned to face the rising of the sun at the beginning of this Great Year. This is a very romantic notion, but unfortunately the facts do not support it: it is impossible to state with any accuracy when the Age of Leo began.

THE AGE OF CANCER

8000–6000 B.C.

With the proliferation of settlements, the importance of the family and the home became paramount; and, as becomes the sign of Cancer, the role of women became more defined. No longer were they as likely to have to help fend off marauding wild animals or join the men in hunting for food to scrape together an existence. The milder climate encouraged the

depicting the Great Mother have been found dating from this time. They show her as great-breasted and full-bellied, the epitome of beauty in a time when fecundity was all, and well-padded females were more likely than their skinny sisters to last through the winter.

development of basic agricultural skills: the hunter-gatherers became farmers and fishermen, and their womenfolk perfected the domestic arts and concentrated on motherhood.

It was a time of great fertility, as reflected in the widespread worship of the Great Mother and the religious observance of the seasons of the year and phases of the Moon (Cancer is ruled by the Moon – see The Ruling Planets). Many figurines

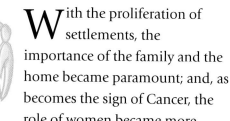

Many modern anthropologists believe that people in those days were totally ignorant of the basic facts of conception and probably believed that women were the sole progenitors of their offspring. This bestowed an air of great magic and mystery on women, hence the intense fervor of early goddess worship.

There was also widespread veneration of the Moon at this time, partly because of its very Cancerian link with the cult of women.

The polar influence of earthy, Saturnine Capricorn introduced elements of caution and constraint to the early settlements. Life, always precarious, was usually short – the average lifetime was only about 30 years.

THE AGE OF GEMINI

6000-4000 B.C.

By now Mankind had recovered from the trauma of the Ice Age and was beginning to develop intellectually, as becomes the Age of Gemini. Ruled by Mercury (see The Ruling Planets, page 36), Gemini is the sign of communication and self-expression, of quick-wittedness and movement. Consequently, this was the era when the first known alphabets were formed and the art of writing was standardized within several civilizations, including those of Egypt and China. Some people believe – as befits a time of movement – that this was when the wheel was invented, enabling people to expand their horizons, both literally and figuratively.

Due to the polar influence of Sagittarius, it may also have been the time when early, horselike animals were first tamed and put to work. Because Man was now relatively mobile, human nature, unfortunately, demanded that he become covetous and quarrelsome. Consequently, this Age saw the beginnings of larger-scale territorial battles. Bows and arrows were probably invented at this time, again thanks to the polar influence of Sagittarius.

Gemini's ruling planet, Mercury, governs all matters connected with commerce; and it was during the Age of Gemini that trading began in earnest between far-flung settlements. Thanks also to the adventurous Sagittarian influence, these trade routes may have encompassed vast tracts of land and even the oceans. This was a time of enormous expansion and discovery.

THE AGE OF TAURUS

4000-2000 B.C.

This is the age of the greatest builders in history, when astonishing temples and pyramids were constructed on both sides of the Atlantic: in Egypt, Crete and Sumer to the East; and in Central and South America to the West. The precision and solid, Taurean beauty of these giant buildings remains unparalleled to this day; and the mystery of their true purpose is still unsolved. However, what is certain is that they were built to last, a typical Taurean trait.

This was also the time of the great bull cults of the Minoans on the island of Crete and in Babylon and Egypt. Murals in the very ancient ruined city of Knossos, in Crete, depict lithe female acrobats entertaining the court by leaping over the heads of bulls. In Egypt at this time, the bull was venerated as the physical embodiment of the father god, Ptah, and of Osiris, the dying-and-rising consort and half-brother of the mother goddess Isis. Bull bones were discovered in the pyramid at Dashur. It is thought that a bull was sacrificed as a gift to Osiris, then buried in state to represent him. He was then believed to rise again three days later, as Osiris did in legend.

Bulls were venerated throughout this period as embodiments of strength, virility and stamina; and although they were eaten and used as beasts of burden, they were also honored as noble beasts.

The polar influence of Scorpio – the sign of occult secrets, death and rebirth – was particularly strong at this time in Egypt, where the priests intoned instructions over the embalmed bodies of the newly dead on how to navigate the perils of the afterlife. It is often said that the ancient Egyptians were obsessed with death. But the truth is that they constantly celebrated life – in parties, festivals and revelry. They saw death as a natural rite of passage to a new spiritual life for which Mankind ought to be prepared.

Ruins of the ancient city of Knossos in Crete

THE AGE OF ARIES

2000 B.C.-0

The Age of Aries was the age of conquest, of pushing back the boundaries and striking out for new land and new adventures. Arian physicality was embodied in the Greek cult of the male body, while the emphasis on beauty and strength is clearly seen in the sculpture of the time.

The most striking example of Arian energy and ambition was surely that of Alexander the Great, the Macedonian king and military leader who conquered most of the then-known world by the time he was in his early thirties. Then, reputedly, he wept because there was nothing left for him to conquer. Single-handedly he changed the world, leaving behind an ineradicable legacy. He chased the hated Persians from Egypt and, after his premature death in 323BC, left the land of the Nile to his general, Ptolemy, who founded a Macedonian dynasty of pharaohs. So began the Greek occupation of that mysterious land, which only ended with the suicide of Queen Cleopatra in 30 B.C.

Later, the Age of Aries saw the rise of the Roman Empire, which was characterized on the one hand by the establishment of many of the precepts of western civilization and, on the other, by relentless brutality.

The polar influence of Libra was exemplified by the development of the democratic ideal in Greece, and the rise of formalized justice in both Greece and Rome.

Alexander the Great, conqueror of the world who reputedly wept because he had nothing left to conquer

THE AGE OF PISCES

1-2000 A.D.

Synchronized, perhaps coincidentally, with the birth of Jesus and the rise of Christianity, a century or so later, came the Age of Pisces. The early Christians used the secret symbol of the fish to signify Jesus' name.

The beginning of the Age of Pisces also coincided with the rise in popularity of the cult of Isis throughout the Roman Empire. Her temples have been discovered as far north as Paris. She was known as "stella maris," Star of the Sea, and was the patron of sailors and navigators. For nearly four centuries her cult, in one form or

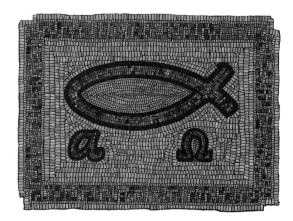

The Virgin Mary with the infant Jesus, whose symbol was the fish
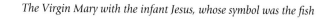

another, was a serious rival to Christianity.

The Piscean qualities of compassion and forgiveness were characteristic of both of these religions.

Pisces can be evasive and, at worst, deceitful, and the last 2000 years have witnessed an astonishing series of half-truths or downright lies: from the continued insistence that the Earth was flat (even though the principle that it was round had already been expounded) to the machinations of the early Church, which was determined to twist the original Gnostic teachings and customs into something more misogynistic, callous and mundane. With the danger of a spread of scientific and other knowledge, which had long been the preserve of the Church, came the pressure to cover up and conspire in order to control the masses.

The polar influence of Virgo can be seen in the worship of the first, or Virgin, aspect of Isis and similar goddesses such as Diana and, later, the Virgin Mary. The extension of the cult of virginity can be seen in the insistence on priestly celibacy and the demonization of pleasure.

THE AGE OF AQUARIUS

2000-4000 AD

The New Age begins with a celebration of the Age of Pisces and, hopefully, a serious and honest appraisal of its successes and failures. Then, it is time to move on – and there is no better influence under which to do so than Aquarius.

The last hundred or so years have seen an extraordinary upsurge of Aquarian idealism and the burning desire to change things for the better. This process accelerated rapidly as the twenty-first century loomed ever closer. In the West, at least, women finally won the vote, medical and social breakthroughs mean that many hitherto fatal illnesses can now be eliminated and most pain is easily treatable. Thanks to better housing, diet and education, the average life expectancy is still shooting upwards. Women need no longer be crushed by endless childbearing, thanks to reliable contraception. The breakdown of old class barriers means greater equality in education and career opportunity. Rape and child abuse are now treated as serious crimes. And powerful organizations such as the United Nations attempt, though not always successfully, to keep the world safe. But, perhaps, the character of the Age of Aquarius has been most strikingly exemplified by pushing back the frontiers of space exploration and beaming back to Earth images from the surface of Mars – including the much-discussed "face" seen above.

However, no one doubts that these and many other examples of recent progress can be matched by countless instances of terrible injustice and the phenomena of social breakdown. It may be thought that the Aquarian revolution could not come at a better time. But, since the influence of each Great Year is felt many years before it technically comes into effect, there may be a suspicion that many of these modern ills have happened because of the Age of Aquarius.

It is also worth considering what form the polar influence of Leo will bring to our brave new world. Will it mark an era of new paternalism, perhaps even benign dictatorship? Powerful forces are at work, politically and astrologically, which are already making themselves felt in the societies of the West. Increasingly, democratic governments are demonstrating, time and time again, that they do not hesitate to use the iron hand in the velvet glove. So far, they have acted only against criminals or those who threaten human rights in many parts of the world. This is an interesting development, for it exemplifies a mix of Aquarian freedom and the demonstrations of strength for which Leo is famous. But will it stop there? How far will Aquarian idealism and Leonine power take us?

This is not an easy balance to maintain, and the road ahead into the heart of the new Great Year may well be rocky.

Only time will tell.

33

THE GENDERS

Traditionally, the twelve signs of the zodiac are divided into masculine and feminine, although of course both men and women are born into each.

The characteristics were assigned to the genders eons ago, well before women's liberation or political correctness, and may now seem old-fashioned to many.

THE MASCULINE SIGNS

The masculine signs are Aries, Gemini, Leo, Libra, Sagittarius and Aquarius. Masculine traits tend to be accentuated in the Fire signs, which are Aries, Leo and Sagittarius.

Masculine signs are dominant, assertive – often to the point of being pugnacious – and extroverted. They are natural leaders and rulers, showing fiery initiative and are fiercely protective of others in their care. They are pioneers and visionaries, conquerors of new lands and the first to achieve great things. They tend to tackle things themselves and can be impatient with others who are less assertive.

Negatively, masculine signs can be egotistical, arrogant and cruel, and dismissive of the needs and feelings of others. They can be trouble-makers and rebels – violent, belligerent and inclined to subversion.

THE FEMININE SIGNS

The feminine signs are Taurus, Cancer, Virgo, Scorpio, Capricorn and Pisces. Feminine traits tend to be accentuated in the Water signs Cancer and Pisces.

These signs present gentler, more passive qualities. They are the carers and nurturers, inclined to take a back seat and worry over the well-being of others. They are artistic and in tune with their intuition, and may be psychic. Self-evidently, these are the motherly, sisterly signs, with all the attendant positive and negative characteristics. They tend to be the power behind the throne, rather than movers and shakers; although many are great achievers, especially in the modern, more egalitarian world, where their qualities of leadership are encouraged.

Negatively, the feminine signs can be fussy, possessive, mean-spirited, vindictive, cringing, clinging and over-emotional.

Aquarius, the sign of the coming age, is endowed with both masculine and feminine traits, although it is traditionally categorized as masculine.

THE RULING PLANETS

Until the eighteenth century, astrologers knew only the planets of our solar system that could be seen with the naked eye: Mercury, Venus, Mars, Jupiter and Saturn. (For the purposes of astrology, the Sun and the Moon are also counted as planets even though the Sun is a star and the Moon is the satellite of Earth.) Uranus was discovered in 1781, Neptune in 1846 and Pluto was first seen in 1930. Many astrologers believe that the existence of other heavenly bodies – such as the rumored Vulcan, which hypothetically exists within the orbit of Mercury – is about to be confirmed. Astrologers will then have to agree which signs these "new" planets will rule, and what human characteristics their discovery will accentuate.

THE SUN

The Sun, around which nine planets and their satellites revolve, is the life-giver of our solar system. Without it, everything would die. It is about 93 million miles (150 million kilometers) from Earth and is so large that approximately 110 Earths could fit inside it.

Many ancient civilizations worshipped the Sun, seeing in its brightness the potential perfection of Man. Zeus, Helios, Mithras, Ra, Atum and Aten were just some of the many Sun gods who were venerated millennia ago. Lucifer, now seen as synonymous with Satan in the West, was originally a beneficent Sun god. His name simply means "light-bringer," or illuminator of the spirit. The goddess Diana was known as "Diana Lucifera," and Mary Magdalene was called "Mary Lucifera" by the early Gnostic Church, in honor of their power to illuminate the souls of men. It seems that Luciferans were not the evil Satanists of popular imagination, but were in reality adherents of a Gnostic belief system that celebrated personal knowledge of, and enlighten-ment by, the light of God. Gold and kingship are associated with the Sun, the ruler of Leo and archetypical sign of royalty, nobility and worldly achievement.

Its fire inspires loyalty, *joie de vivre* and ambition. However, Sun-subjects can be ruthless, patronizing and overbearing, and their fire can die very quickly, leaving them lazy and downcast.

The day that was originally sacred to the Sun was, of course, Sunday.

A scarab, a symbol of solar power

Lucifer the light-bringer

THE MOON

The Moon orbits the Sun while it also circles the Earth approximately once every 27.5 days. The Sun's illumination gives the illusion that the Moon grows and diminishes in size or waxes and wanes, producing the three major phases of New Moon, Full Moon and Dark of the Moon. When the orbiting Moon completely masks the Sun, it creates the spectacular phenomenon of a solar eclipse. This is now thought to have limited astrological significance; although once, like the Moon itself, it was believed to have a major effect on human life.

The Moon does have a major role to play in the drama of life on Earth, though. It causes tides to ebb and flow, and induces certain types of behavior in animals. The hatching of baby turtles, for example, takes place under a Full Moon. Many animals become restless and aggressive at this time. Research strongly suggests that human beings are similarly affected. Indeed, the term "lunatic" comes from the Latin luna, meaning Moon. Some people believe that sleeping in the light of the Full Moon helps women regulate their menstrual cycle. Some research indicates that the Moon also affects plant life, both on land and in the depths of the oceans.

In mythology, the Moon is traditionally associated with women, whereas the Sun is honored as a very male god. The Moon is the Queen of Heaven, a title also given to the Egyptian goddess Isis and, later, to the Virgin Mary. The Moon is associated with magic,

spells and seduction, which is why the other great lunar goddesses Circe and Hecate are considered to be enchantresses. So strong was the distrust of the latter's power by the early Church that she became associated with Hell.

The ancient Egyptians also had a Moon deity, the goddess Tsukiyomi.

The Moon was the first heavenly body to be reached by manned spacecraft. In 1969 Neil Armstrong became the first man to step on the surface of the Moon, famously declaring it to be "One small step for Man ... a giant leap for Mankind." As he planted the Stars and Stripes in the lunar dust, the Moon belongs, technically, to the United States.

Cancers are ruled by the Moon, which is believed to make them emotional, caring and nurturing, although they can become easily distressed and possessive. The Moon is traditionally associated with silver.

The sacred day of the Moon is Monday.

38

VENUS

Our nearest neighbor in the solar system, Venus, is 160 million miles (260 million kilometers) from Earth, and is usually visible at night. Venus takes 225 days to orbit the Sun.

Venus has always been associated with beauty, harmony and love. The name comes from the Roman goddess of love, who also governed cosmetics, clothes and all finery and luxury. The negative side of Venus is expressed in venereal diseases, which were once

Hathor, Egyptian goddess of love and beauty

thought to be caused by an excess of Venusian influence.

The Greek name for Venus was Aphrodite, while the Egyptians worshipped several love-and-beauty goddesses – Isis, Hathor and the cat-headed goddess, Bast. In Christian iconography the nearest saint to Venus – although of course the Church has never celebrated female sexuality – is Mary Magdalene. In Scandinavia, the goddess of love was Freya, who gave her name to Friday.

Venus rules both Taurus and Libra, endowing them both with an appreciation of beautiful things and a lusty love of sex. Both seek harmony – Taureans, with their need for stability, hate anything that rocks the boat, while Libras' distaste for confontation underscores all their relationships.

The sacred day of Venus and most similar goddesses is Friday.

The cat-headed Egyptian goddess Bast

MERCURY

This tiny planet, the nearest to the Sun, is just 3000 miles (4880 kilometers) across, with a year of 88 days – the second-fastest-moving heavenly body after the Moon.

Mercury was the name of the Roman messenger god, ruler of communication, whose great energy always kept him on the move. To help him travel quickly he had little wings on his ankles and helmet. In Greek mythology he was Hermes, who gave his name to the legendary body of learning known as the Hermetica – which inspired thousands of great names over the centuries, from Leonardo da Vinci to Sir Isaac Newton. Although many scholars once believed that Hermeticism originated with the Greeks, there is increasing evidence that they had merely adapted much older Egyptian wisdom.

The Egyptian version of Mercury was Thoth, god of wisdom, healing and time. Known as "Thrice-great Thoth," he was worshipped in the form of an ibis-headed man. His secrets were jealously guarded in temples specially dedicated to him in ancient Heliopolis, and passed on only to initiates who had proved worthy of them.

In Scandinavia, the messenger god Loki was also a trickster. So was the Native American Heyeohkah, the mocking version of the creator god, who nevertheless showed kindness and compassion to Mankind. All the mercurial gods share the same dual nature. They are both trickster and friend of the human race.

Mercury gave his name to quicksilver, the beautiful and unusual liquid metal, which – being a cumulative poison – is also deadly. It was of enduring fascination to generations of alchemists who sought for centuries to turn base metal into gold.

Gemini and Virgo are both ruled by Mercury. Typical Geminis are truly mercurial – quick-witted, fast-talking, energetic and volatile. There can also be an element of the trickster in them.

Virgos are great communicators, but at a slower pace than Gemini. They think before they speak and can be immensely entertaining, with a highly developed – often self-deprecating – sense of humor.

The twentieth century, with its unprecedented advances in communication – from the transmission of the first radio signals to the Internet – has been an archetypically Mercurial epoch.

The sacred day of Mercury is Wednesday.

Left: *The Roman god Mercury*
Right: *The Egyptian god of war, Seth*

MARS

M ars is the fourth planet beyond the Sun. Due to its extremely elliptical orbit, Mars can pass as close to the Sun as 129 million miles (208 million kilometers) and takes 687 days to circle it.

Mars was the Roman god of war, from whom we derive our word "martial," although the preferred cult among soldiers of the Roman Empire was that of the Persian sun god, Mithras.

The nearest equivalent to Mars in Greek mythology was Ares, who is featured in many epic poems. He was seen as the destroyer, which perhaps explains his lack of cult worship. Possibly, like the Egyptian Seth, he was seen as a god too dangerous to invoke. In India, the destroyer was female – the many-armed goddess Kali, who tore men apart in her bloodlust.

The Egyptians had no god of war as such, but worshipped Horus, the hawk-headed son of Osiris and Isis, who represented courage and valor, Sekhmet, the ferocious lioness-headed goddess of revenge and mighty Seth, god of destruction and the implacable enemy of Osiris and Horus.

Known as the "red planet" because of the color of its dusty, eroded, lava-strewn surface, Mars recently became the subject of much excited controversy when pictures taken of its surface in the 1970s were re-examined. It was noticed that they seemed to reveal the existence of artificial structures in the Cydonia region. There appeared to be vast, five-sided pyramids, a gigantic "amphitheatre" and – most dramatic and exciting of all – a "face" (See Aquarius, The Great Year, page 33). Usually described as Leonine, this massive "structure" looked out into space – as if intended as some kind of a message for us. But pictures sent back to NASA by the Mars Global Surveyor in the late 1990s revealed that the "face" was no more than a trick of the light – or was it? Amid claims of conspiracy and cover-up, Mars continues to guard its secrets jealously.

Arians are ruled by warlike Mars, as are highly assertive Scorpios (although the latter are now also ruled by Pluto).

Mars gives Aries its fiery zeal, its explosive temper and courage that often amounts to foolhardiness. It bestows on Scorpio its red-blooded sense of drama and angry passion.

Tuesday is sacred to Mars.

Mars, Roman god of triumph in war

JUPITER

A far-distant 484 million miles (778 million kilometers) from the Sun, the planet Jupiter measures a massive 90,000 miles (145,000 kilometers) across. It is the largest heavenly body in our solar system, although much of its mass is composed of hydrogen and helium. It has 16 moons, two of which, Ganymede and Callisto, were discovered by the Italian astronomer Galileo Galilei in 1610. Jupiter naturally emits radio waves, which have confused and temporarily excited amateur astronomers who frequently think they have finally made contact with extra-terrestrial beings!

Jupiter was the Greco-Roman god of plenty, also known as Jove or, in ancient Greece, Zeus. He was the protecting father god of the city of Rome. The Egyptians had no god of plenty, but sometimes the Earth god Geb, and Ptah, the father god, were worshipped for their beneficence. In many cultures it was the fertile Earth Mother who bestowed all material blessings on her children, so the seasons of the year became associated with her waxing and waning fecundity.

Traditionally deemed a "lucky" planet by astrologers, Jupiter is the ruler of Sagittarius, and is associated with joy, plenty, philosophy and all manner of academic study. Happy-go-lucky and naturally disposed to be optimistic, Sagittarians do seem to embody the air of cheerful expectancy conjured up by the image of Jupiter. They accept that anything can happen but have little fear for the future, feeling instinctively that fate will take care of them, and it usually does.

Jupiter's sacred day is Thursday.

Zeus, the Greek father god

The winter Solstice, time of the festival of Saturnalia

SATURN

At 74,600 miles (120,000 kilometers) in diameter, Saturn is the second-largest planet in our solar system. It is 887 million miles (1427 million kilometers) away from the Sun, which it takes 29 years to orbit. The largest of its 12 moons is Titan. Saturn is surrounded by many hundreds of rings, which are composed of chunks of rock and ice.

The god Saturn originally governed the agricultural arts and skills, but later he gave his name to one of Rome's favorite festivals – Saturnalia, in which the dark of winter was enlivened with music, dancing, feasting and more than a little lechery. This usually took place at the winter solstice of December 20-21, although when the Christians took over and sanitized the feast day of Saturnalia, it was moved to December 25 to encompass other pagan festivals, including the celebration of the birth of gods such as Dionysus.

Because Saturn was once thought to lie at the remote edge of the solar system, it has come to represent coldness, distance and limitation. Many of the old astrologers were repelled and frightened by Saturn, a view reflected in the adjective "saturnine" – meaning gloomy, taciturn and somewhat sinister. However, we now know that Saturn does not mark the edge of the planetary system, and astrologers no longer consider it to be totally negative in its influence on Mankind.

Saturn rules Capricorn (and, more controversially, Aquarius), bestowing the mixed blessing of great karmic lessons on those born under the sign of the Goat. It can bring restrictions in its wake, and can make its subjects inclined to be narrow in outlook. It is also the bringer of tenacity and the wisdom that comes from learning the hard way.

The day sacred to Saturn is, of course, Saturday.

The Roman festival of Saturnalia

THE
MODERN
PLANETS

URANUS

F our times the size of Earth, Uranus was discovered in 1781 by William Herschel. It is nearly 1785 million miles (2875 million kilometers) from the Sun, which it orbits every 84 years. Uranus is surrounded by many rings and has four moons.

In Greek mythology, Uranus was the son of the Great Mother, from whose incestuous mating were born all the creatures of the Earth. He was caught by Saturn, who came at the head of an army, and vengefully castrated. From his severed testicles grew the goddess of love, Aphrodite.

Uranus is associated with abrupt upheaval, like the Tower struck by lightning in the Tarot pack. His rule of sudden and ruthless change highlights the impermanence of life and the way in which all of Man's greatest achievements and material

wealth can be swept away in an instant. This is fate at its most dramatic.

Astrologically, Uranus governs Aquarius, bestowing the ability to be forward-looking, original and idealistic. The negative aspects of Uranus as a ruling planet are its tendency to make Aquarians too eager to sweep away the old, to be shocking and to seek "kicks" in unusual and even dangerous ways.

This planet is now increasingly seen as the "cult" ruler of futuristic fantasy, such as science fiction and of space exploration.

Uranus has no sacred day.

Aphrodite, who grew from the severed testicles of Uranus

NEPTUNE

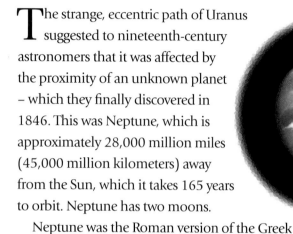

The strange, eccentric path of Uranus suggested to nineteenth-century astronomers that it was affected by the proximity of an unknown planet – which they finally discovered in 1846. This was Neptune, which is approximately 28,000 million miles (45,000 million kilometers) away from the Sun, which it takes 165 years to orbit. Neptune has two moons.

Neptune was the Roman version of the Greek god of the sea, Poseidon. He was often depicted as a bearded man rising from the depths clutching a trident, the symbol of his power. Interestingly enough, he was ruler of the ocean in relatively male-dominated societies; but in Egypt – which was comparatively egalitarian – it was a goddess, Isis, who governed the sea. She herself was often pictured sailing across heaven in her sacred barque, and was known as "Star of the Sea," a title later given to the Virgin Mary.

Poseidon was said to be the name of the city or main island of Atlantis, the legendary continent that many believe sank beneath the Atlantic Ocean

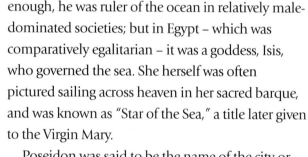

Poseidon, Greek god of the sea

around 10,000 B.C. A highly advanced civilization, for which many technological wonders have been claimed, it was destroyed by a volcanic eruption – some say as divine retribution for the wickedness of its inhabitants. The survivors then went their separate ways, bestowing their great knowledge upon the peoples with whom they settled. As a direct result of their intervention, the Great Pyramid of Egypt was built. This was an engineering feat so mysterious that it cannot be repeated even today. Many other wonders of the ancient world came into being as a result of the same influence.

No one knows for certain where Atlantis was located or if it really existed; but modern researchers have variously situated it near Bermuda, in the mid-Atlantic, in the Mediterranean, Antarctica and Cuba.

Astrologically, Neptune is associated with artistic expression, especially dancing and poetry – and also with illusion. The planet can encourage fine creativity, but at the same time mislead the unwary into the dead end of illusory activities such as gambling or obsessive daydreaming.

Pisces is ruled by Neptune. Pisceans, dreamy, artistic, indecisive and sometimes even deceitful, reflect Neptune's curious power. There is an element of insubstantial promises about Neptune, like wishes in fairy stories. They may come true, but often in a cruelly deceptive way.

Neptune has no sacred day, but by association with the Moon, which rules the sea, Monday may be considered a suitable candidate.

PLUTO

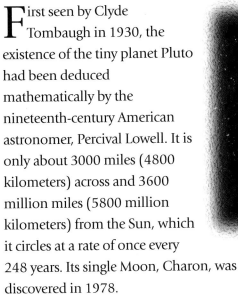

First seen by Clyde Tombaugh in 1930, the existence of the tiny planet Pluto had been deduced mathematically by the nineteenth-century American astronomer, Percival Lowell. It is only about 3000 miles (4800 kilometers) across and 3600 million miles (5800 million kilometers) from the Sun, which it circles at a rate of once every 248 years. Its single Moon, Charon, was discovered in 1978.

Pluto was named after the ancient Greco-Roman god Pluto ruled the Underworld, which the souls of the dead reached in a ferry that crossed the River Styx, and from which no one ever returned. He was associated with dread, inevitability and doom. However, the Egyptian version, Osiris, who ruled the Duat (the Egyptian "otherworld"), represented the endless cycle of death and rebirth. Man could rise from death to become, like the Pharaohs, literally a star in the night sky that followed the Sun across the sky during the day, while his soul remained on Earth to be reborn. In many ancient mythologies the Underworld was visited by courageous goddesses – such as Ishtar and, in some stories, Isis – to rescue their beloved god-consorts. Afterwards, they returned to the world of the living. There was also Persephone, who in Greek mythology was kidnapped and taken down to the Underworld by its god, Pluto. On the orders of Zeus, she was sent back up to Earth for six months of the year. Her return was understood to mark the start of spring, and her sojourn in the Underworld typified winter.

Astrologically, Pluto is associated with the dark, unconscious mind, with secrets and karmic liabilities. With Mars, the ninth planet now co-rules Scorpio, endowing that sign with its passion for the occult (meaning "hidden") and for plumbing the depths of the psyche.

There is no day sacred to Pluto, but by association with Mars, Tuesday could be eligible. Saturday, the day of Saturn, is also a formidable contender.

Ishtar, one of the courageous goddesses who dared visit the Underworld in order to rescue their beloved god-consorts, and returned safely to the world of the living

THE
QUALITIES

In addition to the influence of gender, the elements and the
planets, each sign of the zodiac is affected by having an
intrinsic quality – Cardinal, Fixed or Mutable.

CARDINAL

Those with a strong Cardinal quality to their chart are, traditionally, supremely ambitious and perhaps somewhat ruthless in getting to the top. They are bursting with ideas and dynamic in pursuing their goals, especially where their careers are concerned. They see themselves as achievers and winners: every day is a challenge that they willingly accept. Their sense of determination inspires others, although they themselves will continue to take the lead and initiate every new project. They can be dismissive of lesser mortals. Cardinality also represents new beginnings.

THE CARDINAL SIGNS

Aries: Arians are volcanic in their desire to get ahead and achieve great things. They will not stand for any opposition. Energetic, forceful and competitive, they rush headlong towards their goal and are not above devious behavior in order to get their own way.

Cardinality. But many Libras use their pleasant, "anything for a quiet life" manner in order to achieve their ambitions, for example lulling potential rivals into a false sense of security. They can be surprisingly assertive and ambitious.

Cancer: At first sight, this sign does not seem to fit the classic profile of Cardinality, being too unassertive and introverted. However, many Cancers are courageous and determined fighters, although usually on behalf of others – especially their children.

Libra: Again, these indecisive and decent individuals do not appear to fit the bill of

Capricorn: Like the Goat of their sign, Capricorns will react with fury if anyone attempts to domineer them. There will come a point when they erupt, put their heads down – and charge! They also harbor strong, long-term ambitions, which they determinedly pursue, even though it may take years to achieve them. Many Capricorns are not happy in a competitive situation and will do anything to end it – but only by winning.

FIXED

Individuals born under a Fixed sign have an inherent disposition toward tradition, convention and stability. They hate change and often refuse to adapt to new circumstances. These people are not happy taking the initiative or being in situations that require a quick-fire response. Fixed signs also tend to have conventional, conservative opinions and find it hard to move with the times. However, they do tend to be reliable and down-to-earth.

THE FIXED SIGNS

Taurus: Strong, stubborn and traditional, Taureans are the people who translate the great plans of others into solid, three-dimensional reality. They are at ease with customs that are hallowed by age, and have great respect for old-fashioned values. They are loyal, patriotic and unhappy with any challenge to the status quo.

Leo: Those born under the sign of the Lion believe that they have a natural nobility and that they are leaders of men. Their innate laziness, however, makes them disinclined to stir from any comfortable situation, be it a job, a life partnership or a particular house. They hate change for its own sake and, despite their ambition, they lack the necessary stamina to fight their rivals to the bitter end.

Scorpio: Although highly emotional, those born under this Water Sign know their own mind and react strongly, even violently, against challenges to their position. Many of their opinions were formed in youth and will remain the basis for much of their adult decision-making. Often unable to adapt or see alternative points of view, Scorpios take everything very personally.

Aquarius: At first sight, this progressive, idealistic sign would seem to be the antithesis of Fixed. However, many Aquarians are remarkably set in their ways, even though those ways may seem unorthodox. For example, there are still many Aquarian hippies eking out a living in communes. They are the backbone of what might be called the New Orthodoxy, espousing anything that fits their idealism and rejecting everything that does not.

MUTABLE

*Those born under the Mutable signs are always
on the move, either physically or mentally, forever seeking
fresh fields and new pastures. They are restless, versatile and
flexible, hating routine and any form of strict discipline. These
individuals can have butterfly minds, endlessly alighting on new
enthusiasms, fads or crazes, then dropping them just as quickly
and moving on to the next thing. Mutable people can be
unreliable and irresponsible, and are rarely self-disciplined,
although they are often extremely charming.*

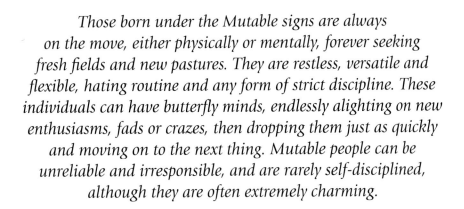

THE MUTABLE SIGNS

Gemini: Creative and persuasive, Geminis personify Mutable qualities. They loathe restriction of any kind and tend to despise more solid citizens. Forever seizing opportunities, they are quick-witted and articulate, and can be very amusing. Extremely gregarious, they are unhappy alone or in the same unchanging environment. They often lack depth.

Sagittarius: Always on the move, always with an eye to the next project, lover or ambition, Sagittarians are very Mutable individuals. They become unhappy, sometimes to the point of becoming ill, if they are restricted or expected to conform. Sagittarians are delightful people with unbounded energy and a relentless curiosity about life, but they frequently lack the energy necessary to follow projects through to their completion.

Virgo: Excellent communicators, Virgos make amusing and pleasant companions, revealing a sharp wit and a sense of the absurd. However, their Mutable qualities are tempered by being an Earth Sign, which restrains their flights of fancy and makes them essentially realistic. Surprisingly, perhaps, they are not completely put off by change and can adapt very well to new situations and challenges.

Pisces: Emotional, insecure Pisces are creative and intuitive, but often seem a little adrift in the everyday world. They seek peace, harmony and love, and can tend to have an unrealistic view of life. This longing for harmony is often all that gets them through, because a negative side of this sign is the ease with which Pisces lose incentive and take refuge in escapism and illusion.

SIGNS
AND
SYMBOLS

Most people are familiar with the zodiac "zoo" – the collection of symbols
that represent the twelve signs. They are not random images, but accurately
reflect the characteristics traditionally assigned to each sign and contain
a wealth of secret knowledge about its true nature.

𝓔ach sign of the zodiac is represented by a symbol – the twin fish of Pisces, for example. No one is sure exactly when or why the symbols were chosen, although some authorities believe they date from Sumeria or Mesopotamia, some 4000 years before the birth of Christ. The priest-astrologers of the ancient world were the first to impose recognizable patterns on the great constellations – Leo the Lion being one example.

Today, seeing such shapes in the stars may seem fanciful. But thousands of years ago imaginations were more poetic, and many myths were told of magical animals, such as the dragon, which had strange powers to influence Man's everyday life.

Although the ancient Egyptians left few astrological records, they were almost unique in antiquity for worshipping archetypal, animal-headed gods. However, these strange hybrid gods – half-man, half-animal – were worshipped as aspects of one god. Contrary to the general belief that the Egyptians were idolaters, their religion was basically monotheistic. Each statue represented an aspect of the one true god. Parallels are to be found in Hinduism and in the role of the different patron saints of the Catholic Church, who "rule"

or protect various human activities and endeavors.

Since they were established, the signs have remained unchanged; although there was a move in the Middle Ages to change the sign of Aquarius into the sign of John the Baptist – presumably because of the connection with water. If this suggestion had been taken up, we would now be about to enter the Age of John the Baptist. (See The Great Year.)

The twelve signs of the Zodiac do seem particularly appropriate on the whole, and accurately reflect the archetypal character of typical Sun Sign types. The great Swiss psychoanalyst Carl Gustav Jung (1875–1961) believed that, deep in our psyches, humanity shares a collective unconsciousness – a set of archetypal images which, at a profound level, we all understand. The signs of the zodiac are but part of this pool of images, conveying eternal truths to our unconscious minds, whether we consciously know it or not.

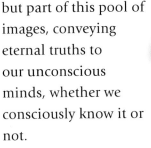

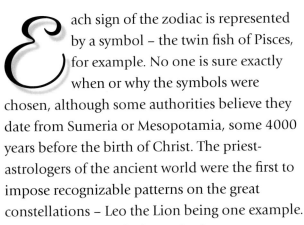

ARIES

The Ram

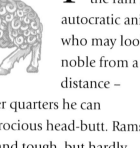

Protector of his harem, the ram is an alert, autocratic animal who may look noble from a distance – but at closer quarters he can deliver a ferocious head-butt. Rams are strong and tough, but hardly lovable. Those pale blue eyes seem cold and bereft of feeling, yet somehow always charged with danger. Rams often seem like coiled springs: all that energy winds them up to the exploding point when they either furiously fornicate with the ewes in their flock or cause trouble elsewhere. And once they begin to attack, there is no stopping them: after all, they gave their name to that ubiquitous war-machine of the ancient and medieval worlds – the battering ram.

In ancient Egypt, the Sun god Amun-Re (or Amun-Ra) was represented with a ram's head. Hundreds of statues of the god in his ram form line processional avenues at the great temple of Karnak.

The ram was seen as a symbol of fertility, and was often shown wearing a beard – standing for kingship and virility. Even queens were expected to wear false beards on ceremonial occasions to indicate their sovereignty.

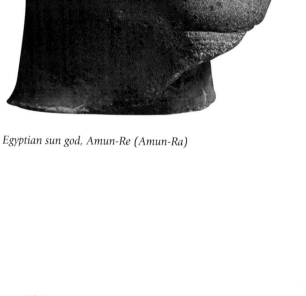

Egyptian sun god, Amun-Re (Amun-Ra)

TAURUS

The Bull

The bull can be wild, raging and dangerous, or content to stand in his field, eating and watching the world go by. Think of the difference between the elegant, doomed bulls of the Spanish bullrings and the domestic American version – lumbering, dull and almost too heavy to move. The bull does not usually have the sexual voracity of the ram.

The quiet, stolid air of many bulls can be misleading. Many picnickers have discovered to their cost that the overweight beast idly chewing the cud in the corner of the field has a nasty temper and can move like a train when he wants to. Once mobilized, bulls have extraordinary strength and courage. They also have a certain innate dignity.

In the ancient world, the bull was venerated as a symbol of sexual potency and strength, especially in the Minoan civilization on the island of Crete, where bull-leaping was a sacred sport (see The Great Years). A sculpture of giant bulls' horns was set up at the boundary of the necropolis of Knossos, where it still stands overlooking the valley.

In Greece, the king of the gods, Zeus, once transformed himself into a bull in order to kidnap and rape Europa.

In Egypt, too, the bull was a sacred animal. In the Middle and New Kingdoms the bull was venerated as the dying-and-rising god Osiris, who was, like Jesus, born on December 25 in humble surroundings. He, too, died on a Friday and rose again three days later. The bull was also seen as the living form of the god Ptah Seker Asari. During the latter stages of the Greek and Roman occupation of Egypt, the bull represented Serapis, another dying-and-rising god very similar to Jesus .

A sculpture of giant bull's horns stood at the boundary of the necropolis of Knossos, where bull-leaping was a sacred sport

The Egyptian god Osiris, twin of Isis

GEMINI

The Twins

The celestial twins of Gemini are the Greco-Roman semi-divine characters Castor and Pollux. In recent years, research has demonstrated the amazing similarity between the lives of many twins, even if they were separated at birth. Not only do they share the same mannerisms, likes and dislikes, but they also often make the same life-choices, even marrying people with the same names and on the same dates. Then, the same number of years later, they divorce them and marry new spouses, also with the same names! This almost paranormal phenomenon is by no means uncommon, suggesting either that forces other than genes are at work, or that our understanding of the material carried by genes, and the way they work, is far from complete. Conversely, however, the closest possible type of duos – Siamese twins – can show marked differences in predilections and behavior. One may smoke while the other hates tobacco, for example. It is, therefore, fortunate that with modern surgical skills it is possible to separate some Siamese twins and give them their own individual lives.

In the ancient world, twins were believed to have magical powers, perhaps because of their natural telepathic abilities. The twins Romulus and Remus were believed to have founded ancient Rome in 753BC.

The name of the great Meso-American god, Quetzacoatl, means either "feathered serpent" or "magnificent twin."

In ancient Egypt, there were several sets of twins in the pantheon of gods, including Geb, god of the Earth, and Nut, goddess of the Sky, and the more famous Isis and Osiris, with their darker counterparts, Nepthys and Seth.

The duality of twins represented the eternal fight between light and darkness, good and evil.

Above: *Romulus and Remus, founders of Rome, who were suckled by a she-wolf*
Left: *Nepthys, twin of Seth, and dark counterpart of Osiris*

CANCER

The Crab

The Crab is perhaps the least appropriate symbol in the zodiac. Whereas the small scuttling sea creature is a loner and scavenger, Cancers are passionate about their families and immediate circle of friends. They can become upset and depressed if denied their company. More than any other sign, Cancers need others in order to fulfill themselves and to satisfy their innate urge to be of service.

Crabs live half their lives in the water and half on the land; and, in a figurative sense, this is true of those born under the sign of Cancer, for they bring an intense awareness of the submerged, subconscious realm into the light of everyday reality. This, though, does not always make for an easy life. Too often, Cancers feed off the psychic, intuitive and feminine aspect of the hidden mind and turn it into a constant demand for emotional satisfaction. However, the more well-balanced Cancers have learned to tame this side of their character and to use their unique insights for the good of others.

Cancers possess all the typical Water Sign's emotional intensity, which is further enhanced by being ruled by the Moon. Their moods often ebb and flow like the tides, and they frequently allow themselves to be carried away on a wave of feeling, trusting to fate that no harm will befall them.

Like the crab, those born under this sign tend to put up a protective front when their loved ones are threatened, or in order to conceal their own soft-heartedness. Some Cancers become so frightened or embittered by life that they take to hiding behind their shells most of the time.

Of course, crabs, no matter how tiny, are liable to give nasty nips with their claws, especially if cornered. This aptly describes the normally amenable Cancer, who is nevertheless given to lashing out hurtfully if put on the spot.

There are no known mythological associations, but as the crab, in one form or another, was known to all ancient cultures, it may be assumed that its characteristics were generally agreed to fit those of the typical Cancer.

Recently, there was a move to change the name of those born under this sign from Cancers – because of the connotations arising from the disease of the same name – to "Moon Children," but this failed to catch on.

Cancer is ruled by the Moon and is strongly associated with feminine qualities, particularly intuitiveness. The Moon in the Tarot also represents these qualities and speaks of things that are hidden

LEO

The Lion

Lions are magnificent beasts – strong, athletic and noble. They can be excellent hunters, although it is the lionesses who usually do the lion's share of the work. Sometimes even the King of the Jungle stoops to stealing the kills of others. They are good protectors of their pride, but can be irascible – chasing off those who challenge their male supremacy. They can even kill their own offspring, should they have the temerity to be demanding or too playful.

Throughout history, because lions have always represented kingship, ferocious strength and nobility, their image has often been incorporated into heraldic devices such as banners or shields. The archetypal appeal of the beast can be seen in powerful adopted names such as "Lionheart" for King Richard I of England and "The Lion of Judah" for emperors of Ethiopia.

In the so-called "black art" of alchemy, which was outlawed by the Church, the lion represented the uncontrolled forces of nature in the real world.

In ancient Egyptian mythology, Sekhmet, the lioness-headed goddess, was the avenger and protector of her worshippers. The daughter of the great sun god Ra, her name meant "powerful" or "mightiest," and her other titles included "Lady of the Flame," reflecting Leo's archetypal association with fire.

The story goes that Sekhmet was instructed, in the name of her father, to punish Mankind for its waywardness. But once unleashed, her vengeance far outstripped his intentions and nearly destroyed the world. The only way she could be halted was by tempting her with rivers of beer – which she drank. Afterwards, she fell asleep, fortunately forgetting to annihilate Mankind. But Sekhmet had a gentler side and was very popular among those who needed courage in their endeavors.

Lioness-headed Egyptian goddess, Sekhmet

Because she answered the prayers of a certain Pharaoh, granting him triumph in battle, he raised over four hundred statues to her in Egypt. To this day, there are more statues of Sekhmet than of any other Egyptian deity, many of which are in western museums. She is now a great favorite with New Agers.

VIRGO

The Virgin

T he symbol of innocence, the Virgoan sign also, conversely, represents the time of harvest, when the seed sown was finally reaped, a symbol of fertility. This apparent contradiction derives partly from the old confusion of the word "Virgin" with young woman – the original Greek word for the "Virgin" Mary in the New Testament simply meant a girl – and partly from associations with pagan goddesses.

All major goddesses who were represented in human form – such as Demeter, Diana, Ceres and Isis – were believed to have three main chronological "aspects": virgin or young woman, then mother and finally old woman or crone. These synchronized with, and were symbolized by, the New Moon, the Full Moon and the Dark of the Moon. However, unlike the Virgin Mary, whose status is unchanging, these goddesses moved fluidly from one aspect to another, thus symbolizing all aspects of womanhood. Some were worshipped in one aspect only – Isis was usually the Mother, for example – but they were understood to be rulers over all female experience, which is why they were so beloved of their women worshippers.

The Greek goddess Demeter

LIBRA

The Scales

The only inanimate object in the zodiac, the Scales represent the eternal struggle to achieve balance and justice. Modern scales can be very high-tech, usually with a single weighing pan, and do not adequately convey the essence of balance as did the old double-pan version.

The Scales have a profound association with the concept of justice – as exemplified in the statue of blind Justice holding the scales outside London's Old Bailey criminal courts. But once again, this concept originates in the mythology of ancient Egypt.

In Egyptian mythology, the soul was believed to undergo extraordinary adventures in the Underworld after leaving the body. The central event in this journey of the afterlife was the weighing of an individual's heart in the balance by the goddess Ma'at, the ruler of human and divine justice. She carefully weighed the hearts of men – which, the ancient Egyptians believed, encompassed a lesser "soul" – against the feather of truth, which was her own symbol, as a measure of their goodness on earth and their right to enjoy eternal life with the gods.

Egyptian priest-judges always wore masks of Ma'at when pronouncing their verdicts in legal cases.

Ibis and the Egyptian goddess Ma'at, ruler of human and divine justice

SCORPIO

The Scorpion

These tiny, armored creatures are greatly feared, yet few of them possess a sting that is serious, let alone fatal. Image is all to a Scorpio! Sometimes, however, they are so eager to attack enemies with their venom that they overreach, and actually sting themselves. This should act as a dire warning to vengeful, dark-hearted Scorpion types!

Originally, the symbol for this sign was the Phoenix, the magical bird of mythology, which was consumed in fire and rose from the ashes as magnificent as ever. This is very much the positive side of Scorpio.

There are many mythological and magical associations with the Phoenix. He was intimately involved with the transformative aspects of alchemy, and often represented the cycle of incarnation, death and rebirth. The Phoenix also occasionally symbolized the many dying-and-rising gods of the ancient world. These included Attis, Osiris, Tammuz, Adonis, Dionysus, Mithras and, last of all, Jesus himself. Their deaths were associated with the coming of winter, and their rebirth with the renewal of nature in the spring and with reincarnation. Every year, there were great festivals to celebrate the death and resurrection of these gods – which were eventually appropriated by the early Church and became the Christian celebration of Easter.

Mithras, one of the many dying-and-rising gods of mythology

SAGITTARIUS

The Archer or Centaur

The Archer was the mainstay of ancient armies. Poised, strong-armed and alert, with his eye constantly on the far-distant target, the arrows flew swiftly from his bow. Although some may have fallen short, many hit the bullseye – rather like the myriad ideas and ambitions of a typical Sagittarian.

Energy, virility and even a certain dreamlike surrealism distinguish the symbol of the Centaur – who is often also shown with bow and arrow. The Centaurs were ubiquitous in Greek mythology, where they were often depicted as being particularly sexually voracious. For example, in the story of the rape of the Sabine women by the early Romans, it is the Centaurs who carried off the women.

Sometimes Centaurs were associated with Pan, the hooved nature god of the ancient world, whose musical pipes could lure the unwary into the deepest woods. There, they would become so disoriented that panic ensued. Indeed, this is where our word "panic" derives from. Pan was also linked with unashamed sexuality, and his statues were often depicted with erect phallae. In ancient Egypt, he was known as Min, who was also shown as ipthyphallic.

Pan was believed to have been killed off by the coming of Christianity. One story tells how a mysterious voice could be heard moaning "Pan is dead!" – but the modern pagan movement, both in Europe and the United States, has seen a return to his worship and a new respect for nature.

Pan, the great Nature god

CAPRICORN

The Goat

The goat is a highly adaptive creature who can – and often does – eat just about anything. He can also live just about anywhere, even in some very hostile environments.

The goat is usually a pleasant, amenable beast, getting on well with its own kind, other animals and humans alike – and producing delightful milk. Goats can be difficult, however, as any farmer who keeps them will attest. They can also be very destructive. Goats frequently appear to come from nowhere to land a very painful butt on the particularly tender areas of humans.

In Christian countries, the goat has had a bad reputation as an associate of the Devil. During the witchcraft hysteria that began in fifteenth-century Europe, it was believed that witches flew on their broomsticks to unholy Sabbats, or meetings with the Devil, in which their evil master appeared as a gigantic goat. This was said to represent the worship of the Goat of Mendes (or Memphis) in ancient Egypt, for which there is little or no evidence. Later, this idea was amended: the Satanist High Priest was said to wear a mask of the Goat of Mendes while presiding over filthy – that is, sexual – rites in his master's name. Modern researchers have found no evidence that such ceremonies ever took place.

Witches on their way to a Sabbat

AQUARIUS

The Water Carrier

Usually depicted as a young man pouring water from his vessel, Aquarius evokes feelings of compassion, refreshment and rest after a hard struggle. There is also the resonance of a constant flow of ideas or good fortune.

Travelers across the arid wastes of life feel their hearts lift up at the sight of the water carrier; they are refreshed and perhaps inspired by him, reinvigorated before resuming their journey. It is a potent and appropriate symbol.

In ancient times, the Egyptian goddess Isis was the water carrier: she was often depicted as holding two jars, constantly pouring a stream of life-giving water from one to the other – an image that became incorporated into the symbolism of Temperance, in the Major Arcana of the Tarot cards (and, in some packs, also in the Star).

For thousands of years before the building of the Aswan Dam in 1960–4 , Egypt was totally dependent on the River Nile for its livelihood. Water was deemed to be very precious, which is why only royalty and certain priesthoods had their own pools, and why water was the central element in their sacred ritual of baptism. They had practiced the rite of confession of sins and the symbolic cleansing by immersion many centuries before John the Baptist (who had his headquarters in Alexandria in upper Egypt) took it into Judea.

John the Baptist. A movement in the Middle Ages to rename the sign of Aquarius after him came to nothing

In the Middle Ages, there were moves to rename this sign "John the Baptist," but they failed – perhaps because it would have been too confusing or because his feast day, on June 24, does not fall within the span of Aquarius.

Astrologers are uncertain about exactly when the Age of Aquarius will transpire. Some believe it has already dawned, while others believe it will not begin for another two or three hundred years. However, whenever a new Great Year arrives, its influence is always felt many years beforehand. Either way, therefore, we have already begun to feel the effects of the Age of Aquarius.

PISCES

The Fish

The symbol of Pisces is two fish, sometimes apparently tied together, constantly swimming against each other and wasting their energies. Even if they are free, one is set to go one way while the other forever journeys in the opposite direction. It is an apt symbol for this often contrary, dual Water Sign.

Fish are notoriously difficult to catch – otherwise there would be no sport in fishing. They symbolize the elusive, unpredictable characteristics of those sometimes slippery customers born under the sign of Pisces.

However, fish also go deep, sometimes to the very bottom, plumbing the depths. In dreams, water always symbolizes the hidden emotions and darkest secrets of the unconscious mind, with which many Pisceans are intuitively in touch.

The fish was an early symbol of Jesus: "fish" in Greek was made up of the same letters as his name. In the first days of Christian persecution under the Roman Empire, the sign of the fish, scrawled on walls and doors, told fellow-believers in which houses they could take shelter.

Above: *Mary Magdalene, the original "Fisher of Men"*

Left: *Jesus, whose symbol was the fish*

Many of Jesus' male disciples were originally fishermen: Simon Peter, the founder of the Christian Church and the first Pope, was affectionately known as "the Big Fisherman" because of his unusual height. Like many of the dying-and-rising gods of his day, Jesus was known as "the Fisher of men." However, few today realize that this was a title that, according to the many gospels not included in the New Testament, was originally given to his close companion, Mary Magdalene, by Jesus himself.

THE SUN IN ARIES

(March 21 – April 20)

Sun Sign: ARIES

Sign: THE RAM

Ruling Planet: MARS

Gender: MASCULINE

Element: FIRE

Quality: CARDINAL

Compatibility: TAURUS AND VIRGO

Non-compatibility: LEO, GEMINI, LIBRA AND AQUARIUS

Sun Sign Arians are feisty, straightforward and adventurous. Blessed with abundant energy and drive, they have no time for laziness or prevarication and make excellent motivators, whether in the workplace or at home. Keen-witted, they see straight to the heart of a problem, cutting away all the unnecessary detail and distractions, and are much admired for being quick on the uptake. They are idealistic, eager to defend the underdog and impulsively drawn to many campaigns for the betterment of humanity, even if these campaigns are lost causes.

The first sign of the zodiac, Aries represents springtime, the burgeoning of new life and a great upsurge of energy and optimism. They have a childlike belief in miracles, in things turning out right – perhaps at the last moment, just before disaster strikes. Often, though, this blind faith is justified. Positively aspected Arians can be very lucky. There is an attractive naïveté about them, a marked lack of deviousness or pessimism, and an ability to find energy and resources inside themselves when everyone around them is burned out. If they believe in something, they will harness all that Martian zeal and go for it, without worrying about the consequences.

Negative Arian characteristics arise out of their driven nature. Often, they seem cold and afflicted with tunnel vision. To them, the end usually justifies the means, even if the way to the top involves methods that are ruthless or otherwise questionable. They are childishly egocentric, extremely demanding and liable to throw violent tantrums if denied their own way. Always leaping before giving even the most cursory look around, Arians often find themselves in deep trouble. They then become hurt and bewildered at what they see as the blind force of fate singling them out for undeserved punishment. "Why me? I was only trying to help!" is a typical Arian response

when things fall apart because of their own miscalculation or inappropriate behavior.

Arians are disarmingly frank; and in their eagerness to let everyone know exactly where they stand, they can be very hurtful and over-blunt. They are good with words, but all too often they use them as weapons and can be cuttingly sarcastic and dismissive. Profoundly self-centered, they rarely bother to see themselves as others see them; and this is the hardest lesson for them to learn, often at great cost to themselves and those around them. Born under the archetypal fire sign, Arians can burn up and burn out with equal ease, destroying even their loved ones as they blaze their way through life. Many people find badly aspected Arians hard to know and even harder to love, especially when they are well on their way up the ladder of success. It is then that they use any and everyone as stepping stones.

APPEARANCE

Typical Sun Sign Arians tend to be angular, slim people in early life; although they may fill out later. They have a flushed complexion and brown or reddish hair. Rarely graceful, they seem awkward and ill at ease in their bodies, with particularly sharp elbows and knees.

HEALTH

Traditional Arian areas of weakness are the eyes, head, teeth and upper jaw. Always in a very big hurry, they often have a fast metabolism – which keeps their weight down; but the constant speed has its drawbacks, and they are prone to stress. They suffer badly from tension headaches.

Though usually far too motivated to either notice illness or give in to it, they may be suddenly felled by feverish ailments or accidents, to which they are particularly prone due to their haste and carelessness.

Their Arian impetuousness makes them neither good patients nor natural nurses, and they rarely follow a course of medication or treatment through to the end. This, unfortunately, causes relapses or recurrences of the illness. If given a choice, they may change doctors or types of treatment in mid-stream, not because of indecision, but out of impatience. Arians are not good with pain. The slightest twinge worries them out of all proportion to its danger, but they rarely have time to be hypochondriacs. They demand quick fixes or none at all. For this reason, they tend to favor conventional medicine, deeming alternative or complementary therapies too time-consuming and uncertain. Why waste time boiling up Chinese herbs or meditating when you can pop a pill?

CAREER

Arians are made for adventure, whether it takes the form of dealing with "futures" on the money markets or hacking their way through the Amazonian rainforest. Their energy and disregard for their own safety or comfort makes Arians, both male and female, pioneers at heart, willing to put up with enormous difficulties and setbacks for the sake of reaching their goal.

As long as they can be in charge, a star in their chosen field, they are generous and inspiring to work with. However, once they are questioned or crossed, their bad temper can make them difficult

– even dangerous – colleagues. Well-aspected Arians are public-spirited, as long as they can make tangible improvements and see results quickly. They are impatient with anything requiring diplomacy or long, drawn-out committee work. With Mars as their ruling planet, many Arians are drawn to the armed services, where they often achieve high rank and distinguish themselves under fire. They can also express this side of their nature in the police, the Scout movement or paramilitary organizations.

Arians hold strong political and religious views – at worst to the point of fanaticism. They can be either extremely right- or left-wing, or they can slip easily into the role of missionary with regard to their chosen religion. They have the dubious honor of making excellent cult leaders.

Anything involving long-term planning is anathema to Arians, and money-making is usually incidental to their ambitions. Typical Arians, who find materialism and luxury disconcerting, are better at making money for others than for themselves.

They are ill at ease with boring and repetitive jobs, seeking to express themselves as individuals whenever possible. They thrive on challenges, and have an enviable capacity to shut out background noise and concentrate on the job in hand. They can be enterprising and excellent motivators of a workforce, but once they are expected to be second-in-command or knuckle down to unappealing tasks, their performance drops sharply.

They find it hard to back down or apologize, although they are usually direct in most of their dealings. However, if they are forced to say sorry, don't expect sincerity from them!

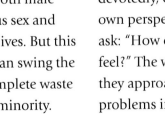

Arguments will be frequent, although male Arians are quick to make up with chocolates, flowers and romantic gestures – such as a trip to the theater or a weekend break. Always demanding, Arians will expect, rather than give, support; although they can be motivated to save a relationship if their hearts and sexuality are really engaged. Under their pomposity and bluster, they can often be very vulnerable. The wise partner soon realizes that they need to be constantly encouraged and praised, perhaps even "babied" through any crisis.

Hot-headed and devil-may-care, Arians often put themselves and others in all sorts of danger. Never go exploring caves with a lone Aries. All the same, they can be charming, if irresponsible, parents. Some may even find themselves being treated like teenagers by their own children; and they may be the cause of despair for the more cautious and sober members of their family throughout their lives. Although they will love their spouses, parents and family devotedly, everything begins and ends with their own perspective. Arians rarely ask: "How do you feel?" The way they approach problems in the family inevitably begins with: "I think… I feel… " When their sarcasm or thoughtlessness reduces their loved ones

RELATIONSHIPS

Passionate and incurably romantic, both male and female Arians tend to need joyous sex and close relationships throughout their lives. But this is a sign of extremes: the pendulum can swing the other way. Some Arians find sex a complete waste of time – although they tend to be a minority. Typical Arians find the bedroom either an adventure playground or a battlefield, and they love sexual experimentation, although their basic egocentricity can make them too demanding and selfish as lovers. Incompatibility is often more about a partner's occasional need to sleep rather than a view of the sex act itself.

to silent fury or hurt bewilderment, Arians find themselves rudderless, without the resources or people skills to put things right. Fortunately, they rarely sulk, seeking above all to get things out in the open and to let others know exactly where they stand – even if this means adding further to

partner belongs to one of the Earth signs, Taurus or Virgo. Their ruling planet, Venus, is the perfect balance to Martian extremism, softening a tendency to see life as a series of all-or-nothing challenges. Taureans are traditionally no-nonsense, solid individuals who are conservative

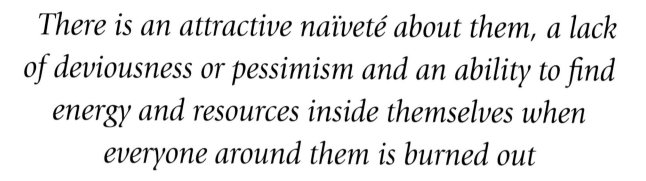

There is an attractive naïveté about them, a lack of deviousness or pessimism and an ability to find energy and resources inside themselves when everyone around them is burned out

an already hurtful situation.

When romance dies or a loved one disappoints them in some way, Arians can appear to be cruelly dismissive, often reacting by completely cutting the "culprit" out of their life, as if shutting a door on the relationship and throwing away the key. Always looking forward to the next project or lover, they rarely indulge in nostalgia or sentiment; and they can seem to discard lovers, friends and family without a backwards glance. Any slights cast on them and their integrity will meet with raging fury, followed by cold disdain. Arians are unlikely to give second chances or sit down and think about the motives or problems of other people.

and restrained. Fortunately, they often have a secret admiration for more flamboyant characters, and can fall deeply in love with Arian fire. Virgos can be considerably more organized than Arians, which is no bad thing. However, their introversion and tendency to keep their emotions under wraps can be either intriguing or, at worst, deeply irritating to the average Arian.

Although there are always notable exceptions to the rule, another Fire Sign, Leo, is far too similar in character and disposition to be a life mate for an Aries. They would constantly be fighting to be at the center of attention. Air Signs – Gemini, Libra and Aquarius – all too often succeed in fanning the Arian flames, while Cancer, Scorpio and Pisces are either too "wet" and wimpy for Aries, or they pour too much cold water on all those magnificent Arian plans.

IDEAL PARTNER

Arians need support, encouragement and bringing down to earth – with a bump, if necessary – so their ideal life

Compatibility in Relationships

Aries
Fire meets fire with fellow Arians, and a clash of egos may cause far too many problems for a happy life.

Cancer
Home-loving Cancers may offer stability but cause too many scenes. Sometimes it works, though.

Libra
Gregarious and fun-loving Libras can suit Arians, but the Ram's ambitions can be too self-centered.

Capricorn
Repressed, inhibited Goats may hero-worship Arians, but this combination won't last for long.

Taurus
Calm, dignified and stolid Taureans can give madcap Arians the status and stable home they seek.

Leo
Two volatile Fire Signs together do not make for a happy life. Some Leos are big enough to compromise.

Scorpio
Aries will be fascinated by the deep, unfathomable Scorpian but life will prove too intense for comfort.

Aquarius
Crusading Aquarians can all too often succeed in clashing for the center of attention with pioneering Arians.

Gemini
Geminis tend to be too flighty – and often too wily – for pioneering Arians' long-term plans.

Virgo
Orderly, down-to-earth Virgos can ideally complement Arian fire, as long as they are not too secretive.

Sagittarius
Arians and easy-going Sagittarians do get along but in the end both will go their separate ways.

Pisces
Dreamy and emotional, Pisceans will often find it hard to give Arians the emotional freedom they need.

THE ARIAN CHILD

Spontaneous and demonstrative, Arians always remain childlike, sometimes even childish. When they are small children, they can delight and exasperate their parents more than most. They are free with their affections but also particularly unruly and headstrong. They are given to foot-stamping, tears before bedtime and truly

Criticism and punishment need to be handled sensitively because Arians are inclined to give up if humiliated or rejected. Constructive criticism and constant encouragement, on the other hand, can produce extremely high standards of achievement. Arians always live up to others' expectations. Because of their self-centeredness and adventurous spirit, they need clear guidelines for behavior – the earlier the better. Arians have a

> *They are given to foot-stamping, tears before bedtime and truly spectacular temper tantrums if not allowed to have their own way*

spectacular temper tantrums if not allowed to have their own way. Nevertheless, they also have respect for authority and react very favorably to appeals to their self-esteem such as: "Who's mommy's brave soldier, then?" Arians are in many ways admirably independent and energetic. Foolhardy to a fault, however, they are always suffering from cuts and bruises – and more than their fair share of broken bones – so they need to be carefully supervised, especially on vacations.

paradoxical love of rules and regulations; and once they understand what acceptable behavior is, they will usually comply with it.

Highly competitive and combative by nature, Arians are not easy siblings to live with; although boys can become brave protectors of their little sisters. Sharing toys and treats will always be a problem, and the imminent arrival of a baby brother or sister must be discussed with the greatest sensitivity, or the sense of outrage and rejection can scar an Aries for life.

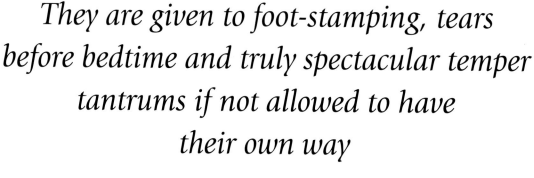

Classic Aries Leonardo da Vinci and some of his moments of inspiration

Famous Arians

Leonardo da Vinci
Muddy Waters
St. Francis Xavier
Elton John
Peter Ustinov
Marlon Brando
Hans Christian Andersen
Johan Sebastian Bach

Harry Houdini

Marlon Brando

Otto von Bismarck
Rene Descartes
Helmut Kohl
Romulus (Founder of Rome)
Leonard Nimoy
Joseph Pulitzer
Severiano Ballesteros
Clarence Darrow
Casanova
Harry Houdini
Wilbur Wright
Modest Mussorgsky

THE SUN IN TAURUS

(April 21 – May 21)

Sun Sign: TAURUS

Sign: THE BULL

Ruling Planet: VENUS

Gender: FEMININE

Element: EARTH

Quality: FIXED

Compatibility: ARIES, TAURUS

AND SCORPIO

Non-compatibility: AQUARIUS

AND SAGITTARIUS

Sun Sign Taureans are reliable, responsible and affectionate, with strong artistic leanings and a winning way with money. Methodical to a fault, Taureans prefer to stick to well-established plans, rather than change or adapt, and are excellent homemakers and builders of secure families. They are patient, determined and possess enormous reserves of strength and common sense. The "salt of the earth", they are always there, towers of strength in a crisis. They are strangers to Arian-style tantrums or impulsiveness. Taureans love routine and rarely question rules and regulations, possessing a natural inclination to respect authority and take orders. Taureans are Establishment figures through and through. For example, in one London publishers' strike, over 80 percent of the strike-breakers were Sun Sign Taureans. London, with its love of tradition, pomp and ceremony, is a very Taurean city. Excellent seconds-in-command, they do not often aspire to be the top of their chosen profession; although there are many Taureans who are musical stars, such as Cher, Shirley Maclaine and Barbra Striesand. Natural talent in the performing arts will often take them to the top of the ladder, but many Taureans in more conventional lines of work, such as banking or manufacturing, are too afraid of change to pursue the glittering prizes with any real and lasting ambition. One of their most typical characteristics is the tendency to plod through life, content with an unremarkable existence as good citizens and the builders of a stable society.

Warm-hearted and loving people, Taureans seek above all to create a happy family. Their home is always their castle, however humble it may be. They love to surround themselves with beautiful things, often doing without rather than having to settle for second-best. Frequently "hands on" hobbyists, they are enthusiastic about decorating and home improvement, although the pace of progress may be slow. One of their most negative traits is indolence, the ability to switch off and do absolutely nothing – except perhaps eat, drink and make love.

The sensualists par excellence of the zodiac, Taureans love all forms of self-expression – except perhaps sports and self-indulgence. They turn being pampered into a serious art form. They love being touched or massaged, and can suffer real feelings of deprivation if denied the joys of love or being touched. They are sensual eaters, who pick up food with their hands and greet every dish with an appreciative "Mmmm."Gourmands rather than gourmets, Taureans do sometimes become food faddists, seeking out the perfect olive oil or wild mushroom with fanatical single-mindedness. They can also

become knowledgeable wine buffs.

Taureans are prone to fierce possessiveness and to making unreasonable accusations, seeing serious liaisons in the most light-hearted and innocent of banter. Jealousy can provoke sudden outbursts of fearful rage, when they charge like a bull at a gate, in blind fits of fury. However, Taurean negativity is mostly expressed in dullness, stubbornness and resistance to change. Taureans can be "Old Fogeys" at any age.

APPEARANCE

Often short to medium height and stocky, Taureans' delicate hands and feet reveal a strong artistic streak. Although archetypically broad-shouldered, they often have a small behind. As the years go by, their lifestyle virtually guarantees increasingly generous padding. Their eyes are bright and soulful, and their voices can be musical and sexy. They move gracefully, surprisingly light on their feet, with the assurance of a dancer. They move slowly, however in a measured fashion and at a steady pace.

HEALTH

Too much food and wine inevitably takes its toll, and Taureans are often inclined to suffer from obesity and its associated health problems. In some cases, they can find themselves hopelessly addicted to both food and alcohol; although it will cause them great pain to admit it. Traditionally, Taureans suffer with their throat and necks, which is a grave affliction to the many professional singers under this sign.

They avoid solo sports, preferring team games; although many Taureans enjoy golf – that great Establishment pastime. Physically strong, they can suffer greatly from the stress caused by any of the major life changes, such as moving house or the death of a loved one, although they will find it very hard to express their emotions.

Stoic and reserved, Taureans often leave visiting the doctor until they can no longer carry on. Sometimes, this has life-threatening results. Even so, they make good patients, obeying doctor's orders and causing nursing staff no problems. They can be competent, if unimaginative, nurses

themselves, and are willing to work long hours at tedious jobs without complaint. Most Taureans are content with conventional medicine, although the more bohemian types will occasionally experiment with complementary therapies such as acupuncture.

CAREER

Taureans have a wide spread of potential careers, from money matters – accounting, tax collecting and banking – to the arts, building, fashion or gardening. Intensely practical people, Sun Sign Taureans are happiest when creating something tangible and lasting, be it a house, a landscaped garden, a painting, sculpture or a piece of haute couture. A fixed Earth Sign, they are good at putting down roots and maintaining their stability against the ravages of change. If they are trapped in uninspiring office jobs, they will transfer their creative cravings to their leisure time – often keeping up several hobbies, from amateur opera to prize-winning rose-growing.

But there is no getting away from the fact that Taureans are often content to sit out their entire working lives in dull jobs, never really attempting to seek promotion or change to something more demanding. Methodical and thorough, they will duck out of going the extra mile that is so attractive to bosses, and might not show enough of the initiative that pinpoints someone destined for success. Taureans are the career uniformed policemen who rarely rise above the rank of sergeant or the publisher's personal assistant rather than a top-rank editor who snatches up best-selling authors. They are the box office manager rather than the star on stage. Having said that, though, there will be few personal crises and personality clashes in the office. Time-keeping will be flawless and absenteeism will be almost nil. Gritty, dogged and strong, Taureans will rise to tackle any major crisis, from a bomb blast to a flood – their sturdy shoulders ever ready to carry the burdens of others, both literally and figuratively.

RELATIONSHIPS

Taureans like to know where they stand, so they can carve out a distinctive role for themselves that will last, unchanging, throughout the years. In a family situation, they like to know where they come in the pecking order. Though they may fume

of which is likely to drive non-Taurean partners nuts with boredom. But on the other hand, Taureans are very generous and hospitable entertainers, so visitors will always be made welcome. Taureans invite any chance to show off their beautiful home and garden. Business wives born into this sign often score the highest points

Taureans seek harmony and peace above all – "anything for a quiet life"

with jealousy over a rival sibling's favored place in their parents' affections, they will often suffer in silence, keeping their emotional burden to themselves all their lives. Taureans seek harmony and peace above all – "anything for a quiet life" being one of their favorite sayings – but they can suffer real emotional hardship just to keep the peace. Sometimes, this results in an explosion of rage in inappropriate circumstances, puzzling those who witness it. However, this is the explosion of the long-simmering volcano, rarely having a direct link to the events of the time.

Loyal, devoted Taureans need to make real efforts to keep their relationships fresh. They possess affection, even passion, in vast amounts, but this can easily become bogged down under the weight of complacency. They may forget to speak words of love or keep themselves in attractive shape, or use those little romantic touches that make all the difference. In classic fashion, once married and settled down, Taureans tend to "let themselves go." Sometimes their obsession with their home can make them disinclined to stir out of it, even to take part in family celebrations or vacations, all

in entertaining overseas visitors, leaving a lasting impression of culture and almost effortless hospitality.

Even when ill or feeling down, Taureans will struggle to do what they consider to be their duty, and this makes them attentive parents – always being present at School plays and PTA meetings. They will also keep their children on schedule with homework and studying for exams.

Conscientious and dutiful, they are eager to look after elderly parents and organize the best kind of assisted living if necessary. They are focused on providing for the future and usually have sound pension plans and insurance. They will often be insured up to the hilt for every conceivable eventuality. Though life can be unpredictable, Taureans would rather live without hassle than actually make a claim.

They will stubbornly cling to a way of doing things that even they admit is long outdated. This can be extremely irritating for loved ones who want to move on to more exciting territory. Taureans are suspicious, even frightened, of spontaneity, and need to be advised well in advance of any plans, even for happy social events. Surprise parties and sudden trips are not for them, and any break in their carefully

Compatibility in Relationships

Aries
Dashing Arians add sparkle to the life of the more prosaic Taurus. They can have long, successful relationships.

Taurus
Fellow Taureans make for safety, convention and stability. So it can work, but it won't be very exciting.

Gemini
Taureans are often attracted to easy-going and sociable Geminis, who can be too daring for this to last.

Cancer
Well-behaved, stolid, reserved Taureans can find Cancerian scenes just too much to take – but can learn to cope.

Leo
Egocentric Leos often charm Taureans, but sooner or later there will be a huge, disastrous – and final – showdown.

Virgo
Earthy and very organized Virgos attract Taurean, but this combination can prove too predictable for both.

Libra
Libras, also ruled by Venus, seriously attract Taureans. Libras' outlook is too cool, though.

Scorpio
Opposite sign Scorpios fascinate Taureans, but there may be too much murkiness for convention-bound Taureans.

Sagittarius
All that energy and irresponsibility charm but ultimately horrify steady Taureans, who prefer pensions to penury.

Capricorn
The unadventurous Goat can find happiness with a stolid Bull but sooner or later a red cape will appear.

Aquarius
To Taureans, unconventional Aquarians can often seem to have come from another planet. No chance!

Pisces
Excessively emotional, clingy Pisceans can be a very definite turn-off for salt-of-the-earth Taureans.

maintained routine needs to be discussed and thoroughly hashed out if it is to stand any chance of happening. Generally, however, Taurus is a sign remarkably free of irritating habits.

Taureans make charming company, being careful never to interrupt, make insensitive comments or become aggressive. However, if provoked into an argument about religion or politics, they may stridently defend the belief system with which they grew up, often becoming very heated. They are far happier at conventional social gatherings than at anything wild, and will react nervously, with evident disapproval, if good taste is not maintained. On the rare occasions that they do make a social gaffe, they will be overcome with horror and apologize profusely - perhaps not so much because they have hurt someone's feelings but because they have upset the status quo. Taureans of both sexes make ideal "no strings" escorts. In most cases, the terms "lady" or "gentleman" fit their style perfectly.

IDEAL PARTNER

Typical, stolid Taureans who seek emotional and material stability could do a lot worse than spend their lives with another Taurus, although sparks will fly should both

these obstinate natures clash. They are inclined to be faithful and carry the same values and tastes throughout life, and so make a perfect match. However, this marriage of similarities may not be the most stimulating, because the challenges they set each other will be strictly limited. With both Earth Sign sets of feet firmly on the ground, life will be safe but predictable.

If Taureans want a little magic in their lives, they should go for their opposite zodiacal sign – the intense and magnetic Scorpio, whose smoldering charm often proves fascinating to the sign of the Bull. Profound and often interested in occult mysteries, Scorpios provide the antidote to bovine dullness; but their secretive nature is puzzling to the straightforward and honorable Taurus, and their esoteric interests can upset Taurean conventionality.

Arians, with their fiery energy, can also provide opposite characteristics that create a balance – even though this is often rather tense. In addition, the Ram's tendency to wander, physically and sexually, will not meet with the steady Taurus' approval, although they may secretly admire them for it.

Because of their home-loving and stoical nature, Taureans are the best providers of the zodiac and are second only to Cancers as homemakers. They can, therefore, turn many of the most unpromising relationships with diverse signs of the zodiac into lasting love matches, with few real complaints.

Traditional Taureans can all too easily become worried and upset by those who mock their own values and traditions, so they should be wary of becoming too enamored of the more rebellious sort of Aquarius – for all their many charms. Nor is the sensible Taurus likely to find much joy with happy-go-lucky Sagittarians, who are never particularly eager to discuss the

household accounts or put something away for a rainy day.

THE TAUREAN CHILD

Quiet, reserved and often timid, typical Taurean children know how to keep their views and opinions to themselves. This type is rarely naughty and perhaps even something a "teacher's pet." They obey every parental rule, never being too demanding. They can be stubborn, though, and even their respect for authority can quickly evaporate if their most cherished beliefs and habits are threatened. Some Taurean children will even argue with school principals if they are defending their right to live life at their own pace and in their own way. Sometimes the victims of bullying, they can shock their tormentors by declaring that enough is enough and turning the tables. This is when the quietly grazing bovine turns into the raging bull, and anyone and everyone in the way had better beware! Conversely, another Taurean type can become the bullies themselves, using brute force to intimidate smaller and weaker children; although they are usually too lazy to keep up a lengthy reign of terror.

As siblings, they are often fair-minded and amenable; but their basic acquisitiveness and lack of spontaneity may cause problems in the nursery. Children who are inclined to covet others' toys and are disinclined to be spontaneous are not the best playmates.

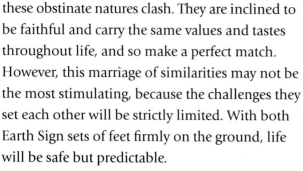

They, too, can be ragingly jealous of a new baby brother or sister – being wildly possessive of their mother's attention, although they often react favorably to being given the role of protector to the new addition to the family.

Pope John Paul II
Queen Elizabeth II
Charlotte Brontë
Cher
Barbra Streisand
William Shakespeare
Sigmund Freud
Emperor Hirohito
Karl Marx
Robert Oppenheimer
Eva Peron
Sergei Prokofiev
Sugar Ray Robinson
Bertrand Russell
Socrates
Rudolph Valentino
Malcolm X
Bing Crosby
Antony Trollope
Florence Nightingale

William Shakespeare

Rudolph Valentino (with co-star Vilma Banky in Son of the Sheik*)*

THE SUN IN GEMINI

(May 22 – June 21)

Sun Sign: GEMINI

Sign: THE TWINS

Ruling Planet: MERCURY

Gender: MASCULINE

Element: AIR

Quality: MUTABLE

Compatibility: AQUARIUS

Non-compatibility:

TAURUS, CAPRICORN

AND VIRGO

Sun Sign Geminis tend to be jack-of-all trades and masters of none – or at least few. Quick-witted, versatile and adaptable, they love word-play and jokes, and are often extremely witty and amusing companions – the life and soul of the party. Expert communicators, they are confident public speakers with enviable timing and panache, and are excellent at networking or bringing shy or diverse people together in social or business situations. The dual sign of the zodiac, Geminis need more than one project on the go at the same time, and require constant intellectual and social stimulation. Variety is not just the spice of life, it is life itself for typical Sun Sign Geminis. They can easily become bored and restless – "twitchy" and nervy if nothing interesting is going on, or if their mind is not being fully engaged. But even though this is a sign noted for its sharp mind and mental fluency, it can suffer from a very short attention span and lack of concentration and stamina. Geminis are inclined to do things in short, sharp bursts and display intense enthusiasm – although a day later they may have completely forgotten that they had ever

declared any interest at all in the subject.

Versatile and adaptable, they are quick to turn apparent disadvantages into personal successes; although long-term plans tend to bore them and routine scares them away. As for living alone, it's simply not on the agenda. A Gemini must at least have someone else to share ideas with – hopefully someone with the good sense to bring them down to earth from time to time. Gregarious and often actually frightened of being alone, they love constant interaction and feedback, seeking endless challenges in all areas of life.

Their major flaws are superficiality and manipulativeness. Ruled by Mercury, their quicksilver minds rarely alight on any one subject long enough to absorb the finer points. They can also be very guileful, sometimes to the point of being accomplished liars and even con artists. The tricksters of the zodiac, Geminis are constantly looking out for number one, regardless of the cost in human terms. They are frequently cold-hearted and uneasy with the gentler emotions. You will hear them complain of weariness during major charity campaigns sooner than any other sign of the zodiac. The fact is that Geminis are very uneasy with deep emotions. When faced with strong feelings, they tend to take refuge in flippant remarks, sarcasm or logical analysis. Their

energy-intensive natural foods such as bananas and dried fruit. They are particularly sensitive to the ill-effects of smoking, and should never even consider taking it up – their lungs are delicate and are the

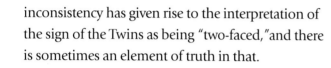

Aquarians understand the Geminian restlessness and drive, but add their own gentleness and more profound idealism

inconsistency has given rise to the interpretation of the sign of the Twins as being "two-faced," and there is sometimes an element of truth in that.

APPEARANCE

Wiry and bursting with nervous energy, Geminis tend to be tallish and slim, with indeterminate color hair, which many of them dye to dramatic effect. When at rest, they can appear rather mousey and insignificant; but once they are animated and enthused by life, they light up from inside and can have real star charisma. They have small, narrow hands and feet, and quick, sometimes theatrical, gestures. They are Peter Pans, maintaining a youthful appearance to the end; although some of it may eventually come from the surgeon's knife.

HEALTH

Prone to nervous prostration, Geminis need to guard against "burn out" and discipline themselves to get enough sleep and eat regular meals. Because they burn up so much energy, it suits their metabolism to eat little and often, especially

first organs to suffer from any debility.

Sun Sign Geminis find regular exercise routines a bore, and should maintain a varied program of sports and martial arts, which will help balance their energies and promote greater powers of concentration.

CAREER

Although many Geminis are successfully self-employed, they find working alone absolutely unacceptable because they need the motivation and feedback of a workplace – preferably a very busy one. The ultimate charmers and communicators, they are particularly suited to media work - especially the ephemeral world of television and advertising copywriting, where their talent for catchphrases can really shine. Fashionable and chic, Geminis are good at creating an impressive image, which allows them to be all the more persuasive in making sales pitches. Indeed, typical Geminians are *the* salespersons of the zodiac. They enjoy challenges, but feel trapped by deadly routine or too many rules and regulations. A lack of variety can ultimately cause them enormous stress. Many are authors or journalists, often writing two books at the same time or several different articles for a variety of publications. However, don't expect too much depth or an impressive array of facts and figures. Details slow Geminis down: they would rather pay a researcher well above the going rate than sift their own way through a mountain of reference books. They are often skilled in speed-reading and fond of quick fixes, instant answers and immediate responses, which is why they are also naturally computer literate. Surfing the net is second nature to typical Geminis – once they are online, they can be reluctant to communicate in any other way.

Other suitable jobs for Geminis include switchboard operating, tour guiding, legislative lobbying, theater managers, theatrical agents, acting, modeling or anything that involves using personality and persuasion. They also make excellent conjurors and illusionists – sleight of hand and sleight of mind being much the same to them.

Unfortunately, Geminis make good career criminals, having the gift of the gab and the ability to lie very convincingly. Many swindlers were born under the sign of the Twins, and even upright Geminian citizens can rarely resist the opportunity to stretch the truth – usually very humorously. Never forget that Geminians can charm the birds out the trees and then sell them a used car, before persuading them to lie down in the casserole dish and cover themselves with gravy.

Bosses will often be impressed by Geminian energy and initiative, and by their easy assurance and confidence. But their fast talking and often careless reports - completed just before the deadline – can cause problems. Geminis find the old-fashioned idea of "jobs for life" too dreary for words. They often jump from one position to another well before they can be shown the door.

RELATIONSHIPS

Geminis who grow up in emotionally conservative families are themselves uneasy with kissing and cuddling, and can actually become distressed by others encroaching on their personal space. But they enjoy being in a lively household and seek partners with strong opinions and marked preferences – at least it's something to discuss and argue over. Talking is always the Gemini's favorite hobby; although listening has to be an acquired skill. They will stay up late into the night talking or strike up conversations with casual acquaintances. Even the normally reserved British have an easy, happy-go-lucky attitude to strangers if they are born under the sign of the Twins. Many Geminis have relatively few real friends and dozens of acquaintances, which they often insist on bringing back home for dinner or drinks, perhaps at an inconvenient time for the rest of the family.

Geminis are eager to make relationships work, but tend to be too egocentric and outgoing to ever really know what makes their partners tick, or why they are unhappy. All too often, it comes as a terrible shock when they discover the note on the mantelpiece and half the wardrobe emptied of clothes. When they moan, "Why didn't s/he tell me s/he was unhappy?" our Gemini honestly has no idea what they did, because they were too busy talking to notice.

Often, Geminis content themselves with playing the field for many years before settling down, being rather proud of their image as men or women behaving badly. Naturally afraid of commitment or any depth of emotion, the prospect of love for life terrifies them. Others throw themselves into their careers, which they use as an excuse for not having a partner or even wanting a close relationship. On the other hand, they can be effusively, even sloppily, affectionate with their pets, over whom they can become extremely protective. The uncomplicated loyalty of dogs particularly suits the Geminian temperament, whereas the lofty detachment of cats can be rather disconcerting. Traditionally, though, talking birds are the perfect Geminian pets – clever, wily, quick-witted and with a

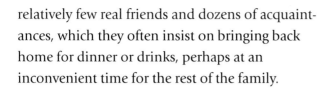

capacity to be funny, although one sometimes suspects it is at your own expense. Geminis have a multitude of annoying habits, which can add up to major relationship problems. Top of the list is their insistence on dropping everything for some wild idea that they have failed to think through, and which will end in misery or disaster. And it can be strangely unsettling to try to communicate with someone who does at least three different things at the same time – one of which is always talking on the telephone. (Mobile phones were invented for Geminis.) If you're looking for a nice, reliable partner who is always there for you, forget your Geminian charmer, who considers being half an hour late to be on time. (Go for a Taurus instead.)

THE GEMINIAN CHILD

Traditionally, it is often said that Geminis have unhappy childhoods, without much love or affection, and sometimes actually a traumatic upbringing. Obviously, this is a very sweeping statement, which must be true of many children from other signs of the zodiac. Yet Geminis can easily feel nervous and out of place, especially when too young to have developed social skills. They need lots of love and encouragement, to be given space to be themselves, and to express their energy and creativity. Forever starting a project, hobby or enthusiasm – but rarely staying the course – Geminian children need a firm hand to get anything off the ground. Parents should encourage them to finish each task before starting the next, although this may be a difficult task in itself. From an early age, they should be introduced to the idea of searching around for information, using libraries and making enquiries, so they learn the value of facts and figures to give their schoolwork some depth. At school and college they will always do better in tutorials and discussion groups than in written work. And they may easily become distracted,

So they should be gradually introduced to the idea that a lone walk along the seashore – perhaps with a dog or two – is actually pleasurable and restorative.

Geminian children may not be good sharers or team members, but their capacity for fun and being the life and soul of the party will endear them to most other youngsters - even though they may not make real friends very easily. Parents should try to ensure that they are not too flighty in their friendships.

IDEAL PARTNER

Because they often stick their head in the clouds, Geminis need a planner, someone who is careful with money. Taureans are too plodding and Capricorns far too pessimistic. Typical Sun Sign Virgos, though they can be far too analytical and organized, can do the trick if softened with other planetary influences. Perhaps, curiously, it is another air sign – Aquarius – which is ideal for them. Aquarians understand the Geminian restlessness and drive, but add their own gentleness and more profound idealism. Together, they make an excellent team, and can even work happily together, either in business or for charity. Geminis need someone who is fairly thick-skinned and independent, someone who can cope with their sudden changes of plan, spontaneous outbursts and the chaos that can come as a result of trying to do a multitude of things at the same time.

more than most, by the drama group or the university newspaper. Unsuited to more ponderous subjects such as philosophy and history, Geminis excel in languages, literature, information technology, media studies and journalism. However, many will drop out in favor of more convivial pastimes, such as becoming stand-up comics or cocktail waiters in fashionable bars.

From an early age, Geminian children should be encouraged to have a great deal of sleep. They careen through life at such a breakneck speed that they rapidly use up all their reserves and become severely run down. They should be made to spend some time winding down before bedtime, to help quell their racing minds and prevent the onset of chronic insomnia, to which this sign is particularly prone. Fresh air and solitude – which they naturally dislike – is necessary for everyone, even a Gemini.

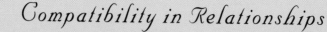

Aries
Feisty Arians may seem glamorous, but underneath they are far too serious and self-absorbed for Geminis.

Cancer
Cancerian emotional blackmail and frequent tantrums will send Gemini fleeing. Calmer Crabs might last.

Libra
Both real charmers, Geminis and Libras can seem to have something special, but they won't be soul mates.

Capricorn
The austere Goat may view easygoing and plausible Geminis with suspicion and – justifiable – cynicism.

Taurus
Taureans all too often fall for the famous Geminian charm, which will finally be too superficial for the heavyweight Bull.

Leo
High and mighty Leos can be magnificent lovers but, all too often, there will be a major personality clash.

Scorpio
Scorpios' glamour will fascinate Geminis and there may be a real sexual buzz, but tears in the end.

Aquarius
Geminis can fall for the challenge of life with a true Aquarius – in a big way – and find lifelong happiness.

Gemini
Fellow Geminis know only too well each other's wiles – so this usually won't work for long.

Virgo
Geminis can find the more sociable Virgos good company, but they will soon tire of them.

Sagittarius
This will be a fun relationship with wild times and big plans, but it won't make for a settled, cozy home.

Pisces
Geminis have little patience for the often difficult, emotionally intense and rather contradictory Pisceans.

Famous Geminis

Bob Dylan
John F. Kennedy
Marilyn Monroe
Isadora Duncan
The artist formerly known as Prince
Sir Edward Elgar
PC Faberge
Jean-Paul Sartre
Judy Garland
Che Guevara
Marquis de Sade
Anne Frank
Bob Hope

Marilyn Monroe

John F. Kennedy

Henry Kissinger
Paul McCartney
Cole Porter
Grigori Rasputin
Bjorn Borg
Al Jolson
Sir Arthur Conan Doyle

THE SUN IN CANCER

(June 22 — July 22)

Sun Sign: CANCER

Sign: THE CRAB

Ruling Planet: THE MOON

Gender: FEMININE

Element: WATER

Quality: CARDINAL

Compatibility: TAURUS AND WELL-ASPECTED LEOS

Non-compatibility: CAPRICORN AND PISCES

Sun Sign Cancers are the most family-centered of the zodiac. Fiercely protective of their loved ones, they are nourishers and care-givers at heart. Loving, demonstrative and tender-hearted to the point of sentimentality, they attach great importance to anniversaries, trinkets and trips down memory lane. They are unashamedly feminine and even male Cancers tend to be care-givers. Cancers are also in tune with their true self and in touch with their intuition. They are often psychic and can be intuitively wise, but distrust cold academic logic and analysis: book learning for its own sake is not for them. Unlike fellow Water Sign Pisces, Cancerian dreams are rarely vague and otherworldly, focusing instead on creating images of success and happiness for those they love. Though often without driving ambition for themselves, they yearn passionately on behalf of others. They are artistic, practical and excellent homemakers. The world outside rarely offers anything to eclipse the attraction of coming home, especially home to the family, and even lone Cancers lavish time and money on creating their ideal nest.

However, those born under the sign of the Crab are great worriers, constantly fretting about the health and safety of their family and friends. As far as Cancers are concerned, if someone is a few minutes late, something bad must have happened to them. Their constant fussing can drive others to distraction. So can their tendency to be overemotional and sentimental, eyes brimming with tears for the slightest reason – whether real or imagined. Cancers take offense easily, often going off in a huff. They tend to fall out with others and then keep their distance. They may not speak to those who have ruffled them, sometimes for years on end.

Cancers are nothing if not tenacious. They hang on to a relationship, belief or cause with their crab's claws, even when it causes them pain. For them, it is enormously difficult to let go and move on. They are constantly looking back and can wallow in nostalgia, even though the past was not the Golden Age or romantic dream they seem to imagine. Cancers are very good at creating their own myths and turning humdrum lives into fairy stories, even if it requires a willingness to stretch the truth. Anyone who tries to make them face facts is answered with outrage, denial and a storm of hurt tears.

Being too emotional makes Cancers moody, withdrawn and even secretive. Sometimes they can sulk for days, without anyone being able to find out why. Since they are virtually telepathic, they find it hard to understand that others may not necessarily share their intuitive gifts.

Cancers are both loving and loyal, but can often be unsure of themselves and somewhat timid socially, preferring to give someone else the limelight. They will, however, shine at providing the refreshments after the star has done his or her turn.

APPEARANCE

Cancers are often smallish, with round "moon" faces and a tendency to put on weight. This applies especially to women who may have what used to be described as a "motherly figure." These Earth Mother types have abundant, shiny hair, soulful eyes, and they are economical with their gestures. Another Cancerian type is thin and nervy, with reddish hair and more extroverted behavior in social situations.

Some people born under the sign of the Crab become so sour through bitterness and worry that it is reflected in the permanent downturn of their mouths, their prematurely lined faces and their cold, dissatisfied expressions. On the whole, Cancers move as little as possible, and only a real emergency will make them do so swiftly.

HEALTH

Cancers, the archetypal couch potatoes, are happiest slouching in front of the television. Exercise is generally anathema to them, but they can be encouraged to take part in family walks. The ladies might be persuaded to join the "family" at an all-women weight-loss group. Being a Water Sign, Cancerians can excel at watersports; and even the most exercise averse among them will willingly take the plunge if

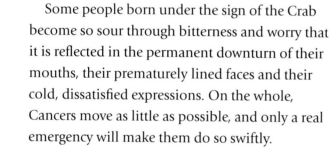
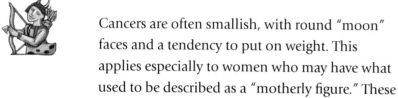

there is a swimming pool nearby.

Cancerian weaknesses include their digestive systems, where all that worry can wreak havoc, causing heartburn, colitis and ulcers. Women tend to suffer from breast problems and water retention, but both men and women become very distressed by all illnesses, trivial as well as serious. They tend to become hypochondriacs, always visiting the doctor – on behalf of family members as well as themselves – and buying over-the-counter remedies. Many Cancers are fascinated by holistic or alternative therapies, and can spend a fortune working their way through them. It is important to stress that those born under the sign of Cancer are not more likely than any other sign to develop the illness of the same name, but of course it is always a good idea to have regular health checks.

CAREER

Being naturally sympathetic, practical and nurturing, Cancers make excellent nurses. They understand how unsettling illness can be, and easily relate to their patients. They are naturals with children, especially tiny tots, and make memorable primary school and special needs teachers. Here their immense reserves of patience are often rewarded with remarkable progress. Their ability to sympathize with others who are in difficulties also attracts them to counseling and charity work. They can often be found working as volunteers on telephone hotlines, perhaps as suicide or AIDS counselors.

Cancers are also the mainstay of help for the homeless and like to make donations for far-off victims of famine. They cannot bear the idea of anyone going hungry, and are the first to react to television images of skeletal babies in the Third World. However, although they are excellent at "hands-on" charity work, they can often be far too sensitive and thin-skinned to work for any length of time in famine areas or with war victims. Most, with some notable exceptions, simply could not take the scale of the misery, nor the sights and smells of atrocities, of Man's inhumanity to Man.

Reliable and responsible, they make good co-workers; but they can equally run their own small businesses. This is where being so organized with money helps. Cancers also make imaginative cooks and caterers; although they prefer to see people's reactions to their dishes, rather than remaining behind the scenes in the kitchen. Because of their love of the past and tradition, you may find some Cancers working in museums especially mothers, find that hard to accept. Cosseted and over-protected, the children of typical Sun Sign Cancers can grow up timid and unadventurous or, conversely, become rebels.

Cancers cling. Female Crabs often refuse to accept that a boyfriend doesn't love them any more or that they will not even consider marrying them. With their over-romanticized image of love and marriage, it is inconceivable to them that the man in their life does not also want the cottage with roses around the door and two-point-four children playing with grannie in the garden. Long after any hope of reconciliation, Cancers are still trying to revive the long-dead embers of a relationship. They don't seem to realize that their endless scenes of tearful entreaty only succeed in pushing their beloved further and further away. They also cling to old-fashioned values, and even non-religious Cancers still expect to be virgins on their wedding night. They may also expect their bride or groom to be equally unsullied.

Many Cancers do not realize that they have the power to lash out and hurt others, though almost never in a physical way. When they are on the defensive – and they often are – Cancers can hit back with very cruel words, often dredging up old secrets in order to inflict the greatest hurt. If faced with this aspect of their behavior, they will either utterly deny it or berate themselves for being so wicked. On such occasions it is better not to press for a rational discussion. When Cancers are blinded by emotion they will never see

and libraries, or in the antiques trade. They also make tenacious researchers, especially if tracking down genealogical data or some fact of local history. They may have problems, though, with modern technology. Some are actually technophobes, something which can greatly hamper the progress of their chosen careers.

RELATIONSHIPS

Cancers make relationships their business, but they are sometimes not quite as good at it as they think. They make loving parents, sensitive lovers and generally docile children. However, Cancers tend to smother their children, suffocating them and others with their endless fussing and their inability to accept that people need their own space and freedom. Children need to have their own lives, but Cancerian parents,

reason. Perhaps when they have calmed down, the topic can be raised in a more constructive manner. But even then it will have to be handled very sensitively. Many Cancers can take constructive criticism, especially those whose professional training, perhaps in nursing or counseling, makes them more amenable to it. However, it is hard coming from loved ones, and often causes deep family or marital rifts. Cancers long for an atmosphere of love and harmony to prevail in the home. However, they take every little criticism personally, and brood on it – possibly even for years – so that the hurt goes deep and is constantly fresh in their minds, while everyone else has probably forgotten it.

IDEAL PARTNER

Cancers should stay clear of typical Sun Signs who cannot cope with emotions, especially Capricorns, who tend to be wintry in the expression of their feelings. Best for them are steady, grounded types such as Taureans, who can be very happy to create a nest with these traditional homebodies. They also understand the need to keep a firm hand on the bank balance, and this combination creates an almost ideally secure background in

Compatibility in Relationships

Aries
The fire and dash of Aries appeals, but they have little time for Cancerian emotion. It might work, but not for long.

Cancer
Though they have much in common, two emotional blackmailers under the same roof can make for disaster.

Libra
Life can be easy for a while. Libras value their independence too much to hand it over to a Cancer.

Capricorn
True Goats will never understand the Cancer's need to discuss emotion, which will frighten them off for good.

Taurus
This is a perfect match: both are home-makers and respecters of family values. They will enhance each other's life.

Leo
Cancers can worship Leos and make fine homes with them. With enough compromise, an excellent match.

Scorpio
Flashy Scorpios may infatuate Cancers, but the price is too high to pay. One drama queen is enough!

Aquarius
Home-loving Cancers feel threatened by real crusading Aquarians, who want to change their settled world.

Gemini
Self-seeking and specious Geminis can be charm itself, but soon they'll never be a lifelong partner.

Virgo
This combination can work, though Virgos may be puzzled and upset by Cancerian outburts and contradictions.

Sagittarius
Cancers want to own their beloved's body and soul – the last thing a Sagittarius will ever agree to.

Pisces
Both Water Signs can be tearful clingers, which is not the best recipe for lasting love or mutual respect.

which their children can grow up and fulfill their real potential.

Idealistic Aquarians and canny Virgos can also fit the bill, although they may find Cancerian

grasping side of the Cancerian nature should be nipped in the bud early in life – sharing toys and treats should be encouraged. Discipline can be hard for parents of Cancers to maintain,

The children take everything so much to heart and can become very distressed

emotionality very hard to take.

Proud Leos, however, could find Cancers supportive. Cancers may idolize them, easily falling into their role as nurturers rather than leaders. Badly aspected Leos can be overbearing and badly aspected Cancers sniveling martyrs, which makes a bad mix. However, most are well-balanced enough to make the combination work.

THE CANCERIAN CHILD

Hypersensitive and moody, the Cancerian child will be mommy's boy or daddy's girl from the cradle. Even so, they will love both parents to distraction and live in fear of being abandoned by them, or even left alone. It is important for the adopted Cancerian child to be told as early as possible about his or her background. Leaving it until they are older may cause emotional upset.

Cancers are inherently untidy, and this is made worse by their inability to throw anything away. Hoarding is second nature to them, due partly to a grasping streak and partly to their extreme sentimentality, which invests every little item with enormous emotional significance. This

especially if one or both of them are Crabs themselves, because the children take everything so much to heart and can become very distressed even when mildly reprimanded. By far the best way of coping with them is by appealing directly to their love and loyalty. Punishments do not need to be severe – just sending the children to their rooms while the rest of the family enjoys an evening together can produce immediate and heartfelt remorse.

Many Cancerian children are placid souls and, while not especially witty, can be amusing and imaginative.

Cancers are often timid and can develop a marked inferiority complex. Perversely, they become almost proud of this complex in later life, using it as an excuse not to take risks or improve themselves, intellectually or materially.

These children find it exceptionally hard to cope with bereavement, whether it is the death of a pet or a family member. They will see it as a betrayal of love, an abandonment, and may easily become severely traumatized and profoundly angry with the departed. They should be encouraged to talk about their feelings.

Teenage girls born under this sign will be especially moody at the time of the Full Moon, and bursting with nervous energy when the Moon is new. Wise parents will take this into account.

Famous Cancers

Alexander the Great
Diana, Princess of Wales
Rubens
George Orwell
O.J. Simpson
Meryl Streep
Louis Mountbatten
Emmeline Pankhurst
Marcel Proust
Arnold Schwarzenegger
Julius Caesar
James Cagney
Louis Armstrong

Diana, Princess of Wales

Ginger Rogers
Jean Cocteau
King Henry VIII
Arlo Guthrie
Arthur Ashe
Nelson Rockefeller
Ernest Hemingway

Julius Caesar

THE SUN IN LEO

(July 23 – August 23)

Sun Sign: LEO

Sign: THE LION

Ruling Planet: THE SUN

Gender: MASCULINE

Element: FIRE

Quality: FIXED

Compatibility: CANCER,

AQUARIUS AND VIRGO

Non-compatibility: SCORPIO

AND GEMINI

Sun Sign Leos are powerful, ambitious, and protective – truly the kings of the jungle. Ruled by the Sun, they are outgoing and optimistic, their sunny disposition often inspiring lesser mortals to greater efforts. They are the party animals of the zodiac, dynamic and uninhibited, believing they can achieve whatever they set out to do. New York is the perfect city for a Leo. As natural leaders, they love being on top, their innate reserves of energy and self-confidence helping them to overcome any setbacks. To Leos, integrity and dignity are as natural as breathing. Warm-hearted and often extremely generous, they love company – especially if they are the center of attention. Their enthusiasm is contagious, especially when it comes to motivating others in more creative endeavors. Well-aspected Sun Sign Leos are intrinsically faithful partners and loyal friends, and extremely loving in a very demonstrative, expansive way. When life is good for a Leo, everyone in their circle benefits in some way.

Conversely, when Leos are crossed and their integrity or self-esteem is challenged, they can fly into towering rages – which may soon evaporate, but they can leave those at the receiving end shaken to the core. It is easy for Leos to become overbearing. Sometimes they seem to demand worship from those closest to them, without realizing that respect must be earned. Some Leos are out-and-out bullies, taking advantage of any weakness in others; many can be domineering and unapproachable, both at work and at home. They can also be extremely dogmatic and ruthless in pursuing their particular ideology, giving no thought to the differing beliefs and lifestyles of others. Weakness or illness irritates this type and

provokes them into unkindness, even cruelty. Even the lesser Leonine tyrants can be amazingly pompous, often speaking on a one-to-one basis as if addressing a formal meeting, and inevitably patronizing those they consider to be their inferiors. Badly aspected Leos are often male chauvinists or racists, in much the same way as their fellow Fire Sign, Aries. However, the Lion's bigotry arises out of a basic lack of tolerance of any threat to his or her leadership.

Even Leos who appear to be quiet and restrained have all the virtues and flaws of the typical, expansive Lion. If you want to see Leos turn from pussycat into magnificent, terrifying king of the jungle, just injure their pride or treat them with contempt. Then the seemingly docile tabby shakes out its mane and growls.

APPEARANCE

The major characteristic of the Leonine appearance is gloriously abundant hair, often reddish or tawny colored, a true mane, wavy and untamed. Leos have "big hair" to match their personalities. They tend to be dramatic and prone to the occasional bad day, when nothing works out and the Sun that rules them is blotted out by a haze of gloom. Slow and deliberate in speech and movement, their bearing is regal and dignified. They tend to have a direct stare, which can be unnerving, and curiously wide or upward slanting eyes, giving them an unusual and rather theatrical appearance. Their complexion is youthful, but also somewhat sallow. When suntanned, they look far more stunning than any other sign. They dress in the best of taste, but are too impatient to drag endlessly around the shops, contenting themselves with one or two good outfits, in which they know they can stop the traffic.

HEALTH

Leos tend to suffer from heart trouble: their lion hearts take so much stress, both emotional and physical, that sooner or later they will have a health scare and become very heart-conscious, though usually late in the day. Until that moment, however, they tend to indulge their love of high-fat luxury foods and good wines, as befits their innate regality. They also tend, for the same reasons, to put on weight, but rarely attempt to do anything about it for very long, although expensive health farms and intensive pampering will certainly appeal to them. They may be far too lazy to follow a regular exercise program; but by employing personal training instructors, they can be weaned off the sedentary life. Anything that requires ugly sweating in a group of lesser mortals is absolute anathema to them.

Leos also suffer from back and spine problems, made worse by their tendency to be overweight and their lack of exercise. However, they can ease their discomfort by doing regular stretching exercises and visiting the chiropractor or osteopath.

CAREER

Leos are happiest and most effective in any career where they can give orders or be the center of attention. Being second-in-command or a humble team member is not for them, and their irritation at working – as they see it – for and with fools will not make for a happy workplace. When a Leo is upset, everyone soon knows about it. Teaching gives them the opportunity to take charge and also to express their creativity and pass on their often considerable wisdom to the next generation. Leos are often the teachers who make a lasting impression on the children in their care. They may tend to have mood swings and can be irascible one minute, but capable of

Even Leos without that overwhelming urge to see their name in lights need to feel that what they do is of real value, that their contribution is meaningful. Despite their desire to show off, Leos are fair and meticulous in keeping agreements. They expect others to be the same.

Whatever they do, they expect their attention to be fully engaged, and to be constantly praised and given positive feedback. They can't do any job for long, especially something routine or tedious, without bursting out and opting for something that offers to fulfill their considerable potential. Never take a Leo for granted, or expect them to work away without any recognition. Bosses with Leo employees should be particularly careful – Leo the Lion could be after their jobs.

making the whole class rock with mirth at some joke or anecdote the next – all acted out with great gusto and a complete lack of inhibition. Their enthusiasms can inspire pupils for life, although they can also destroy the confidence of more timid children – such as Sun Sign Cancers – with too much over-hearty teasing and the occasional outburst of titanic temper.

Leos have a natural bent for the theater and the performing arts. This is why they are so much at home in the acting and singing professions, and are often excellent dancers. They are never content to take just any part that comes along, but will use these more humble occupations as a means to an end – to progress to higher things. Working with these potential stars of the show is not easy. Leos can be tiresome as one of an ensemble, and constantly seek to upstage the others – even at the expense of the show as a whole or at the expense of personal feelings. Other flamboyant Leos find fulfillment in the glamour industries of fashion, modeling and design, anything, in fact, which is luxurious, impressive and has panache.

RELATIONSHIPS

Leos make wonderfully sociable companions, amusing, urbane and expansive. They tend to have a large circle of friends, many of them close and many for life. If they can afford it (and often even if they can't) they will pick up the tab in restaurants or host lavish parties. Gregarious and charming, they rarely live alone, even if it means sharing their home with several cats and dogs, to whom they are devoted.

Leos are usually fairly easy to live with, although they do expect others to live up to their own high standards as they cannot tolerate failure. They often expect life partners to be almost as ambitious as themselves. Leos love luxury and the best of everything, and tend to be snobbish. Status means everything to certain extreme Leo types. Because of this, they may even choose to live in an area where they don't really feel at home simply because it is stylish or "up-and-coming." A Leo is usually nobody's fool, but they can make easy prey for real estate agents with impressive properties for sale. They are not obsessively tidy and prefer a cozy home where they can relax and enjoy family life. Although they love the planning stages of interior design and home decorating, they are far too grand and lazy to get their own hands dirty. They are quite happy to pay for someone else to do the work.

Leos suffer from a certain dichotomy. Though they frequently lay on the charm thickly, they can be ruthless at the same time – a combination of the appealing and appalling. Male Leos can be surprisingly lazy, often giving up a project for the sake of time off or changing to something else quite abruptly. The lioness, however, is almost always on the alert, whether it is for the perfect red lipstick, for the bargain of a lifetime, the dream man or the big break that leads to success. These are qualities which can disrupt a happy home, but once they are accepted as congenital in Leos, other zodiac signs are more or less able to live with them.

Though Leos are passionate and faithful lovers, they can still look elsewhere if their partners betray them or injure their over-developed sense of pride. These partners tread on dangerous ground if they laugh at an inappropriate moment, or even try to provide comfort and understanding at difficult times in a Leo's sex life – worse still, if they show Leos up in any way, however minor. Apart from failure, what Leos hate most is boredom and pessimism. Anyone gloomy and uninspired by nature will not last the course with a typical Sun Sign Leo. They relish the chance to laugh and be sociable, and to wine and dine their loved ones. They really enjoy lavishing romantic gifts on them. In return they expect to be showered with compliments and praised to the heavens. Although they can often see through the more crude type of insincerity, flattery will get you almost anywhere with a Leo.

Leos can be difficult parents. They try very hard to enter into the child's world by playing rambunctious games and acting out bedtime stories at great length – and never mind if their partners are just longing for the little dears to go to sleep. It is in the nature of the Lion to want to be in control where children are concerned. This is why they are interfering, bossy and often extremely demanding. Unfortunately, the Leo parent can destroy the confidence of delicate flowers and totally fail to understand their more introspective children, who may be very grateful for the drama lessons and birthday parties for 200 with a famous conjuror for entertainment, but would really rather stay home and read a book.

Compatibility in Relationships

Aries
Matching fire with fire – and ego with ego – is not a good recipe for a harmonious and loving relationship.

Cancer
This is an enviable partner-ship: more well-balanced Cancers can make a happy nest with a beloved Leo.

Libra
Libras and Leos are mutually attracted, but the Scales dither too much for decisive, opinionated Leo.

Capricorn
Any initial attraction will soon wear thin due to the Goat's innate distrust of Leonine extravagance.

Taurus
Steady, feet-on-the-ground Taureans can make it work with Leos, but too often there will be a spark missing.

Leo
There can never be two kings in the same jungle. One will be forced to back off or sub-mit. Not a happy pairing.

Scorpio
There will be great sex and memorable times, but the intensity will cause too many problems in the long term.

Aquarius
Leos can make a effort with big-thinking Aquarians, but they may need more support than is forthcoming.

Gemini
Good times will be enjoyed, but difficult-to-pin-down Geminis will not provide Leo with the right home life.

Virgo
More relaxed Virgos can hit it off fairly well with expansive Leos, but most are too inhibit-ed to try.

Sagittarius
All fire and energy, these two will wear each other out with their headlong rush at life and fierce power struggles.

Pisces
This combination makes for a roller-coaster partnership. The water, in this case, is more likely to put out the fire.

There is often an ambivalence in their attitude to successful partners, siblings or children. Leos can be very competitive, although many of them expect to succeed without having to fight against anything other than Fate. To take on anyone else as a competitor makes them feel stressed and threatened.

Leos – male and female – need to be wary of feelings of jealousy creeping in when they are confronted with their children's successes. They will, however, usually take some comfort in the thought that those very successes are in some way part of their own achievement as a parent.

THE IDEAL PARTNER

Leos, especially the men, can make a happy lifelong commitment to the emotional and home-loving Cancer or the supportive, stable Taurus. There will, of course, be problems, for Leos always expect primacy and deference, and even the most martyrly Cancer will sometimes feel slighted by this situation. Gentle, idealistic Aquarians, who may be knowledgeable astrologers and therefore forewarned, can cope better with Leo's excessive demands, although they may not always be there when needed. Aquarians are often too busy with a host of good causes to provide the kind of consistent support that Leos tend to expect from a devoted partner.

As far as Virgos are concerned, the straightforward and usually well-grounded Leos can be complementary partners, since Virgo is the sign of the obsessively organized. However,

aggressive, hitting out both physically and verbally.

Although, at heart, Leos want to be liked, what they really crave is the near adulation of siblings, schoolfriends, parents and teachers. This they see as their unalienable right, whether or not they have earned it. Fortunately,

> *If by any chance praise and encouragement are not forthcoming, Leo children may just give up. Their natural indolence persuades them that the fight isn't worth the trouble*

Leos are often attracted, sometimes with disastrous results, to the fascinating Scorpio or flighty Gemini. Generally, however, Leos are magnanimous and can be adaptable. As long as they are fully supported and loved, they can conduct a successful relationship with almost any sign.

THE LEO CHILD

Leo children are assertive, organized and enthusiastic, and are often independent from an early age. They are able to charm adults with their bright intellects and sunny temperaments. As long as they are given due recognition that their place in the pecking order is at the top, Leos are relatively problem-free as children. However, if their leadership is questioned or others fail to fall in with their way of doing things, they can be extremely bossy and

this tendency can be positively sublimated by solo sports or the starring role in the school play, or simply by being given greater responsibility and a good "talking to" that appeals to the Leo sense of pride and honor. Most Leos, however, are naturally good citizens and may eventually seek prominent roles in their local government or become leading lights in Parent-Teacher Associations.

If by any chance praise and encouragement are not forthcoming, Leo children may just give up. Their natural indolence persuades them that the fight isn't worth the trouble. Often their achievements are in direct proportion to the high or low expectations of their teachers or parents.

If their life is hard, deprived of treats, vacations and luxuries, Leos will feel diminished as people and personally insulted by Fate. Though little demoralizes the sunny Leo for very long, they find physical or financial hardship difficult to bear, and they need extra love and support then. What gets them through is a dream, something to aim for.

Famous Leos

Her Majesty Queen Elizabeth the Queen Mother

Napoleon Bonaparte

Robert Mitchum

Madonna

Robert Redford

Fidel Castro

Leonard Bernstein

Emily Brontë

Coco Chanel

Claude Debussy

Cecil B. DeMille

Robert de Niro

Mick Jagger

George Bernard Shaw

Benito Mussolini

Percy Bysshe Shelley

Sir Alexander Fleming

Dustin Hoffman

Carl G. Jung

Guy de Maupassant

Madonna

Napoleon Bonaparte

THE SUN IN VIRGO

(August 24 – September 22)

Sun Sign: VIRGO

Sign: THE VIRGIN

Ruling Planet: MERCURY

Gender: FEMININE

Element: EARTH

Quality: MUTABLE

Compatibility: PISCES

AND SOME AQUARIANS

Non-compatibility: LEO

AND SAGITTARIUS

Sun Sign Virgos are not necessarily virginal, of course, but they often have the quiet, unsophisticated air of an inexperienced person, which can be deceptive. They are meticulous, tidy and thorough. Typical Sun Sign Virgos keep their own counsel; and although they are frequently profound thinkers, they are essentially practical, with few impossible dreams. These enormously hard-working people are the first to roll up their sleeves and get on with the job – while unrealistic Geminis or hot-air Arians fail to carry through their grand plans. By contrast, it is the Virgos who keep records and undertake research to put flesh on the bones of the ambitious projects of others. The Virgoan social style is quiet and unassuming. A typical Virgoan will never interrupt and rarely holds the floor for more than a few minutes. They listen very carefully, however, and when they do voice an opinion, it is often startlingly intelligent, cutting right through to the heart of the matter. Because Virgos are ruled by Mercury, they are excellent at putting two and two together and seeing connections and inferences others may miss. Their memories are formidable and they can suddenly recall an essential reference from a book they read years ago. This enables them to make the connection with a current project, and the problem is solved. Virgos are often very witty – with a dry, sometimes surrealistic, sense of humor. They have others in fits of laughter. They can also be brilliant mimics, due to their ability to quietly note every mannerism and characteristic of their subject.

And Virgoan jokes linger in the mind longer than most others.

Negative Virgoan traits include a capacity for endless worry, which can cloud their own lives unnecessarily. It also irritates more happy-go-lucky signs. Not only do Virgos fret, they can also be first-class naggers – carping relentlessly about other people's failings and sloppiness. Badly aspected Virgos can be cold, over-analytical and obsessed with detail. They can become totally bogged down with trivia, delighting in what others consider boring facts. At work, for example, Virgos may wax lyrical about new filing systems, and they can be fussy hobbyists, collecting sports statistics or matchboxes. They seem obsessed with routines. Everything must always be done in the same way and in the same order. This type of Virgo will eat the same food day in and day out, go to the same vacation spots year after year. They fret constantly about spending money and keep a record of every purchase in tiny, neat handwriting. Everything must be just so, or they can suffer real distress. Virgos are great ones for inventing rules on the "just in case" principle. For example, they may insist that no one takes drinks into their study in case some gets spilled onto their computer. It makes sense, but it does not seem to occur to Virgos that adults can take that risk. Most people enjoy a cup of coffee while working long hours at the keyboard, but this is not the extreme type of Virgo, who hedges his or her life around with a host of such restricting rules in order to feel safe.

APPEARANCE

Virgos have good bone structure and are often highly photogenic. They are attractive, with beautiful eyes that sparkle with intelligence. They can be vain. Their glossy, thick hair frequently rises from a "widow's peak." When young, they can seem prematurely old, with a wary, watchful expression. But once safely in their mid-30s, they seem to look much the same for quite a long time.

meditation would be good for them. So would going for long walks in the evening and, of course, following a careful diet. Virgos are particularly sensitive to drugs of all types, whether they are prescribed by their doctor or are herbal concoctions, nicotine or alcohol. In such cases, it is sometimes not enough just to cut down. They may have to abstain completely for the sake of their well-being. Virgos are notably fussy about their health, and often carry their

The natural life is best for earthy Virgos. They need plenty of fresh air to blow away the cobwebs and rebalance their energies

It is often said that typical Sun Sign Virgos have protruding stomachs, which can be their only rotund feature. However, some types are very angular. Sometimes the first impression they give is of slow, deliberate movements. Curiously, many Virgos have a slightly unbalanced way of walking, perhaps with a barely perceptible limp. Once animated, though, they can leap into a higher gear, becoming very nervy and quick.

favorite remedies, vitamins and even their own special brand of mineral water around with them.

The natural life is best for earthy Virgos. They need plenty of fresh air to blow away the cobwebs and rebalance their energies. Many choose to be vegetarians, which suits their nervy digestions – although they must remember to include a wide variety of foods in their diet, and take extra vitamin B if necessary. Homeopathic and naturopathic remedies often suit Virgos, and the process of tracking down the right therapies for them appeals to their love of detective work.

HEALTH

All that worry can play havoc with Virgoan digestions. They are often martyrs to their stomachs, and many suffer from Irritable Bowel Syndrome – which greatly embarrasses and inconveniences them. Many also suffer from food intolerances or full-blown allergies. In this case, they should seek good advice from reputable nutritionists. Usually the only answer to their health problems is to learn to unwind. Yoga or

CAREER

Virgos make excellent nurses because they are practical, calm, disciplined and cheerful. Their quiet confidence and efficiency can be very comforting, and their quick wit can lift their patients' flagging spirits. They make caring and effective alternative therapists, too, and are often

columns of figures and computer work. They make superb programmers and are the natural accountants of the zodiac – they can carry the details of all their clients' accounts in their heads. They can also make highly efficient tax inspectors and private detectives, as long as the work isn't too dangerous.

Dogged, analytical and intellectual, Virgos make skilled and inspired research scientists. They rarely let their hearts rule their heads, and some types would show little sentiment toward laboratory animals.

Traditionally associated with the time of harvest, Virgos are happy planning and cooking meals; and they are often found in the catering trade.

Perhaps uncharacteristically, Virgos, who are normally so introverted, can frequently be found in

involved in researching their subject in great depth to add to their knowledge. Virgos also make excellent counselors or social workers. Some love providing nourishing food for the less fortunate members of society.

They love making a contribution, and being of service to any group or corporation, to which they will be unfailingly loyal. They are, however, better as members of a team than as bosses. A Virgo in charge can easily become tediously nit-picking and hypercritical, forever double-checking the work of others and waiting to pounce on any evidence of sloppiness. Untidiness and tardiness are anathema to strongly aspected Virgos, and they can be completely intolerant of other ways of doing things. Like their fellow Earth Sign, Taurus, they love tradition, convention and rules and regulations for their own sake, even when these are outdated and inefficient. Virgos like analyzing and collating and are totally at home with

the theater. They appreciate the chance to cast off their inhibitions and assume another personality on stage. Many actors are actually shy and retiring people. They come to life only when they can hide behind the mask of the character they play. This suits Virgos completely.

Virgos have strong opinions, but sometimes hesitate to express them, and often fear attempting something new – in case it fails and they are thought stupid or incompetent. They can be excellent business partners, however, even in creative endeavors such as writing or computer graphics, where they will provide the common sense and attention to detail that may escape their more unworldly partners. They are particularly good at providing the facts and figures for a book or television documentary, while more creative colleagues translate them into words or images.

Many Virgos are obsessive workaholics, condemning themselves to a life chained to their desk, and ignoring the outside world. Relationships, health and endless opportunities pass them by as they live in constant tunnel vision, totally absorbed in their work. Conversely, there is a type of extremely slothful, unmotivated Virgo, whose self-worth is too low for them to attempt anything without a crippling fear of failure – so they just do nothing and drift through life.

RELATIONSHIPS

Though they are reliable, responsible, eminently sensible and can be happy in a stable relationship, Virgos are often very difficult to live with. These fussy, critical people can make life a misery for more relaxed souls by constant complaints about tidiness or anything else.

Conversely, there is a very untidy and chaotic Virgo, who happily lives in apparent chaos, though they usually know, roughly, where the important things are. Curiously, even this type has an element of Virgoan neatness about them – despite the litter. This type is happiest living the single life, with a small circle of like-minded friends who drop in from time to time for a chat. They love surfing the net, which satisfies their craving for accumulating facts and having a vicarious social life at the same time – and all without moving from their chairs.

If they marry, many Virgos do so more than once, perhaps because they have to learn the hard way all about sharing and tolerance, and because they easily tire of the routine of living with one person. They can be tense in close relationships, which can badly upset their sex lives, and makes it hard for them to become truly intimate with those they love. Some Virgos prefer others to take the lead sexually, although they soon show an aptitude for experimentation and excitement in bed.

Virgos can be irritable with those around them, particularly those who are more physical or devil-may-care. They tend to bring their work home, which does not make for jolly family evenings. However, they take their family responsibilities seriously and can be solicitous for the welfare of wives and families. Although careful with money, they can be generous, and usually remember birthdays and anniversaries. Some extreme Virgos, however, are the penny-pinching type – those who would put the grasping sort of Cancers to

Compatibility in Relationships

Aries
Quick-fire Arians have a certain allure for more timid Virgos, but prove too combustible in the long term.

Cancer
Loving, sympathetic Cancers can hit it off with sensible Virgos, but they will cause too many scenes.

Libra
Romantic, sensitive Libras can make amenable partners for Virgos, but they may lack the staying power.

Capricorn
Virgos appreciate the Goat's measured approach to life and love, but even they need more adventurousness.

Taurus
Both being Earth Signs, they understand each other well, but life can lack that all-important spark.

Leo
Virgos may love to bask in reflected Leonine glory, but can find Leo's overbearing manner ultimately offputting.

Scorpio
Though attracted sexually, straightforward Virgos are scared off by the Scorpio's sharp tongue.

Aquarius
Virgos often admire Aquarians greatly, but their lifestyles are too divergent for lasting bonds to develop.

Gemini
They will enjoy each other's company, but frivolous and flighty Geminis can frighten Virgos away.

Virgo
Though safe, this can be a deeply dull combination. Two Virgos will rarely have a sparkling love life.

Sagittarius
True Virgos are often horrified by Sagittarian fecklessness and their capacity to live for the moment.

Pisces
Something about loving, needy Pisceans can bring out the best in the more supportive, well-grounded Virgo.

shame – and they may live bleak lives and cause misery to those around them. This extreme type may also invent strange ground rules for those living under the same roof, and they will force them to obey, no matter how inconvenient it may be. This form of control mania arises out of fear of disorder.

Virgos may find parenthood difficult. The demonstrative motherhood of Cancers and the robust fathering of a solid Taurus are not for them. Virgos find expressing emotion hard, and are often too absorbed in their world of facts, figures and fussing to give much of their time to their youngsters.

It is only when children are capable of rational thought that Virgoan parents truly come into their own, helping their children to learn the rules of life. Later, when the children are on the verge of independence and young adulthood, Virgoan parents are more than happy to help with finances, find a suitable mortgage, explain the intricacies of pensions and insurance plans, and scrutinize the small print of any financial or contractual agreement. They can make far better grandparents than parents. By that time of life, they may well have learned to relax and to enjoy the spontaneity of having very young children around them.

IDEAL PARTNER

Virgos can find most close relationships something of a trial. But if near opposites attract, they will go for deep, dark Scorpians, whose intensity adds color to their more plodding lives, and whose sexuality can encourage them to lose their inhibitions. Gentle Pisceans, with their soft emotions, can make Virgos realize that they can relax and enjoy home life – although both can be their own worst enemies at times. Some types of Aquarian also bring out the best in Virgo, and madcap Arians can bring a totally different energy into their lives. Here, the relationship may be too fiery to survive, but it will be fun while it lasts. Leos, with their love of display, can help Virgos to discover the joy and laughter they find so elusive. And though Leonine extravagance can seriously worry some Virgoans, the more relaxed of their type can fare well enough with Leo.

Like fellow Venusians of the bovine sort, gentle Virgoans can be disconcerted by banner-waving Aquarians; although they may enjoy deep discussions with them about more serious issues. And again – as with Taureans – the energy and innocence of a Sagittarius may be initially appealing, but the Sagittarian lifestyle is ultimately too unpredictable for steady Virgo.

THE VIRGOAN CHILD

Always fretting and worrying, Virgoan children need to have their self-esteem constantly reinforced. They need to be told they can succeed, and encouraged to be adventurous. Otherwise, they will simply become increasingly timorous and insecure. They need to have their expectations notched up, to be told time and time again that it is a good idea to aim for the top, to have dreams and goals and to fight for them. At the same time, however, goal-setting should be realistic, or they will see through it and never make any attempt at rising to the challenge. The best thing to do is to encourage them to go for gold in their chosen field, or in a subject that is close to Virgoan hearts, rather than forcing them to compete in unappealing subjects. They may enjoy taking part in the school play, or joining a team sport – they can also be extremely loyal team supporters – or helping in an administrative capacity with special interest clubs or charities.

Virgos are neat, tidy children on the whole. They may not present the most creative or promising work, but it will always be legible and clean. They do have a lazy streak, though, but prefer to be kept busy at some clearly defined task where they can see they are making progress. They like being told what to do, rather than taking the initiative; although they should be actively encouraged to think for themselves, perhaps through puzzles and quiz games. They are better at slow, steady course-work and do not usually shine when it comes to sitting examinations.

They can often be found deeply absorbed in the local library, while more boisterous children are kicking a ball around. Because they tend to be tidy, do their homework on time and dislike danger, upheaval or anything that disrupts the normal routine, others may think of them as prigs. Sometimes they are, but in reality they just like a quiet life – making small steps for man, rather than giant leaps for mankind.

Famous Virgos

Queen Elizabeth I
Greta Garbo
Peter Sellers ·
Jesse James
B.B. King
Agatha Christie
Sean Connery
Stephen King
Prince Albert
Yasser Arafat
Lauren Bacall

Queen Elizabeth I

Greta Garbo

Anton Bruckner
Edgar Rice Burroughs
John Cage ·
Maurice Chevalier
James Fenimore Cooper
Antonin Dvorak
Gustave Holst
H.G. Wells
Mary Shelley
Aristotle Onasis

THE SUN IN LIBRA

(September 23 – October 23)

Sun Sign: LIBRA

Sign: THE SCALES

Ruling Planet: VENUS

Gender: MASCULINE

Element: AIR

Quality: CARDINAL

Compatibility: SAGITTARIUS, AQUARIUS AND TAURUS

Non-compatibility: SCORPIO, CANCER AND PISCES

Sun Sign Libras make peace and harmony a priority in any situation in which they find themselves. Natural arbiters and diplomats, they are constantly seeking balance, as exemplified by their sign of the Scales.

Libras are pleasant and companionable, friendly, sunny souls whose ready smile and firm handshake makes them popular and trusted members of society. They are open and unquestioning, attractive and confident. Libras are hard workers, and their search for balance enables them to play hard as well. They often indulge in several hobbies to offset the demands of their careers.

Libras are personable and smart. They are attractive in appearance. Even those odd Libras who are not overconcerned about choosing the right color dress or the most noseworthy aftershave are still clean and presentable. They like to be surrounded by a certain amount of order and tidiness, although they are not fanatical about it; in fact, anything overdone or "over the top" is alien to the Libran temperament. The axiom "Everything in moderation" was probably invented by a Libra. They may occasionally go wild, but their first concerns on "the morning after" are to apologize for any bad behavior and then to set themselves to working off their excesses in the gym.

Conversely, Libras are famous for their hesitation, dithering and inability to make decisions. Sometimes this image is justified; but mostly Libras are simply cautious, preferring to wait and consider their options before committing themselves to an idea, belief or relationship. On the other hand, they can be gullible and credulous, falling for ridiculous schemes. In extreme cases, they can become members of somewhat sinister cults, simply because it is not in their nature to question the motives of others, believing them to be just as open as themselves. "What you see is what you get" is true of most Libras; although their friendliness may be more superficial than it appears. They can give the impression of being totally fascinated by your company, only to have difficulty remembering who you are a couple of weeks later.

Libras are undemanding and "laid back," often to the point of appearing to lack all ambition or drive. But how influential this trait is depends very much on their chart as a whole. True, they are usually happy to take orders and be part of a team; but they have a strong head for business, and can reveal a surprisingly steely streak if their livelihood is threatened. Most need the security of a regular job and a happy home, always seeking to find partners who will balance their own nature. Libras are wildly romantic, though, and sometimes pursue their dreams rather than settle for what they have.

Libras can be unsettling: they are often inconsistent, even contradictory characters. Although they hate rudeness, they can be disconcertingly brash and blunt. Though extremely restless, they don't often express it in a physical way. With such charming people as Libras, it is easy to forget what the symbolism of the Scales implies: balance is transitory, and imbalance, if only slight, is in fact the usual state of affairs. Libras find that life is a constant effort to make the two sides level and make sense of its inherent duality.

APPEARANCE

Sun Sign Libras are rarely unattractive. They are usually handsome or pretty, and both sexes can have charming dimples. They have sweet, open faces with laughing eyes and a devastating smile. Sometimes people fall in love with them at first

the occasional allergy can bring them out in itchy rashes, especially on the face and upper chest.

Libras should learn to pace themselves and do nothing to excess. They should compensate for a trip to the wine bar by working out or going for a long walk in the country. Libras need to drink plenty of water to flush out the toxins from their

Sometimes people fall in love with them at first sight, believing, often wrongly, that the Libran smile-to-end-all-smiles was just for them

sight, believing, often wrongly, that the Libran smile-to-end-all-smiles was just for them. Libras tend to be rounded, though not often plump, rather than angular or skinny. Even overweight Libras have an aura of Venusian charm and beauty. Their hair waves or curls, and is professionally coiffured in the latest, chic style. Even the poorer Libra has an eye for classy outfits, perhaps finding them in thrift shops or at the back of a friend's wardrobe, from where they are charmed into their own. They have an innate sense of style, adding a personal touch to classic suits or evening clothes that everyone is sure to remember.

kidneys, and cut down on salty foods which tend to encourage water retention and high blood pressure. They also need to counterbalance their bouts of frantic activity with yoga, meditation or aromatherapy for the sake of their minds, bodies and spirits. Indeed, Libras need to recognize that humans are more than just physical bodies. For this reason, holistic therapies work very well for them, and spiritual exercises are important for their total well-being.

CAREER

Gregarious, amenable Libras dislike working alone; but equally, they are not fond of suffering under a rod of iron. They like lighthearted offices with a relaxed atmosphere, lots of banter and fun, and appreciate being left to themselves to work at their own pace. Their surroundings are important: gloomy or ugly buildings adversely affect their mental and physical well-being, while touches of style and luxury bring out the best in them. Careers in glamorous industries often appeal

HEALTH

With their roller-coaster emotions, Libras tend to suffer from nervous stomachs and, sometimes, ulcers. They tend to overindulge in food and wine, and that can lead to kidney and bladder problems. Stress also results in classic Libran headaches and migraines. Too much rich food and be thoroughgoing law students, but once they have to present a strong argument as defense or prosecuting counsel, they may be lost. For the same reason, Libran jurors can show a tendency to defer verdicts.

Libras make excellent listeners and are good at giving well-thought-out advice. They love dealing with the public and are ideal for customer services and public relations, and as personal assistants. Many Libras are not particularly ambitious on their own behalf, but they are proud to be associated with sucessful or famous people and organizations.

Though usually steady, Librans can sometimes sulk; and it is not unknown for them to be argumentative. They will assert that black is white, but never allow others to get away with sweeping statements. Libras can, in fact, be almost as nitpicking as Virgos when the mood takes them. They are logical, have a healthy regard for facts and figures and are rarely unrealistic and vague – all of which makes them perfect civil servants, planners and designers.

to Sun Sign Libras – fashion, theatre, television and modeling all provide them with ideal opportunities to express themselves in stylish ways.

Libras make good diplomats, professional mediators and counselors, but can easily become distressed by too much naked aggression. They often find it a terrible shock to discover that there is such a thing as real evil in the world.

Libras are superb at comparing and contrasting – seeing all aspects of a problem or situation and all sides of an argument – which can make them excellent, objective researchers, assessors and evaluators. But they can find it difficult to come down firmly on one side or the other. Libras may

RELATIONSHIPS

Libras often think they are much better at handling relationships than they actually are. They see themselves as so urbane, pleasant and approachable that it comes as a shock when engagements are broken or friendships and marriages fail. Often they are the last people to notice that their partners are flirting with someone else, or the first to miss the hints of tension in a close friendship. Libras can sail through life, unaware of the iceberg that looms closer and never realizing that the name of their ship is Titanic.

Those born under the sign of the Scales may be moody and liable to extreme ups and downs, which can be very difficult to live with. They can be their old charming selves – on a high, laughing in a crowd – when the life suddenly seems to drain out of them, leaving them mean-spirited and sulky. Similarly, their energy levels can soar or plummet within a very short space of time, leaving loved ones with the problem of figuring out what approach to take. They may become too exhausted to go out on a long-awaited special date; and if it's their turn to walk the dog, they might well duck out of it. Yet how can anyone complain about Libras when they can't help working so hard? The Libran attitude is one of surprise if others feel let down, abandoned or lonely, when they see themselves as essentially such decent people.

Loneliness is something a Libra finds almost impossible to cope with. Even when leading a carefree single life, perhaps playing the field, they surround themselves with a cheery crowd – the more the merrier – and barely have a night at home alone. They can keep up a hectic social life for several nights in a row, then suddenly collapse in a heap or cozy up with a good book, the television and supper on a tray. Some Libras manage to keep their social and home lives completely separate, never inviting their friends around but always meeting them in restaurants, bars and clubs — but this is an extreme type.

The overriding purpose of the single Libra is to find his or her soulmate – which they do, repeatedly! Always romantic and whole-hearted, they love the chase, the chocolates and roses, even writing poetry and arranging expensive surprises. They make romance their business, and many a heart flutters in return. Libras really know how to flatter, and will appear to be giving their entire attention to someone – even going so far as to focus their entire lives on their loved one. In many cases, though, they are fooling themselves as well as the object of their passion. Above all, Libras tend to be in love with the idea of love, rather than with a real

Compatibility in Relationships

Aries
They may have fun while dating, but living together soon shows that self-centered Arians are too much for Libras.

Cancer
Initial attraction may not last: Libras are too uncomfortable with typical Cancerian outbursts.

Libra
Dating and sex will be fun but with two Libras together nothing will ever be settled too readily.

Capricorn
Libras' love of wining and dining may upset Capricornian respect for nest-eggs. They have some basic differences.

Taurus
Libras can fall for beautiful and placid Taureans. This is often a lasting match made in the heavens.

Leo
Libras often feel flattered by magnanimous Leonine attention, but the gloss soon wears off.

Scorpio
Straightforward Libras find Machiavellian Scorpios hard to understand but easy to fall in to bed with.

Aquarius
Libras can easily become acolytes of driven Aquarians, but find them too intense for loving life partnerships.

Gemini
In many ways Geminis and Libras are similar, but the Twins' guiles can ultimately prove unappealing.

Virgo
Socially, these signs may hit it off, but cracks soon appear in the relationship because of Virgoan inhibition.

Sagittarius
With one bound they will be free. Sagittarians offer Libras the adventure and daring they crave.

Pisces
Truly difficult Pisceans make life hell for easygoing Libras, although they can get on well at first.

person. Once committed, though, they have no difficulty rekindling those early rapturous feelings with candlelit dinners and romantic early nights in bed.

It is no use expecting Sun Sign Libras to be too sympathetic, despite their charm and apparent warmth. Anyone who pours out their hearts to them will find themselves asked how they contributed to their problems, and what grief they caused the others in the story. It can be a terrible letdown to find the gorgeous, charming Libra suddenly not taking your side. In family relationships this can often seem very near betrayal, when what is expected is partisanship and loyalty. This can sometimes seem like lack of courage, and male Libras can sometimes be seen, rightly or wrongly, as wimps.

Many Libras are, however, kind and co-operative at home; although stress and uncertainty can make them bad-tempered. They will go out of their way to make the home a haven, where peace and harmony prevail; but when teenage children inevitably begin to rebel, they find it hard to cope, and may overreact and worry excessively. Libras love fairness, and as long as they are treated equitably, life with them is easy. Their rule is "Do as you would be done by." They are eager to have a wide variety of friends, possibly from different ethnic and religious backgrounds. Libras thrive on diversity, respecting the right of the individual, and they hate racism, sexism and any other form of prejudice. They are, at heart, politically and spiritually idealistic.

When faced with any unpleasantness, Libras react either by sticking their head in the sand and pretending it isn't happening, or by trying to smooth things over. Sometimes they can be surprisingly tough, though, really laying it on the line with offenders and demanding that they make positive changes to their behavior.

As parents, Libras tend to be kind and imaginative, but not always deeply involved or even particularly sensitive. They can be too superficial and flippant for many children, especially Cancers, Pisceans and some Scorpios. Nevertheless, they will always make an effort to be sociable with their friends, and will fill the house with laughter, fun and boisterous family pets.

in Libras, although Libras can find all that remorseless energy too demanding, and may need to get away from time to time – just to restore their delicate, internal balance.

Libras are also fascinated with the glamour and sophistication of sultry Scorpios, although they may find Scorpios' strange moods perplexing and intimidating. Many Libras should stay away from the more intensely emotional – and occasionally explosive – kind of Scorpio. The more clinging Water Signs, Cancers and Pisces, can make too many emotional demands and scenes for Libras, who, above all, seek peace and harmony.

IDEAL PARTNER

Romantic Libras can get along with almost anyone, from any zodiacal sign – at least to begin with. They tend to like the enthusiasm and unpredictability of Aquarians, whose love of causes (lost or otherwise) may well add the depth that Libras often feel they lack in their life – although they can find the more extreme and overopinionated Aquarians a bit of a turn-off. Peace-loving, gentle Taureans can bring out a Libra's more romantic streak, and many contented marriages between the two signs do last. Happy, adventurous and optimistic Sagittarians tend to bring out the best

THE LIBRAN CHILD

Children born under the sign of the Scales will try very hard to fit in and be accepted. They are eager to wear the latest clothes and own the best computers. Charming and lively, they appeal to their peers and adults alike, and rarely have serious behavioral problems or learning difficulties. Because they are bright and intelligent, Libras often find schoolwork easy; although they sometimes shrink from thinking too deeply about religion, philosophy or the spiritual side of life. They seek approval above all: anything that marks them out as being different is viewed with suspicion; although they can be induced to join unusual groups and societies.

Famous Libras

Augustus Caesar
Edgar Degas
Michael Douglas
M.de Cervantes
Charlton Heston
Jimmy Carter
Sarah Bernhardt
Georges Clemenceau
Montgomery Clift
Dwight D. Eisenhower
F. Scott Fitzgerald
George Gershwin
John Lennon
Eugene O'Neill
Giuseppe Verdi
Lenny Bruce
Oscar Wilde
Bela Lugosi
Derek Jacobi
Arthur Rimbaud

John Lennon

Oscar Wilde

THE SUN IN SCORPIO

(October 24 – November 22)

Sun Sign: SCORPIO

Sign: THE SCORPION

Ruling Planet: MARS AND

PLUTO

Gender: FEMININE

Element: WATER

Quality: FIXED

Compatibility: TAURUS, VIRGO

AND LIBRA

Non-compatibility:

ARIES, LEO

AND SAGITTARIUS

Sun Sign Scorpios are energetic, passionate and exciting. They have a bad reputation among traditional astrologers, but fortunately few live up to their somewhat unsavory image. Most satisfy themselves with being forceful and fascinating, dramatically sweeping through the lives of others like mini-tornadoes. Of course, there are those born under the sign of the Scorpion who seem shy and retiring, but they are few and far between, and even then they will tend to harbor deep, dark secrets. This sign is nothing if not mysterious.

Most Scorpios have a strong sex drive, which may express itself in endless flirting or even power games. Often, though, it is sublimated in a quest for the Great Mission In Life, for finding their personal Holy Grail or plumbing the mysteries of life. Ruled by Pluto, God of the Underworld, Scorpios are concerned with esoteric matters, with the paranormal, mysticism and the afterlife, and often passionately believe in reincarnation. This is not always as negative as it may sound: Scorpios understand the concept that death is always followed by rebirth, and they can rise like the phoenix from disastrous events in their own lives to start again with enormous, positive energy. Disappointment, bereavement, bankruptcy, illness and natural disasters can depress and seem, at the time, to demolish them, but not for long. Soon they are back on their feet, building new lives for themselves and others with amazing cheerfulness and genuine joy at being given the opportunity for a fresh start.

Sun Sign Scorpios have a marked tendency toward jealousy and possessiveness. Profoundly secretive by nature, they often disturb others with their air of mystery, which can sometimes seem just a little contrived. Scorpios are very theatrical, and can use every trick in the book to get noticed at social gatherings: they love to be outrageous and to shock, which they often do very successfully – just for the hell of it.

However, there is a sting in the tail with Scorpios. The full Scorpian fury can be unsettling enough – after all, their other ruler is fiery, aggressive Mars – but to be at the receiving end of their cold, penetrating sarcasm is to be upset for days. Many Scorpios train themselves to be masters of the put-down that is devastatingly witty, but very hurtful. Both male and female Scorpios can be quite caustic when they put their mind to it.

This is a sign of extremes, of black and white, dark and light; this is often reflected in the ups and downs of their lives. These people can be wildly successful one year and bankrupt the next; although it is a process that is likely to be repeated in a curiously predictable cycle. Similarly, they can be utterly loyal and true lovers, but great passion can rapidly turn to hatred and maybe a desire for revenge.

APPEARANCE

Once seen, rarely forgotten, Sun Sign Scorpios are always striking, whether they are stunningly beautiful or not. They have a magnetic, forceful quality which makes people stare – although they may not be sure why. Most Scorpios have a habit of staring penetratingly, and of frowning while listening to others talk. They can move slowly, as

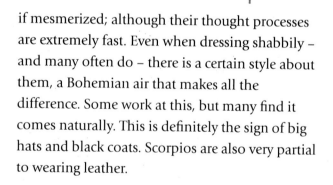

if mesmerized; although their thought processes are extremely fast. Even when dressing shabbily – and many often do – there is a certain style about them, a Bohemian air that makes all the difference. Some work at this, but many find it comes naturally. This is definitely the sign of big hats and black coats. Scorpios are also very partial to wearing leather.

HEALTH

For Scorpios, moderation in anything is for wimps. They throw themselves into orgies of eating and drinking that would shame a Taurean, and often think that they somehow avert the day of reckoning by doing it in style – drinking only champagne, for example, or eating only the best bitter chocolate. But whatever the quality of their indulgences, their lifestyle will catch up with them (usually sooner rather than later) in the shape of stomach trouble, chronic constipation, gall stones, liver and kidney problems, even diabetes. A shocking health scare, however, can be an abrupt turning point for Scorpio, whose ability to live at either end of the spectrum can turn them overnight into the most zealous, proselytizing non-smoking teetotaler or the strictest vegan. Similarly, and just as easily, they can go from sybaritic couch potato to marathon runner – and enjoy both lifestyles with equal gusto.

Traditionally, Scorpios are supposed to suffer from genital problems, and of course some do. But in many cases this is transposed to lower back pain, often caused by too much sitting around and weight gain in middle age.

CAREER

"The Devil finds work for idle hands" was never truer than in the case of an out-of-work Scorpio, whose enormous energy needs to be positively channeled or they may turn to dubious ways of passing the time, for instance, playing around with the Ouija board. However, once a Scorpio is emotionally engaged, there are few more energetic or ambitious workers. They are eager to throw themselves into what is right for them, often working through the night without any idea of the time. It is often said that they are fanatical money-grabbers. They certainly have that potential, but they see money mostly as an outward and visible sign of their dominance in their chosen field, of dramatic success compared to lesser mortals. If their work does not appeal to them, though, they can easily be sloppy and lazy, given to coming back to the office late after lunch.

Scorpios are traditionally associated with jobs that require delving or uncovering secrets, such as mining and detective work; but few actually take up such professions. However, Scorpios tend to have more interesting, even peculiar, jobs than most because of their fascination with anything deep and dark. For example, they can be criminologists, forensic scientists working on murder cases or even writers of detective fiction. Many carve out successful careers in the police force. They can be drawn to "alternative" studies, such as parapsychology, the occult, ancient Egyptian mysteries or piecing together the truth about religion. Many are passionate about conspiracy theories. Even if they have humdrum everyday jobs, Scorpios tend to follow hobbies that reflect their unusual, even bizarre, interests; and they may often find more ordinary people too boring for words.

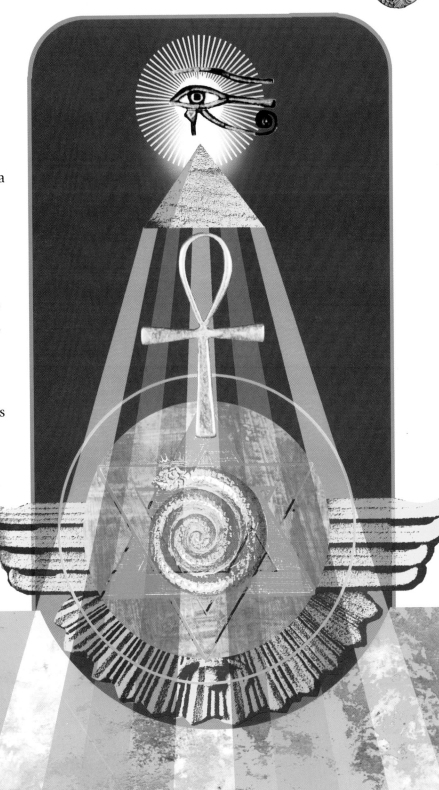

The Scorpian need to go deep also makes them excellent hypnotherapists, psychotherapists and past-life therapists. Scorpios are at home with the unconscious mind, and are less fearful than most people of discovering its dark secrets. They can also find ingenious ways of coping with them. Some Scorpios make powerful psychics or mediums.

Not surprisingly, Scorpios can be rather disruptive in the workplace. They take every little criticism so personally and react with such black and brooding moods – perhaps even flying into dramatic rages – that other, more timid souls will steer clear of them, even when teamwork suffers. They see everything – status, pay and perks – as a reflection of their own worth, and can make formidable rivals. If crossed, Scorpios can be very unforgiving.

They can make demanding bosses, but if their emotions are fully engaged, they can be surprisingly sympathetic and loyal to employees, taking any of their problems or setbacks as a personal challenge. Many Scorpios find life easier when self-employed, although they do like to have regular contact with others. They also need to feel that they are making their mark on the world. Too much time alone can make Scorpios very gloomy.

RELATIONSHIPS

Intense, sexual and demanding, Scorpios are not easy to live with. They are not above using sex as a form of control, although they don't indulge in emotional blackmail as much as Cancers. Many Scorpios are much more interested in the image of sexual conquests than in the act itself.

Depending very much on other factors in the individual chart, Scorpios can throw all their energies into chasing often highly unsuitable people, and will continue to pursue them when it is obvious that there is really no point any more. They won't take no for an answer, refusing to believe that anyone could reject someone as fascinating and sexy as themselves. There is another element in this scenario, though. Scorpios often believe in fate or karma, and once they've got it in their heads that the object of their affection is meant for them, they ignore every indication to the contrary. Because of their tendency to use sexuality to control others, Scorpios see seduction as a form of possession, and believe that, however reluctant the object of their desire may be, one day their view will prevail. Often, though, they are not as promiscuous as their reputation suggests and yearn to be involved in a passionate love affair that will transcend the humdrum world.

Scorpios can be very vindictive and vengeful. Never expect to walk away from a romance with a Scorpio unscathed. Not all Scorpios will necessarily bring down their full wrath upon those who have offended them – though they will fantasize about it.

They make demanding parents and can put too much pressure on their children. On the lighter side, though, they can be rather witty. Sometimes, Scorpios find it hard to give their children the necessary space to be themselves, and can be sticklers for tradition and discipline. Even so, they can learn to relax and be fun parents; it is a good idea for them to participate in lots of activities with their children in order to lighten up.

Compatibility in Relationships

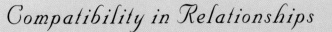

Aries
Arians may bring a breath of fresh air into the claustrophobic world of the Scorpio, but they can be too demanding.

Cancer
Devoted Cancers are too normal for quirky Scorpios, and their emotional highs and lows get short shrift.

Libra
Scorpios often fascinate Libras, and they can enjoy very passionate sex, but Scorpios are just too dark.

Capricorn
Capricornian repression has little appeal for sexually adventurous Scorpios and may lead to frostiness.

Taurus
Perhaps curiously, Scorpio's opposite sign can prove very appealing and make a long-term relationship work well.

Leo
Relationships will be passionate and sex exciting, but Scorpios do not take kindly to Leonine attempts to dominate.

Scorpio
Fellow Scorpios often get on well, having the same unusual interests, but may fall out of love too easily.

Aquarius
Scorpios often respect the causes espoused by Aquarians, but can find them too involved in "boring" politics.

Gemini
Flighty, wily Geminis can charm Scorpios – but not for long. In the end, they're just too shallow for Scorpio.

Virgo
The more sociable Virgos can be complementary partners, but not if they embody Virgoan obsessive tidiness.

Sagittarius
Scorpios find these wild children very charming, but do not go for the insecurity or lack of permanent lifestyle.

Pisces
Both signs are complex and intense with extreme demands. Lasting and loving relationships are unlikely.

IDEAL PARTNER

Scorpios, with their love of drama, may often be attracted to their own sign for that reason alone. It rarely works out, though, because of the Scorpio's temperamental nature and all the scenes that go with it. There also may not be enough real love.

Underneath a Scorpio's theatrical exterior is someone who just wants to be loved and made to feel normal. Their polar sign, Taurus, can give them just what they crave – material and emotional security. Virgos, too, share the ability to calm Scorpios and make them relax, often winning them over with their wit and charm. Well-balanced Libras also share the capacity to humor Scorpios and see beyond the image to the real, needy person inside. Arians, Leos and Sagittarians, however, can be too caught up in themselves to take the time to understand the complex Scorpio and are more likely to compete for the limelight. Scorpian leanings toward the world of the unexplained can make them gravitate towards the more psychic Pisceans, but it rarely works out because Scorpian intensity combined with Piscean emotionality is not a good recipe for enduring love.

THE SCORPIAN CHILD

Scorpian children are natural loners, brooders and worriers. They like to sit alone pondering over adult questions, and that can alarm their siblings and parents alike. They can become very religious at an early age; and although there may be nothing at all wrong with the belief system itself, they should be weaned away – gently and uncritically – into more active pursuits,

and encouraged to play with other children. It goes against the nature of Sun Sign Scorpios to be completely open and "natural." They will always have their secrets and dark passions. Sometimes it does more harm than good to try to persuade a Scorpian child to join in more boisterous pursuits. So – on the principle that if you can't beat them, join them – it might be a good idea to accompany them to the Egyptian galleries in the museum and investigate the mummies together. You could also put them in charge of the Halloween festivities, which could have been invented for Scorpios. If they are at all inclined to take up an active hobby or sport, it is unlikely to be run of the mill.

When distressed or unwell, Scorpios tend to go very quiet, retreating into their own world, to the bewilderment and hurt of their loved ones. They can bottle up all sorts of profound feelings; sometimes it even comes hard to let their parents know what they really want for their birthday. Somehow they just can't articulate something passionately desired – even while knowing that if they say nothing, they are unlikely to get it. For their happiness and future health, they should be encouraged to open up and share at least some of their secret hopes and fears.

Although Scorpios often feel low and retreat into a gloom, this state of affairs tends to be short-lived, and they soon spring back into life. Because of their enormous reserves of energy and courage, and also their capacity to recover quickly from both mental and physical illnesses and setbacks, Scorpios are excellent people to have around in tough times.

Once again, it is their underlying conviction that Fate is on their side that sees them through. Even as children, they can be surprisingly adult, suddenly snapping out of their introspection to take charge in an emergency.

Famous Scorpios

Prince Charles
Theodore Roosevelt
Marie Antoinette
Richard Burton
Edward III
August Rodin
Jamie Lee Curtis
Evelyn Waugh
Charles Atlas
Albert Camus
Stephen T. Crane

Vivien Leigh

Marie Antoinette

Marie Curie
François Mitterrand
Pablo Picasso
Vivien Leigh
Erwin Rommel
Martin Luther
Cheiro (Palmist)
George Patton
Paul Joseph Goebbels

THE SUN IN SAGITTARIUS

(November 23 — December 21)

Sun Sign: SAGITTARIUS

Sign: THE ARCHER OR CENTAUR

Ruling Planet: JUPITER

Gender: MASCULINE

Element: FIRE

Quality: MUTABLE

Compatibility: AQUARIUS

AND LIBRA

Non-compatibility: CANCER,

SCORPIO AND TAURUS

Sun Sign Sagittarians are some of the most likable folk around: open, optimistic, enthusiastic and tolerant. Their ruler, Jupiter, is traditionally supposed to be lucky, and this largest of all the planets in the solar system does seem to bestow very positive opportunities on Sagittarians. This is possibly because their attitude actively invites such opportunity. Exuberant and often restless, Sagittarians are adept at inspiring and encouraging more pessimistic and cautious souls – although they can be appallingly foolhardy, getting themselves into some worrying situations. Usually, though, they get themselves out again without much trouble.

Many people born under the sign of the Archer find it hard to concentrate for very long on any

one subject unless it captures their imagination, and then they can give their whole self to it for hours. Their keen and restless minds are always looking to the future, trying to be one jump ahead – and often succeeding in being at least two. The joyful Sagittarians have an infectious joy and curiosity, and are an interesting blend of the studious – happy to sit with their books for long periods of time, totally oblivious to the outside world – and the very physical, for they are essentially outdoor types. No wonder then that many astrologers believe Australia to be the ideal Sagittarian country.

Sagittarians are often interested in philosophy and religion, although they rarely become bigots or fanatics. They love discussing their ideas, often late into the night, and are happy to share their home with a large number of very diverse people as well as animals, of which they are very fond.

Excessive Sagittarian energy can be disconcerting, though. People born under this sign tend to jump from job to job, lover to lover and home to home. Some may never settle, remaining life's gypsies to the very end. Most Sagittarians are natural backpackers at some point in their lives. Other people may find this restlessness disturbing, especially the more staid, security-minded materialists, such as Taurus or Virgo, whose home is their castle. They fail to understand why anyone would want to leave it. Sagittarians tend to see their home as more of a tent which they fold, metaphorically, before stealing away on their latest adventure.

Sagittarians can take this footloose-and-fancy-free attitude much too far, though. It can easily degenerate into almost mindless optimism and

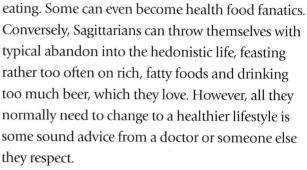

irresponsibility, and make them rely on impossible scenarios to get them out of trouble. They make compulsive gamblers, seeing Lady Luck constantly beckoning. Others may try to tell them she is merely a mirage, but to Sagittarians she is tantamount to a religious vision.

APPEARANCE

Sagittarians come in several types, including the super-athletic. The men can have enviably wide shoulders and slim waist and hips, while the women may be bronzed and muscular. They have quick, determined mannerisms and darting, piercing eyes that are always likely to flash with laughter. While not particularly fashion conscious, Sagittarians can look trendy. Whatever their age, they favor youthful styles, but take care to add their own personal touch to each ensemble. Some Sagittarians are rather eccentric in manner and convey bizarre first impressions.

HEALTH

With such unbounded energy, Sagittarians often fail to look before they leap and, as a result, suffer quite a few bruises, pulled muscles and broken bones. What they need to do is channel and balance their mental, physical and spiritual energies. Many find yoga, Tai Chi and meditation of great benefit. Sometimes, they themselves become teachers of these arts. Sagittarians need to feel that they are in control of their minds and bodies, and like to plan an exercise regime and diet that is right for them. Some, however, may be totally unconcerned with what they eat and drink. They will happily refuel on any old junk food; but most, especially in later years, take an interest in healthy

eating. Some can even become health food fanatics. Conversely, Sagittarians can throw themselves with typical abandon into the hedonistic life, feasting rather too often on rich, fatty foods and drinking too much beer, which they love. However, all they normally need to change to a healthier lifestyle is some sound advice from a doctor or someone else they respect.

Traditionally, the hips and thighs are problem areas for Sagittarians. Perhaps all that distinctive twisting and twirling puts a strain on them. So it is a good idea to have physiotherapy or osteopathy at the first sign of trouble.

CAREER

Sagittarians go for anything that gives free rein to their adventurous spirits. They will never persist with any job that limits them, so they don't go far in large corporations or the military, where there are too many rules and regulations, and where they find it hard to express their individuality. Similarly, dull, claustrophobic offices make Sagittarians feel uncomfortable. While rarely truly

ambitious, Sagittarians like to see the fruits of their labors and enjoy being appreciated. Sometimes they will rise to the top of their chosen profession without much effort. Making money is usually of secondary importance to Sagittarians. They are not seriously materialistic, and although they enjoy a few home comforts and the freedom which money can bring, on the whole their working lives are focused on deeper matters. Many find fulfillment in study, becoming lifelong students and university teachers, or take up bookish pursuits in their spare time. Sagittarians make excellent publishers. They love the look and feel of books, as well as their content – and some even set up their own generally successful publishing companies. However, typical Sun Sign Sagittarians can be far too restless and disorganized to spend months, perhaps even years, actually writing a book. They would need a very efficient and diplomatic literary agent on hand to constantly support and nag them. Even

then, they could miss the deadline by months.

Many Sagittarians lack staying power. They may have a wonderfully inspired idea that they fully intend to turn into a concrete result; but in a very short space of time they forget all about it, become disillusioned, and turn their attention to the next tempting project. Sagittarians need to be brought down to earth gently, and can work well with the right sort of tactful, organized business partner, especially one who gives them space to be themselves.

Another area in which Sagittarians traditionally shine is religion. Many a sleepy village has been rudely awakened by the arrival of the new Sagittarian vicar, with his or her energy, idealism and desire to "clean house." Even when the more conventional parishioners do their best to clip the wings of these assertive newcomers, the Sagittarians will continue to bring a breath of fresh air into their lives, whether they like it or not. Apart from the pastoral aspect of their vocation, Sagittarians find ministering to the

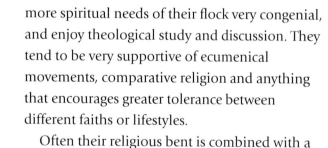

Traditionally, Sagittarians make excellent athletes, and many make it to the top, although they do need the strong guiding hand of a tough coach. They need to be disciplined and made to follow a regular training routine, or all that energy will be dissipated and their talent wasted.

Sagittarians often love horses, and in fact most animals. They find great fulfillment in equestrian sports, either as keen amateurs or as professionals. In some respects, they are rather similar to these big, nervy and powerful animals, and can easily form a strong, lasting bond with them. Sagittarians are natural horse whisperers.

RELATIONSHIPS

Since Sagittarius is a Fire Sign, people born under it are highly sexed, and have no time for prudishness or conventional attitudes.

However, they can be considerably less eager to settle down for life with one partner, and tend to take their time deciding which of their many lovers is their soulmate. Some never decide, and go bowling off through life happily solo, but always surrounded by a large circle of lovers, friends and admirers. As free spirits Sagittarians need very understanding partners who can cope with abrupt changes of plan. Often those born under the sign of the Centaur need to gallop off to fresh fields and new pastures, if only for a few days, to recharge their batteries. More often than not, they will want to be alone

more spiritual needs of their flock very congenial, and enjoy theological study and discussion. They tend to be very supportive of ecumenical movements, comparative religion and anything that encourages greater tolerance between different faiths or lifestyles.

Often their religious bent is combined with a desire to help their fellow man. They may be naturopaths and osteopaths or "hands on" healers and spiritualist mediums. Some are enthusiastic psychic researchers, traveling great distances to investigate ghosts and poltergeists, rarely frightened by even the most dramatic case of things that go bump in the night. Once they have fully researched the case, Sagittarians will then give powerful, inspirational talks to packed audiences and great acclaim.

Compatibility in Relationships

Aries
Aries will usually try to dominate fellow Fire Sign Sagittarius – which will only drive them further away.

Cancer
The famous Cancerian compassion and talent for homemaking is wasted on these free spirits.

Libra
Libras and Sagittarians are a good match, inspiring and supporting each other. Physically very compatible.

Capricorn
Sagittarians find austere Goats difficult to understand. Their caution is anathema to the untamed Sagittarian spirit.

Taurus
Tame, conventional Taureans often prove too stodgy for idiosyncratic and sometimes eccentric Sagittarians.

Leo
The Leonine energy and verve is attractive to fiery Sagittarius, but sooner or later they will clash.

Scorpio
Dark Scorpios often try to ensnare charming Sagittarians, but intense physicality doesn't mean enduring love.

Aquarius
This can be the perfect match. Both signs have little regard for the establishment or convention.

Gemini
Superficially on the same wavelength, but Geminis play too many games for innocent Sagittarians.

Virgo
Steady, organized and repressed, Virgos are the complete opposite of unrealistic Sagittarians.

Sagittarius
Fellow Sagittarians will get on well and fuel each other's madcap schemes. Romantic, yes. Practical, no.

Pisces
Sagittarians have little time for self-indulgent scenes, so touchy Pisceans are unlikely to make good life partners.

while they are doing it. Restless and claustrophobic, they cannot bear any form of restriction, and often react angrily when their chosen lifestyle is challenged, or when their partner demands to accompany them on their adventures.

On the whole, Sagittarians are not good at marriage, even though there are some who seek to spend all their time with the one love of their life. Many more content themselves with being serially monogamous, perfectly faithful to wife or husband until it is time to move on.

Many Sagittarians, on the other hand, prefer to live alone, cheerfully surrounded by the chaos of solo living, but very much at the center of a busy social and love life. They enjoy it when friends, family and lovers drop by.

Basically, Sagittarians are good, kind people who hate unpleasantness and injustice. Any disharmony in the home or elsewhere distresses them, and often the only way they can cope with it is by running away. This tendency makes them unpredictable in relationships, and rather feckless and unreliable parents; although they can be hugely popular with children because they are very childlike themselves.

IDEAL PARTNER

Most Sagittarians prefer to have a range of partners, from all signs of the zodiac. But when they do settle down, they need to spend their lives with easy-going and tolerant, but organized, people who make few demands and who are not particularly jealous or possessive. This is something of a tall order, but certain Aquarians and Libras fit the bill. Those who are definitely not compatible with

Sagittarians are weepy, clinging and insecure Cancers; dark, intense and manipulative Scorpios; and reactionary, jealous Taureans.

THE SAGITTARIAN CHILD

Sun Sign Sagittarian children can be a strange mix of oddball and sporty. Inquisitive, charming, quick-witted and active, they can seem like a dream to teachers or parents, but there is an underlying insecurity and waywardness in them which can cause problems.

They find the restrictions of school an immense bore, and can resort to playing hooky simply to escape into the fresh air. Although their concentration is good when their interest is fully engaged, Sagittarian children can find it hard to focus on less congenial subjects and need a firm hand with their studies. Often they don't see the point of pursuing their education beyond the normal span of around twelve years, and yearn to travel the world, experience other lifestyles and meet as many diverse people as they can. Yet once they have had their fill of travel and discovery, Sagittarians will happily undertake further education or throw themselves into a studious hobby such as local history research.

Sagittarians can be rather eccentric, which separates them from their peers. They can often charm their way out of potential bullying, however, and their prowess at sports is a powerful deterrent to anyone who thinks they must be wimps just because they like reading.

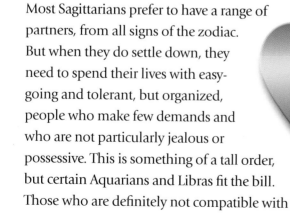

Sagittarians are uncomfortable with emotional intensity or cruelty, whether directed at themselves or others. They cannot cope with Cancerian possessiveness or with heavy-handed brutality, whether physical or verbal.

Famous Sagittarians

Uri Geller
Steven Spielberg
George Eliot
Louisa M. Alcott
Jane Austen
Catherine of Breganza
Walt Disney
Charles Chaplin
Winston Churchill
Joseph Conrad

Benjamin Disraeli
Bruce Lee
Edith Piaf
Ludwig von Beethoven
Jimi Hendrix
William Blake
Henri Toulouse-Lautrec
Gustave Flaubert
Mark Twain
John Paul Getty

Winston Churchill

Jimi Hendrix

THE SUN IN CAPRICORN

(December 22 — January 20)

Sun Sign: CAPRICORN

Sign: THE GOAT

Ruling Planet: SATURN

Gender: FEMININE

Element: EARTH

Quality: CARDINAL

Compatibility: TAURUS

AND VIRGO

Non-compatibility:

SAGITTARIUS AND ARIES

Sun Sign Capricorns are disciplined, methodical, sensible and sensitive. If that makes them sound excessively cold and boring, the truth is that they can be. But often they show remarkable ambition, kindness and gentle, often self-deprecating, humor. Traditionally, their ruling planet, Saturn, is concerned with the tough lessons of life: illness, restriction, old age and death.

Modern astrologers realize that this picture is far too gloomy. While Saturn can be a tough teacher – often repeatedly putting Capricorns through a steep learning curve – it can also galvanize them into action, to get things done, become achievers and climb to the top of their chosen profession with all its attendant status and prosperity.

Capricorns tend to be cautious by nature, sensing pitfalls and obstacles and standing back from problems. This can make them pessimistic and disinclined to move forward: inside they are saying to themselves, not "You might fail," but "You will fail." Some can become so convinced that nothing good will ever happen that their unconscious mind ensures that nothing does. However, the whole point of the Saturnine influence is to present them with a series of challenges that will never actually be too difficult for them to overcome – for those who believe in karma, this is actually an honor. Once Capricorns have come to understand the true nature of their path, it will be easier for them to rise above the mundane pettiness and worries that often beset them.

Sticklers for detail, and methodical to a fault, Capricorns are superb organizers, happy to deal with paperwork and the daily business of life. They are not natural stars like Leos or Scorpios, but usually seek to oil the wheels behind the scenes and make everything run smoothly. They hate untidiness, dirt and mess, whether it is the house or is expressed as a state of mind. Of course, many more sloppy characters consider them irritating and fussy. They can seem joyless and obsessed with doing the right thing, being conventional and often reactionary, with rigid, inflexible, self-imposed rules. But when they let go and relax – even with Saturn as a ruler, this is not impossible! – they are charming, delightful companions, with a wonderfully dry sense of humor.

APPEARANCE

Many typical Sun Sign Capricorns – especially the men – look rather goatish, with prominent noses and angular features. They tend to be on the tall side and somewhat bony, with dark, straight hair. The women are often of medium height, with mousey hair and strong features; although they can have beautiful, serene expressions that give them a particularly attractive air.

Capricorns of both sexes take great care with their appearance, but hate any form of flamboyance, extravagance or eccentricity. They are neat, clean and perhaps slightly old-fashioned. Capricornian females are true ladies – a term that pleases them. They like to have their hair beautifully coiffured once, perhaps twice, a week and regularly tinted in subtle, natural-looking colors. Even young Capricornian females are wary of the latest fads, and tend to stick with the more tried-and-true styles. Capricornian men love collars, ties and formal suits. Their wardrobes usually lack T-shirts and jeans, and even if they do wear them, they look completely wrong.

HEALTH

Capricorns think it bad form to admit to illness, and often force themselves to crawl to work even when they are suffering from really debilitating viruses. They hate what they see as weakness, and continually berate themselves for feeling unwell. This attitude can result in serious problems going untreated – they despise people who "bother" doctors – often making the situation much worse. Their tendency to bottle up emotions can also result in health problems in later life. Research has shown that people who express their anger, disappointment and grief are much more likely to avoid illnesses such as heart attacks – and even some forms of cancer – than those who do not let them out.

Traditionally, Capricornian problem areas are their joints, bones and teeth. There is a tendency toward stiffness and arthritis, although it can be relatively mild. They need to take extra calcium, cod liver oil and evening primrose oil supplements to help their physical flexibility. They should move around more, disciplining themselves to have regular breaks – especially if working long hours at a

computer – because they have a tendency toward Repetitive Strain Injury (RSI), and need to keep their hands and wrists flexible. Although they are inclined to take only conventional medicine seriously, they should at least try alternative therapies. Acupressure and aromatherapy will help to loosen them up enormously, both physically and emotionally.

They should have regular sessions with an osteopath or chiropractor and be sure to visit the dentist regularly.

CAREER

Sun Sign Capricorns are highly industrious and formidably organized, so they make superb administrators. They are happy to sit alone at their desk all day, taking, and often giving, orders by telephone, memo or in curiously formal e-mails. There is a certain haughtiness about them, a detached air that sets them apart from their chattier, more relaxed colleagues and makes them seem intimidating and aloof. They have no wish to be seen as one of the crowd, though. They frequently have their eye on the top job, and are content to work their way toward it in gradual stages. Aiming too high and too soon is likely to be disastrous for a typical Sun Sign Capricorn; although they are unlikely to try it more than once. One bad mistake in business or career, and Capricorns have learned a lesson for life.

Traditionally associated with the Earth, Capricorns are attracted to gardening and environmental issues, and can make stalwart supporters of "green" campaigns, either as a full-time job or a part-time interest.

Rather austere and unimaginative, they make excellent bank employees; although they are perhaps more suited to the old Dickensian days of wing collars and great dusty ledgers than today's relaxed style of "personal bankers" and telephone transactions. They are often career civil servants, rising gradually through the grades to a very high position of respect and authority. Sun Sign Capricorns are very good with money matters and scrupulously honest, which makes them ideal in positions of trust.

Their self-discipline and methodical working style mean that they are happy to tackle the painstaking jobs which others avoid, and they

Compatibility in Relationships

Aries
Fiery, tempestuous Arians may be appealingly different, but this opposite sign will be too cold to attract for long.

Cancer
Cancerian emotion can drive Capricorns mad, although their compassion and loving home have certain attractions.

Libra
Librans' love of the social whirl can cause problems for the more withdrawn and hesitant type of Capricorn.

Capricorn
Two wintry Goats together may not make for much empathizing but sometimes like signs work.

Taurus
Earthy and controlled Taureans have a lot to offer the Goat, and they can bring out the passion in each other.

Leo
Capricorns admire Leonine style and dash, but are fearful of such high-profile egocentrics.

Scorpio
Intrigued by fascinating Scorpio, Capricorn may make a serious error of judgement – and live to regret it.

Aquarius
This combination can work, if only because Aquarians can get on with most people if they are prepared to compromise.

Gemini
Gregarious, persuasive Geminis can charm reserved Capricorns, but the Goat remains distrustful.

Virgo
Calm, self-contained Virgos often make excellent partners for cautious, conventional Capricorns.

Sagittarius
Unfettered by practicalities, Sagittarians seriously upset Capricornian respect for the more traditional way of life.

Pisces
Contradictory and often unhappy Pisceans will bewilder Capricorns, who are scared by overt emotion.

may even choose unpopular careers – as tax inspectors or customs officers, for example. They see duty and law enforcement as of paramount importance, and can unfortunately become overbearing, perhaps even slightly sadistic with lesser mortals who owe tax or are not familiar with rules and regulations. Most Capricorns, have a kind streak, though, and become very hurt at the idea that they might abuse their position of power.

Capricorns tend to have very low self-esteem and see their work as a reflection of the respect they have earned. They love to be pillars of the community; they often take on time-consuming local government work or help out in charities, in addition to having a full-time job.

Lay-offs hit them harder than any other Sun Sign. They take being laid off very personally, seeing "the pink slip" as their own failure, and feel they will never find another job or make their mark in life. Unemployment is always a bleak experience, but to Capricorns it represents the winter of all their hopes.

Of course, many do dust themselves off and successfully start all over again, but the threat of being unemployed always haunts the typical Capricorn like a curse waiting to fall on them.

losing their virginity and can be very timid with the opposite sex.

Capricorns are very rarely easygoing and can, in fact, be rather dour. They need to be encouraged to lighten up. They can be the first to pour cold water on the bright ideas of more enthusiastic family members. Their ultimate accolade is more likely to be "That's good," instead of heartfelt congratulations – an approach that can be discouraging, especially to young children.

Capricorns often marry relatively late in life, waiting until they can afford a comfortable home in an upmarket area. They will spend weeks peering into real estate agents' windows and making calculations about how much they can afford, without ever thinking that a house must be a home and have love, as well as money, lavished on it.

Some Capricorns are constantly worried about money, scrimping and saving even though they earn a decent salary. To them, destitution is only around the corne, and Fate will hand them a place on Skid Row unless they are vigilant and count the pennies every moment of their lives. This is a manifestation of their low self-esteem: the more money they put away, the more respectable they are in their own eyes.

RELATIONSHIPS

Capricorns can be surprisingly passionate behind closed doors – after all, theirs is the sign of the Goat! However, they take a while to warm up, are very cautious about relating to others and tend to be "backward in coming forward." Many Capricorns of both sexes can wait an unfashionably long time before

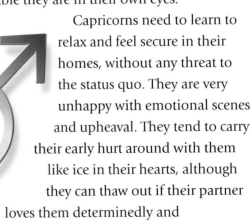

Capricorns need to learn to relax and feel secure in their homes, without any threat to the status quo. They are very unhappy with emotional scenes and upheaval. They tend to carry their early hurt around with them like ice in their hearts, although they can thaw out if their partner loves them determinedly and wholeheartedly, gradually introducing them to the concept of receiving love and all good

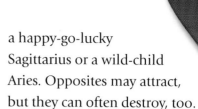

things. They must learn to accept that they are worthy of the devotion of others.

Male Capricorns tend toward stiff-upper-lip reserve (even if they aren't British!), believing that dignity must be maintained at all costs, even in front of their nearest and dearest. Although this can be good for their family, who see them as towers of strength in a crisis, it is less useful for their own health. Capricorns can bottle up a huge backlog of grief and anger, often giving the appearance of coldheartedness at the death of relatives, even of a spouse or parent. They can take refuge behind clichés such as "Life must go on" and "Crying won't bring them back," but inside they are bleeding. Family members should try to encourage Capricorns to discuss their feelings, whether of grief or joy.

Capricorns always try to do the right thing in life. They cannot understand those who rebel against the system, so they hardly make ideal parents for boisterous children or difficult teenagers. But they will always be very proud (in a quiet, unassuming way, of course) of their more timid, studious and sensible offspring.

IDEAL PARTNER

Capricorns need a strong, loving partner who neither whines nor clings, causes scenes or is too adventurous. Intense, dreamy Pisceans rarely fit the bill, and fellow Water Sign Cancers are usually far too emotionally demanding. Earthy Taureans and Virgos, who have a similar fondness for order and neatness, but possess added charm and wit, make possibly the best partners for the wintry Capricorns. It would be a mistake for a typical Goat even to consider a relationship with a happy-go-lucky Sagittarius or a wild-child Aries. Opposites may attract, but they can often destroy, too.

THE CAPRICORNIAN CHILD

Capricorns are rarely happy children. Even if their parents love them to death, the constant fear of losing their father or mother will seriously detract from their happiness. Capricorns are frequently far too fearful and sad, needing endless encouragement to join in the fun, get their hands dirty and have a laugh. Although naturally self-disciplined, they look to their elders and mentors to give them clear ground rules for their behavior, and can be very distressed in an easygoing, irresponsible atmosphere.

Capricornian children need to be given responsibility at an early age so that they can feel they are making a contribution. They should be praised at every opportunity in order to bolster their underdeveloped self-esteem. This is quite safe. There is no danger of Capricorns ever becoming conceited.

Sun Sign Capricorns are always old, even when young children. It is as if they carry all the problems of the world on their tiny shoulders, and they can become very introverted. They should never be bullied or teased, but always gently encouraged to make their contribution, and to make steady, rather than spectacular, success at school. It is also important that they are never compared unfavorably with any of their siblings or the flashy, natural-born achievers in their class. What they like to hear is that everything comes to those who wait.

Famous Capricorns

David Bowie
Louis Braille
Charles Rennie Macintosh
Muhammad Ali
Simone de Beauvoir
Bernadette, Saint of Lourdes
Al Capone
Paul Cézanne
Marlene Dietrich
Oliver Hardy
Martin Luther King

Martin Luther King

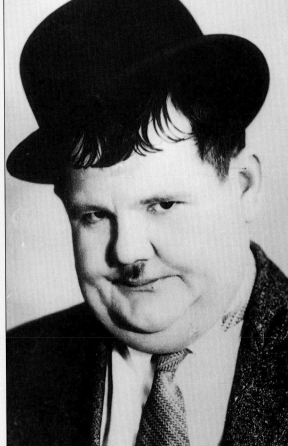

Oliver Hardy

J. Edgar Hoover
Joan of Arc
Mao Tse Tung
Isaac Newton
Michel de Nostradamus
Louis Pasteur
Edgar Allen Poe
Elvis Presley
Henri Matisse

THE SUN IN AQUARIUS

(January 21 – February 18)

Sun Sign: AQUARIUS

Sign: THE WATER CARRIER

Ruling Planet: URANUS AND

SATURN

Gender: MASCULINE

Element: AIR

Quality: FIXED

Compatibility: PISCES

AND CAPRICORN

Non-compatibility: ALMOST

NO ONE –

AT LEAST IN THEORY

Sun Sign Aquarians are friendly, idealistic, independent and humanitarian. That said, they are also the most varied set of individuals within one zodiacal group, so it is difficult to make generalizations about them. However, what is certain is that they tend to be extremely capable, kind, charitable and very forward-looking. After all, the next Great Year (see The Great Year) is the Age of Aquarius, when these people will come into their own.

Aquarians are natural New Agers, born astrologers and vegetarian eco-warriors, always eager to improve themselves and the world around them, and well aware of the spiritual side to life. They frequently hold strong political views, and often mount campaigns against some form of injustice or join groups such as Greenpeace or Amnesty International. Usually pacifists, Sun Sign Aquarians can be relied on to be leaders of the alternative scene and courageous challengers of Establishment values. Many of them also hold strong, but sometimes offbeat, religious or spiritual views, and are fond of philosophical debate.

The brave, free-spirited Aquarians are always true friends to the downtrodden, but find it hard to translate all that "love and light" into close personal relationships. Aquarians may be "New Age huggers," but they are often appallingly bad at creating a loving environment for themselves. For them, charity rarely begins at home.

Though they are good original thinkers and idiosyncratic in many ways, Sun Sign Aquarians can seem eccentric. They will, however, be mostly oblivious to the sly nudgings and criticism of others. Once they have found a lifestyle and, more importantly, a cause to fight for, they will stick to it obdurately. They can be contradictory, though. And they expect others to understand their sudden changes of direction before they settle down again on their chosen life path.

Aquarius is an Air Sign, and those born under this sign need their personal space, both literally and figuratively. They hate limits and react very badly to being told what to do, although they can often be surprisingly dictatorial themselves.

APPEARANCE

Sun Sign Aquarians come in many different shapes and sizes, but they tend to share attractive, clean-cut looks and a proud bearing. They have open, attentive and sympathetic expressions, and a ready smile which shows off their excellent teeth to advantage. Those born under the sign of the Water Carrier tend to be slim, fairly muscular and bronzed in summer. Even those who take no exercise and eat junk food seem to be naturally at ease with their bodies and, fortunately, rarely get fat.

Many Aquarians wear unusual outfits, such as happy hippy gear or floating New Age kaftans, and most would claim to be completely uninterested in something as materialistic and superficial as fashion. However, even those who wear thrift shop rejects somehow manage to look noble and set apart from the crowd.

HEALTH

Aquarians' lungs are particularly sensitive to cigarette smoke and air pollution, so they should be careful to avoid these wherever possible. Similarly, they can suffer from allergies more than most, and should have them checked out by a reputable naturopath.

Traditionally vulnerable to problems with their legs and ankles, Sun Sign Aquarians should take care to wear proper protective footwear when hiking, climbing or exploring caves. Another problem area is their circulation, which they should nurture with brisk exercise (especially in winter), massage, warm baths and daily supplements of gingko, cod liver oil and evening primrose oil.

CAREER

Aquarians can turn their hands very successfully to most things, since they are very determined individuals. They can turn their chosen cause into a career while remaining technically unemployed. In a perverse kind of way, some see living off government handouts as noble, direct action against a repressive capitalist system. Of course, this sort of Aquarius is relatively rare, but they tend to be so picturesque and newsworthy that they frequently get noticed.

Most are hardworking, perhaps even driven, in their chosen field. Many choose rather unusual or esoteric careers – astrology being one of them – and can often be found at New Age festivals, extolling the virtues of a new gadget that they have invented that will ease all aches and pains.

They are best with work that involves them in improving the lot of humanity in some way, and make excellent counselors and advisers, social workers or charity administrators.

Traditionally, Aquarians are non-materialistic people, but this is not necessarily so. They are often rather proud individuals who enjoy social and professional status and all its perks, such as large cars, comfortable houses and expensive long-haul vacations. They enjoy the freedom that comes with money and can often be wretched when it runs out. However, they're not grasping or given to signing up for pension plans and insurance policies when young – like Capricorns or Virgos. They see life as a series of golden

opportunities to make the world a happier place, and if money happens to come their way, so much the better.

Aquarians are independent and logical, and their real talents frequently belie their rather unworldly image. Aquarians value education and often do very well at university; and they travel widely to improve their knowledge of the way others live. With this experience behind them, they are natural problem-solvers, with a strong practical streak and often a marked ability to think laterally. They are forever coming up with astonishingly simple, yet elegant, solutions to apparently intractable problems; and they are not afraid to roll up their sleeves to show how it can be done.

Aquarians make good teachers and are constantly concerned about how their pupils will turn out, helping them along as best they can. They have a real sense of building the future in the here and now, and realize that the best way of building a fair and decent society is by educating the adults of tomorrow.

Despite their rather unrealistic image, Aquarians are surprisingly adept with technology, realizing that it is the way forward. This is the key to their thinking. They rarely look back, and believe that the future is all-important. For them, today's exciting developments will be tomorrow's reality. For this reason, Aquarians are often found working in futuristic careers, such as information technology or researching aspects of dolphin communication.

Aquarians have a great need to push back the frontiers of human knowledge. They see progress as the great challenge, but recognize that there is a price to pay – such as the terrible human and environmental results of the Industrial Revolution. Their brave new world will be caring, compassionate and informed, and they are willing to work hard to ensure that it happens.

RELATIONSHIPS

Aquarians are not good at close relationships, despite all their caring-and-sharing attitudes. They tend to be very wary of emotion, often misconstruing it as mere sentiment that makes irritating demands on their affections. In their minds, they belong to the world, not to one partner or family.

They need tolerance for their peculiarities, and a large measure of independence – so much so that many Aquarians choose to remain unattached, even though they enjoy having a large variety of passionate relationships. In many respects, they are happier with friends and co-crusaders than with life partners; but in that elusive lasting relationship they can finally blossom and turn out to be very loyal.

Often, Aquarians are simply too busy rushing from one campaign to the next to stop and notice the love in someone else's eyes. All too often they mistake a desire for personal closeness as a willingness to carry the banners. However, no one should underestimate Sun Sign Aquarians. They are by no means obtuse, just overly busy. Once they realize they are being pursued romantically, they may be amused or irritated, but are rarely won over immediately.

There is something decidedly superior about Aquarians, no matter how friendly and egalitarian they seem to be, or think they are. They have a detached, slightly quizzical air, and often assume that they are giving humanity the benefit of their expertise. This can make them seem attractively mysterious to some, but it can also be very offputting for others who do not necessarily appreciate being spoken to from on high.

Aquarians often make unusual parents, expressing themselves in slightly oddball activities. Sometimes there is a distinct element of role-reversal: they are the headstrong "child," while their children are the ones who are comparatively prim and proper. Aquarians are always encouraging their offspring to be bold and experimental, and to espouse humanitarian and ecological causes

Compatibility in Relationships

Aries
These two signs share world-saving ambitions and can have powerful sexual magnetism, but it may not last long.

Cancer
Cancers can provide emotional support as long as they are not too clingy or excessively emotional.

Libra
Libras may fall under the Aquarian spell, but it may be hero-worship rather than love that fuels the relationship.

Capricorn
Oddly, staid and cautious Capricorns can succeed in winning the love and protection of Aquarians.

Taurus
Taureans are disconcerted by Aquarian conventionality and rebellion, and will usually steer clear of it.

Leo
Leonine nobility may be appealing, but their grandness cuts no ice with egalitarian Aquarians.

Scorpio
Scorpian interest in deep, mystical subjects appeals to New Age Aquarians, but can be too dark for peace-lovers.

Aquarius
Two world-changing humanitarians must get along – or their egos may be too demanding for this union to work.

Gemini
Aquarians understand the Geminian restlessness and drive, but add their own, more profound idealism.

Virgo
Aquarians may mock safe, steady Virgos' obsesssion with analysis and order as being too retentive.

Sagittarius
These two signs are similarly rebellious and free-spirited, but Sagittarian indiscipline may threaten the grand plan.

Pisces
Dreamy, otherworldly Pisceans can find lasting love with mystical Aquarians, who will overlook their intensity.

almost before they can walk. Sometimes Aquarian parents are so eager to free their children from the yoke of convention that they take them traveling the world, or expose them to unusual home life – in a commune, for example.

Aquarian homes may be neat and bright, and superficially appear much like many other houses in their neighborhood; but there will usually be something different about them. It may just be their large collection of crystals sparkling in every room, the patch of deliberately untended yard that is home to a variety of wildlife, or the solar panels on the roof. However, it is usually the Aquarian lifestyle that differentiates their homes from those of their neighbors. Colorful people are forever coming and going. Their yard will almost certainly be the scene of some interesting activities – Wiccan celebrations of the New Moon perhaps, or the building of a sauna.

IDEAL PARTNER

Anyone who is also an idealistic free spirit will be suitable for an Aquarius. They detest emotional blackmail, so clingers such as the more badly aspected Cancer need not apply. Sometimes they respond well to Pisceans, especially if they have a strong Aquarian aspect in their charts; and the same applies to well-grounded Capricorns. In general, though, Aquarians are so individualistic that they could – at least in theory – settle down with almost anyone. However, although those under the sign of the Water Carrier may well be happy with a long-term commitment, the same may not be true of the other half of the relationship.

THE AQUARIAN CHILD

Children born under the sign of the Water Carrier are friendly and open, and need to be free and independent from an early age. Sometimes, they can be too friendly, and need to be educated about the dangers of talking to strangers as soon as they are able to understand.

No Sun Sign Aquarius will be totally happy in a highly regimented or over-disciplined school environment. "Progressive" schools – run, for instance, under the Montessori system – were made for Aquarians. They need to express their creativity and love of nature, and to become involved in local charities when quite young. Aquarians are superb at inventing new and effective ways of fund-raising, and should be encouraged to take the lead in this at school and in the local community. Their initiative, energy and unfailing good humor are often an inspiration to others. It is also essential, early practice for all the committee work and philanthropy that they will be involved with in later life.

Aquarian children can be worriers, brooding not only about their own problems, whether real or imagined, but also about the state of the world. Troubling news reports can upset them for days, and the parents of Aquarians should take this into account, and treat them accordingly. They have a great need to be taken seriously and should never be mocked or teased. They genuinely appreciate heart-to-heart talks with their parents and positively thrive on family discussions, which give them the opportunity to thrash out problems and plan the way forward. They must feel, however, that their contributions are genuinely valued.

Famous Aquarians

Charles Dickens
Franz Schubert
Paul Newman
Emile Zola
Christian Dior
John McEnroe
Sonny Bono
Humphrey Bogart
Eva Braun
Robert Burns
Lord Byron
Anton Chekhov
Charles Darwin
James Dean
Frederick Delius
Abraham Lincoln
Wolfgang Amadeus Mozart
Ronald Reagan
Franklin D.Roosevelt
George "Babe" Ruth

James Dean

Aquarian genius, Charles Dickens, finds inspiration in his dreams

THE SUN IN PISCES

(February 19 – March 20)

Sun Sign: PISCES

Sign: TWO FISH

Ruling Planet: NEPTUNE

AND JUPITER

Gender: FEMININE

Element: WATER

Quality: MUTABLE

Compatibility: AQUARIUS, PISCES

AND VIRGO

Non-compatibility:

CANCER, SCORPIO

AND CAPRICORN

Sun Sign Pisceans are emotional, dreamy, insecure people with strong creative instincts. Poetic and intuitive, they often seem out of place in the everyday world. All the same, many Pisceans achieve great things. They are kind, sensitive souls, who delight in the happiness and fulfillment of others. Sometimes they go too far in this regard, for they can live their entire lives in the shadow of other, more ambitious people – and never achieve their own true potential. Born under an archetypically feminine Water Sign, Pisceans seek above all to establish peace, harmony and love and can become terribly distressed if they fail to do so, or when others do not share their idealistic visions.

Pisceans tend to view life through rose-colored glasses. In some cases this unrealistic optimism is all that gets them through, because Pisceans can easily become downcast and depressed. Once this happens, all motivation is gone and Pisceans become moody, subservient and weak-willed. Many will do anything rather than face cold, stark reality, finding refuge in escapism of one sort or another. One of their rulers, Neptune, governs illusion; and although this can manifest itself in very healthy, creative ways (see Career), it may cover some forms of addiction.

Like their sign – two fish swimming in opposite directions – Pisceans have a markedly indecisive streak. They may be afraid of offering their own opinions; although, at the same time, they resent it when others take command. This leads to all manner of internal tensions, sometimes resulting in crankiness. Pisceans watch more open, decisive people state their case; and even if they disagree, they don't say so. Then as

time passes they realize what they should have said, and how much difference it would have made. However, they manage to interpret this as the fault of others, and inwardly seethe with resentment.

Pisceans are secretive, and can be deceitful. They may lack the depth and scope of black Scorpionic vengeance, but they can still be nasty. Of course, many are delightful, open people – after all, the full picture of any one character can only be seen at all accurately when the whole chart is studied – but there is almost always an underlying feeling of not belonging, of lacking a voice, of being faceless, which manifests as resentment at the assertiveness of other people.

APPEARANCE

Pisceans tend to be of small to medium height, and quite slightly built; although they can gain weight later in life if they are not careful. They often have strangely rebellious hair, and spend time and money taming it. Pisceans have delicate eyes and, if they are pale-skinned, often need glasses. Typically, Pisceans are strong-featured, with generous mouths and a quirky, slightly twitchy smile. It is as if they are undecided whether or not to join in the fun.

Pisceans are often very chic and take an interest in stylish clothes. Both sexes are usually well-groomed and pay attention to detail. They are rarely eccentric or look out of place, and are uncomfortable with those who do. Female Pisceans often make their own clothes, favoring luxury fabrics such as silk, velvet and satin.

HEALTH

Pisceans are highly-strung, reacting badly to all manner of pollutants, whether physical ones (such as dust, smog and chemicals) or emotional triggers (such as arguments or anxiety). Even psychic "vibes" disturb them. These things can provoke allergies, crippling headaches and many other ailments. To counter these effects, Pisceans should seek protection – either through meditation, prayer or by strengthening themselves through physical exercise. Although not always naturally athletic, they should at least try to walk briskly for half an hour a day or swim three times a week. (Swimming works well for a Water Sign.) Yoga is the perfect exercise, though: it stretches and works the muscles, while at the same time calming and invigorating the soul. Traditionally, Pisceans have trouble with their feet. If this is a problem they should visit their podiatrist regularly, and invest as much as they can afford in good, supportive shoes.

Those born under the sign of the Fishes tend to develop addictions, and should be very wary of smoking and drinking. Pisceans sometimes tend to be hypochondriacs, reaching for the medicine cabinet at the slightest twinge, while others – an increasing number – seek out various holistic therapies. Certainly, they will fare well, on the whole, with acupressure, Chinese medicine and Reiki. However, Pisceans need to realize that many, though not all, of their health problems are psychosomatic and result from their

internalized emotions. They need to find an outlet for them.

CAREER

Pisceans are almost always in touch with their unconscious minds; and once they learn to deal with this effectively, they can become very successful artists. There are many top Piscean painters and poets who obey their inner voice. Many actors, who may be shy and reserved off stage, positively shine once hidden behind the mask of a scripted character.

However, Pisceans are dreamy people and feel threatened by too much structure – which is why the caring professions are excellent outlets for

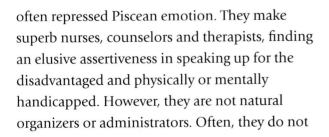

often repressed Piscean emotion. They make superb nurses, counselors and therapists, finding an elusive assertiveness in speaking up for the disadvantaged and physically or mentally handicapped. However, they are not natural organizers or administrators. Often, they do not seek promotion, but are more content to take a back seat and get on with their job. They are very good team members, and can rise to occasions such as major emergencies – as long as someone else is there to tell them, clearly and decisively, what to do.

Because of their own tendency to various forms of addiction, they are especially good with the rehabilitation of addicts – finding the right mix of compassion and "tough love" needed for the program to succeed. They can empathize with cravings, and provide the support the addicts need to overcome their problems.

Many Pisceans find fulfillment in holistic therapies and become qualified in a wide variety

television or films. They love creating a world into which others can step in and lose themselves, even if it is only for a short time. Some Pisceans are cartoonists and animators, while others invent virtual worlds through computer special effects.

Pisces is one of the dual signs, and Piscean restlessness is often assuaged by having more than one job, or by pursuing a career during the

They are particularly attracted to crystal therapy and rebirthing, and make natural dream analysts

of "alternative" disciplines, from acupuncture to hands-on healing. They are particularly attracted to crystal therapy and rebirthing, and make natural dream analysts.

Compassionate Piscean caring also extends to the animal kingdom: many Pisceans are veterinary nurses or helpers in animal rescue centers. Many have a special empathy with distressed pets and a sure instinct about how best to treat their ailments, often using unorthodox methods such as homeopathy. Pisceans have plenty of imagination, but not too much initiative. They hate the boisterousness of programs designed to encourage team bonding and decision-making, but may benefit from them more than most. The glamour professions also attract typical Sun Sign Pisceans, who can be both artistic and moody. They are often found as dress designers, makeup artists and sometimes models, although they are not often individualistic enough for this rather exposed profession. Since Neptune, their ruler, emphasizes illusion, Pisceans make good photographers, and can often be found as set designers for the theater,

day, while enjoying charity work in the evenings and on weekends. Pisceans need to keep busy or they can easily fall prey to self-doubt and depression, and become very irritable.

RELATIONSHIPS

Many Pisceans can be very loving, warm partners for life, although they are too restless to settle without the occasional change of scene. They can be quite flighty, seeking to find self-esteem in the arms of many lovers but all too often failing to do so, even though they long to be loved.

They tend to be easily bored. It is then that they find temptation of one sort or another difficult to resist, or fly into perverse, contradictory moods when they become irritated with themselves and the world around them. As a result, they may strike out at their nearest

Compatibility in Relationships

Aries
Domineering and inflexible Arians find oddball and effusive Pisceans too difficult to live with.

Cancer
At worst, weepy, dramatic Cancers and moody Pisceans make for a nightmare domestic scenario.

Libra
The last thing peace-seeking Librans need is Piscean "baggage" and moodiness. This relationship won't last.

Capricorn
Solid, unemotional Goats find Piscean excesses beyond belief, and won't even begin to woo them.

Taurus
Pisceans' innate moodiness and contrariness can seriously annoy level, well-grounded Taureans.

Leo
Lordly Leos are very sexy and charming, but touchy Pisceans will soon back away from all that ambition.

Scorpio
While these two signs can easily fall for each other, they are far too difficult to make the necessary compromises.

Aquarius
These two signs are soul-mates and made for each other. Aquarian loftiness can easily overlook Piscean angst.

Gemini
There may be a strong initial attraction between these two signs, but party animal Geminis can seem too light.

Virgo
Pisceans can easily come to love Virgos' charm and sense of order. This can be a lasting romance.

Sagittarius
Demanding Pisceans will be hurt and puzzled by the Sagittarian tendency to disappear without a word.

Pisces
A winning combination – the organizational skills of one complementing the dreaminess of the other.

and dearest, often with a deadly accuracy, instinctively knowing how best to hurt those they know well. Pisceans can usually recognize the weaknesses of others and, if cornered, can go after them vindictively. They can also stage huge emotional scenes, although these tend to be over almost as soon as they have begun. The memory, however, will continue to haunt non-Piscean witnesses for some time.

Even so, many Pisceans are truly charming, hospitable folk, who love sharing their beautiful homes with guests, family members and a menagerie of pets. They are justly proud of their homemaking skills and shine primarily as

gardeners, using great imagination and artistry in the landscaping and composition of their land. Pisceans need to get out into the open air, and often love to be near to the sea. Many of them are happiest when living in seaside towns.

Romantic and tender-hearted, Pisceans can easily fall for rogues. Because charm works wonders with them, they are particularly vulnerable to confidence tricksters. If a day of reckoning comes and the flaws of their loved ones are revealed, it is usually more than traumatic for a typical Sun Sign Pisces. They hate having their rose-colored glasses ripped off so cruelly, and can react by striking out at those who dare to do so, before finally accepting the truth. Some never do, though. Occasionally, Pisceans prefer to live with a lie, rather than face the facts.

Pisceans are not always the best of parents, because they are vague and self-absorbed, and need to live their own lives.

Of course many of the more well-balanced Pisceans make excellent parents, creating a loving, stable environment for their family.

IDEAL PARTNER

Aquarians tend to bond romantically with Pisces, although they will not easily endure too many emotional outbursts or any vindictiveness. However, the organizational abilities of Aquarians often complement Piscean dreaminess very well, resulting in a beautiful home and a spiritually aware atmosphere. Two Pisceans together will never get anything done, although their dreams may be truly exciting. Emotions will run too high with watery Cancers. A match with a typical Sun Sign Scorpio is out, too. The nastiness that can arise if things go wrong will be unbearable. However, kind, earthy Virgos can often find happiness with Pisceans; and even, in some cases, lordly Leos will magnanimously allow Pisces to live in their shadow, which may well suit both of them.

THE PISCEAN CHILD

The Piscean tendency toward dreaming and absentmindedness can get many children into trouble at school and also later in life. Parents should therefore encourage them to focus and concentrate as much as possible.

Often Piscean children live in their own fantasy world, and can slip all too easily into stretching the truth. Some may be truly deceitful. The ground rules should be very clear-cut: everyone here speaks the truth. These children need to understand that being straightforward is by far the best way, and that lying is an unattractive social vice.

On the other hand, it is a good idea to channel their undoubted creativity into something more acceptable, such as painting or short story writing, in which they are often near the top of their class. All the same, they need to be taught how to separate fantasy from reality; and any tales they spin need to be taken with a pinch of salt.

It is important to establish trust between parents and Piscean children at an early age, so that there is always an atmosphere of loving support at home. These children need to feel that home is a haven, and that they have a valuable role to play there. This is vital for the development of their self-esteem, and for their future adult relationships. When they are very small, they need strong parenting and the knowledge that they are protected against harsh reality. These are very sensitive, sometimes weak, children, who can react very badly if mishandled at an early age.

Piscean children are not good as competitors, and may easily be overpowered by their siblings. They rarely fight for what they want, usually giving in submissively. They come to idolize a more glamorous or successful brother or sister. Parents should make it clear that they have just as much to offer, in their own way, and should always praise them for their achievements and encourage their siblings to do the same.

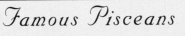

Famous Pisceans

Michael Caine
Mikhail Gorbachev
Jean Harlow
Samuel Pepys
Glen Miller
Alexander Graham Bell
Enrico Caruso

Albert Einstein

Vaslav Nijinsky

Buffalo Bill Cody
Albert Einstein
Bobby Fischer
Yuri Gagarin
Galilei Galileo
Michelangelo
Liza Minnelli
Rupert Murdoch
Rudolph Nuryev
Vaslav Nijinsky
Pierre-Auguste Renoir
Bugsy Siegel
Elizabeth Taylor

MOON SIGNS

So far, we have seen how the Sun influences our outward manner, appearance, major personality traits, career and even our health. The Moon – the second most important body in our solar system – influences our emotions, our inner life and our inherited traits and characteristics. This section of the book provides a summary of the essential characteristics of your Sun and Moon Sign combination and a full chapter devoted to each Moon placement.

FINDING YOUR MOON SIGN

To find out what your Moon Sign is, turn to the charts

on pages 246–253. Then, use the Sun and Moon Sign

Combinations and the relevant chapter to gain an

even deeper understanding of your true character

as influenced by the power

of the Moon.

SUN AND MOON SIGN
COMBINATIONS

*Your Sun and Moon Signs lend a guiding hand to the workings of fate
in your life. They provide an outline of your essential characteristics and
help to shape the way that you will develop. Taken together, Sun and Moon Signs
provide very potent glimpses of your true character and of the kind of life that you will
create for yourself. Although nothing is written in stone, these astrological
signposts point the way to your destiny.*

SUN ARIES, MOON ARIES: Enthusiastic, motivated and quick-witted. Egocentric and impatient. They always aim for the top, seeking the glittering prizes. They can be ruthless.

SUN ARIES, MOON TAURUS: Artistic, sensuous and down to earth. Stubborn and dogmatic. They love tradition but can be fearful of change – even if it's for the better.

SUN ARIES, MOON GEMINI: Bright, articulate, persuasive. Overly sharp tongued and lacking in stamina. Excellent media people, but have erratic energy flow, so need to pace themselves.

SUN ARIES, MOON CANCER: Businesslike, genial and determined. Tough facade hides vulnerability. They carry very old emotional scars and need to open up to a soulmate.

SUN ARIES, MOON LEO: Extrovert, high flyer – the natural stars of the zodiac. Insensitive to others, misses finer points. Often a huge success – thanks to the hard work and loyalty of others.

SUN ARIES, MOON VIRGO: Efficient, logical and analytical. Overcritical and fussy. Can harbor wild fantasies and surprising ambitions – which they should encourage from time to time.

SUN ARIES, MOON LIBRA: Ambitious, balanced, passionate and caring. May be overoptimistic and gullible, but their divine innocence can protect them against many unpleasant situations and people.

SUN ARIES, MOON SCORPIO: Intense, focused and motivated. Can be intimidating and too theatrical. Lots of energy and commitment, but take disappointment very hard. Even so, they bounce back.

SUN ARIES, MOON SAGITTARIUS: Motivating, encouraging, restless and daring. Insensitive and blunt. Something of the eternal child – complete with footstomping tantrums.

SUN ARIES, MOON CAPRICORN: Ambitious, determined and tough. Domineering and cold, but has a surprising capacity to hero worship others – from a safe distance and secretly.

SUN ARIES, MOON AQUARIUS: Idealistic and humanitarian. Tactless and outspoken. Vast resources of energy and resilience and many – often conflicting – goals.

SUN ARIES, MOON PISCES: Confident exterior hides timid interior. Can be something of a zealot. Seeks to wear different masks for different occasions in order to impress.

SUN TAURUS, MOON ARIES: Poised exterior hides raging inner ambition. Opinionated and dogmatic. Can feel taken advantage of and demand apologies where none are required, but often back down if stood up to.

SUN TAURUS, MOON TAURUS: Faithful, musical and creative. Stubborn and temperamental. Committed to maintaining old-fashioned values.

SUN TAURUS, MOON GEMINI: Articulate, witty and excitable, with good ideas. Lacks stamina.

Respects and admires people with organizational skills, and those who are good with money.

SUN TAURUS, MOON CANCER: Caring, home-loving and encouraging. Less secure about own ambitions and may lack drive, but excellent at supporting others and helping them to achieve their dreams.

SUN TAURUS, MOON LEO: Loyal and colorful, dramatic and deliberate. Inflexible and opinionated. Good organizers and natural leaders, although may be inclined to laziness.

SUN TAURUS, MOON VIRGO: Meticulous, orderly and organized. Family-loving, articulate and musical. Hypercritical and often rather dull. Tend to have a hidden poetic streak, and can be surprisingly passionate lovers.

SUN TAURUS, MOON LIBRA: Caring, compassionate and loving. Can be ambitious. Lazy and erratic, but the heart is in the right place. Above all, they seek to be peacemakers.

SUN TAURUS, MOON SCORPIO: Independent, strong and artistic. Inclined to take on too much. Obstinate and inclined to bottle up old regrets and disappointments. Need to open their hearts more to confidants.

SUN TAURUS, MOON SAGITTARIUS: Pious, studious, academic. Intrigued by the idea of adventure. Tend to be lazy, judgmental and dogmatic, but can indulge in flights of fancy and become rather unrealistic.

SUN TAURUS, MOON CAPRICORN: Adept in business, sensible and shrewd. Insecure in personal relationships, but secret romantics at heart. They have a desperate need to be loved and understood.

SUN TAURUS, MOON AQUARIUS: Confident, bright, freethinking, gregarious. Can lay down the law but essentially they are fairly happy-go-lucky and tolerant. Rarely nostalgic – very forward-looking.

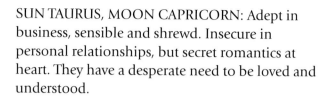

SUN TAURUS, MOON PISCES: Determined and creative, compassionate and caring. Can be gullible and naive, but many see this as rather charming. They have an artsy side to their personality.

SUN GEMINI, MOON ARIES: Interesting, innovative thinkers and excellent in the media. Superficial and sometimes cruel, although they may not realize how much they hurt others.

SUN GEMINI, MOON TAURUS: Patient, intelligent and persistent. Morose and emotionally insecure. Can have bursts of energy and inspiration, which quickly die down again.

SUN GEMINI, MOON GEMINI: Extremely quick-witted and amusing. Tense, glib and lacking in stamina. Can feel very isolated and lonely – even in a large crowd.

SUN GEMINI, MOON CANCER: Communicative, open and homeloving. Weak-willed and possessive – easy to influence. Can become a doormat, although rebelliousness is not unknown.

SUN GEMINI, MOON LEO: Enthusiastic, attractive and creative. Childish and egocentric. Can be very opinionated, but can easily be charmed out of any inflexibility. Moody and erratic.

SUN GEMINI, MOON VIRGO: Adaptable, lateral thinker and rather intellectual. Nervy, lacking in ambition, but tend to admire others who aim for the top.

SUN GEMINI, MOON LIBRA: Flirtatious, sociable and flighty. Pompous and self-congratulatory. Feel threatened by those with strong beliefs or opinions. Need to be centered and calm.

SUN GEMINI, MOON SCORPIO: Deep, possessor of dark secrets and often fascinating. Perverse, vulnerable and lonely. They love to explore the mysterious side of life. Can become hooked on the paranormal.

SUN GEMINI, MOON SAGITTARIUS: Studious, physical and adventurous. Insensitive and outspoken. Can be unrealistic and naive. Need to plan for the future.

SUN GEMINI, MOON CAPRICORN: Media type, good with words, intelligent. Emotionally uncommunicative and cold, but they often cry inside. Often lonely and lost – need a soulmate.

SUN GEMINI, MOON AQUARIUS: Clever and bright, instinctively knowing. Wary of expressing emotions or becoming too deeply involved romantically and sexually. May avoid commitment.

SUN GEMINI, MOON PISCES: Extroverted, fun and very communicative. Inwardly tense and insecure, and in need of romance and sensuality. Intuitive, moody and often somewhat psychic.

SUN CANCER, MOON ARIES: Understanding, businesslike and caring. Over-competitive and restless. Can easily become intense about all relationships, both business and personal. They need emotional commitment.

SUN CANCER, MOON TAURUS: Compassionate, sensual and family-centered, but with a tendency to be rather lazy, sulky and moody. Often need cheering up by friends on fun nights out.

SUN CANCER, MOON GEMINI: Genial, ambitious and quick-witted. Guileful and manipulative, often great plotters and particularly good at revenge.

SUN CANCER, MOON CANCER: Kind, sensitive, upholders of traditional values. Live in the past, are overemotional and possessive. Can become hysterical if crossed. Have a tendency to cut their nose off to spite their face.

SUN CANCER, MOON LEO: Great integrity, passionate and loving. Dogmatic and insecure, but basically kind and compassionate. Above all – need to be understood.

SUN CANCER, MOON VIRGO: Good with illness. Businesslike, hardworking, with good – almost total – recall. Excessive worriers, mean-spirited and penny-pinching, although secretly longing to be wildly extravagant.

SUN CANCER, MOON LIBRA: Ambitious, family-centered and peace-loving. Unrealistic, with little grasp of detail, but can be good at seeing the overall picture. Charming and urbane.

SUN CANCER, MOON SCORPIO: Always after the center stage. Very intense and sometimes psychic. Can suffer from depression and be rather secretive. Great capacity for passionate love.

SUN CANCER, MOON SAGITTARIUS: Family-loving, free-spirited and joyful. Overoptimistic, unrealistic and inclined to daydream. Often charming but feckless. Need to be somewhat more organized.

SUN CANCER, MOON CAPRICORN: Perceptive in business, ambitious and hardworking. Parsimonious and pessimistic, often seeing life in joyless terms. Can have intense, but secret, passions.

SUN CANCER, MOON AQUARIUS: Communicative, articulate and adroit. Manipulative and self-centered, but can work hard for the common good. A good grasp of the long term.

SUN CANCER, MOON PISCES: Psychic, sensitive and compassionate, and a fierce champion of the underdog. Moody and fearful, and inclined to suffer from nightmares. Loving, but emotionally very needy.

SUN LEO, MOON ARIES: Encouraging, enthusiastic and courageous. Domineering and callous, and given to wild tantrums if crossed. However, likely to forgive and forget fairly easily.

SUN LEO, MOON TAURUS: Traditional, placid and dependable. Can sometimes appear boring and stubborn, but can occasionally surprise people by being the life and soul of the party.

SUN LEO, MOON GEMINI: Quick-witted, innovative thinkers – natural leaders. Although inclined to be sharp tongued, insensitive and capable of lashing out without thinking, they are basically kind and well-meaning.

SUN LEO, MOON CANCER: Protective, nurturing and comforting. Over-possessive and hysterical, yet often puzzled and frightened by the emotional needs of others.

SUN LEO, MOON LEO: Successful, individual and a natural star. Domineering and unrealistic, and can ruthlessly exploit others. Charming and inspiring.

SUN LEO, MOON VIRGO: Logical, methodical, kind and decent. Sometimes petty-minded and abrupt, although this cool exterior hides a genuinely compassionate heart.

SUN LEO, MOON LIBRA: Stylish, flirtatious and successful. Egocentric with a tendency to be promiscuous and to abuse the trust of others. Surprisingly bold in coming to the rescue. Something of a hero.

SUN LEO, MOON SCORPIO: Hardworking, theatrical, colorful and witty. Melodramatic and intimidating, with a tendency to ride roughshod over the sensibilities of others. Embarrassed and contrite when this is pointed out.

SUN LEO, MOON SAGITTARIUS: Warmhearted, enthusiastic and adventurous. Impatient, restless, too independent. Great explorers and pioneers. Able to tolerate physical discomfort and help others less fortunate than themselves.

SUN LEO, MOON CAPRICORN: Efficient, traditional and ambitious. Insecure underneath with a great need for demonstrations of affection. Can find it hard to express emotional commitment.

SUN LEO, MOON AQUARIUS: Faithful, honest, fair and idealistic. Opinionated and dogmatic. Need several different outlets for philanthropic urges. Busy and committed.

SUN LEO, MOON PISCES: Kind-hearted, psychic and caring. Easily distressed or distracted, but quick to help others. Can become over-demanding in close relationships.

SUN VIRGO, MOON ARIES: Clever, versatile, adaptable and good with words. Sarcastic and hurtful, but not without some grace and gentleness. Can be very amusing.

SUN VIRGO, MOON TAURUS: Solid, reliable, helpful and good with their hands. Not innovative or original thinkers, but immensely admiring of those who are. Very good supporter of family and friends.

SUN VIRGO, MOON GEMINI: Quick to speak and act, and good at research. Frightened of strong emotion and something of a cold fish outwardly, but secretly desperate to find love.

SUN VIRGO, MOON CANCER: Clever, shrewd, family-loving. Excessive worriers and very possessive. Can be hoarders, being totally convinced that civilization as we know it is about to collapse. Fond of conspiracy theories.

SUN VIRGO, MOON LEO: Honest, enthusiastic and meticulous. Insecure and sometimes unambitious, although they make efforts from time to time to better themselves. Reserved but deep.

SUN VIRGO, MOON VIRGO: Kind, reliable and organized. Petty-minded and can be penny-pinching. Terrible worriers. Good at analysis, investigation and research. Can seem over-intellectual and intimidating.

SUN VIRGO, MOON LIBRA: Diplomatic, organized and good team workers. Indecisive and hesitant, but excellent at seeing all sides of a problem. Sociable and charming.

SUN VIRGO, MOON SCORPIO: Intense, incisive and profound thinkers. Outwardly unemotional and uncommunicative, but a seething mass of hidden feelings. Often harbor lifelong – and sometimes unrequited – passions.

SUN VIRGO, MOON SAGITTARIUS: Open, amenable, gregarious and studious. Impatient and careless, overeager to move on to the next project. Can be impractical and unworldly.

SUN VIRGO, MOON CAPRICORN: Serious, businesslike and meticulous. Self-centered, cold and lacking spontaneity. Need to lighten up and have fun. Emotional commitment is difficult.

SUN VIRGO, MOON AQUARIUS: Independent, philosophical and studious. Insensitive to the emotional needs of others, but determined to live their lives for them – whether they like it or not.

SUN VIRGO, MOON PISCES: Deep, psychic, intuitive and caring to the point of martyrdom. Doormat mentality and over-possessive, but can be very kind, understanding and extremely supportive of others.

S UN LIBRA, MOON ARIES: Excellent in emergencies, pioneering and adventurous. Lack stamina, can be self-centered and unreliable on a day-to-day basis. Often attractive and charming.

SUN LIBRA, MOON TAURUS: Creative and artistic, musical, stylish and practical. Can be lazy and erratic, but once motivated can work hard and become successful. Good homemakers.

SUN LIBRA, MOON GEMINI: Good technical mind, quick, intelligent, practical and innovative. Overdependent on others. Glib and often speak without thinking, tearing through life in a tremendous hurry, rarely finishing anything.

SUN LIBRA, MOON CANCER: Amiable, caring, home-loving and efficient. Too selfless and over-altruistic – and easily walked over by others. Can be naive, but this innocence is very attractive.

SUN LIBRA, MOON LEO: Quick, clever and sharp-tongued. Incurably romantic and melodramatic. Love to be noticed. Can be overextravagant and feckless. Great fun to be with.

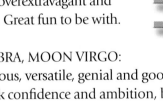
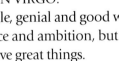

SUN LIBRA, MOON VIRGO: Meticulous, versatile, genial and good with words. Can lack confidence and ambition, but can be motivated to achieve great things.

SUN LIBRA, MOON LIBRA: Charming, stylish and gregarious. Can be slothful and unfocused, although they can certainly move very fast when chasing the object of their passion.

SUN LIBRA, MOON SCORPIO: Forceful, magnetic and sexual. Can be dominating, power-hungry and dramatic, but given to retreating into solitude from time to time to recharge their batteries.

SUN LIBRA, MOON SAGITTARIUS: Good with detail and logical argument. Fair and just, but with a restless spirit that needs many changes of direction. Can ignore the emotional needs of others.

SUN LIBRA, MOON AQUARIUS: Quick-witted, intelligent and strong. A good leader. Can be interfering and arrogant with no time for the niceties of others' feelings. Good at planning.

 SUN LIBRA, MOON CAPRICORN: Tough negotiator, dedicated worker, shrewd and perceptive. Cynical and skeptical, but can be a pushover in love. A great capacity for passion.

SUN LIBRA, MOON PISCES: Intuitive, romantic and creative. Lacking in concentration and inclined to daydream. Apparently spontaneous and childlike, which many find attractive, although there is a manipulative side.

 SUN SCORPIO, MOON ARIES: Intense and brave. Good leaders. Confrontational, aggressive and overdramatic with a strong sense of destiny that drives them to become very successful.

SUN SCORPIO, MOON LIBRA: Purposeful, diplomatic, career-minded and good at mediation. Uncomfortable with close family ties, often preferring to live apart from relatives. Too independent.

 SUN SCORPIO, MOON TAURUS: Dependable, erotic and musical. Stubborn, stolid and sometimes a little dull. However, they can be passionate and occasionally have exotic interests.

SUN SCORPIO, MOON SCORPIO: Passionate, dramatic, assertive and often highly motivated and successful. Intimidating and intense, but can translate this intensity into extreme loyalty, either to an individual or a belief system.

SUN SCORPIO, MOON GEMINI: Quick-witted, intuitive and a good judge of people. Cynical and world-weary, but still determined to enjoy life. Sometimes love crowds; at other times seek solitude.

SUN SCORPIO, MOON SAGITTARIUS: Funny, persistent, well grounded and good at research. Can be erratic and have unrealistic moods. Need to find a sensible pace to maintain workable energy levels.

 SUN SCORPIO, MOON CANCER: Intuitive, magnetic and caring. Moody, suspicious – and frightened – of intimacy. Not an easy type, but once won over tends to become a lifelong friend.

SUN SCORPIO, MOON CAPRICORN: Serious, ambitious and determined. Lacking spontaneity and a sense of fun, but often long desperately to do something surprising. Secretly seek a true soulmate.

 SUN SCORPIO, MOON LEO: Persistent and faithful with great powers of endurance. Inflexible, dogmatic and can be hurtful. Set high standards for themselves and others.

SUN SCORPIO, MOON AQUARIUS: Determined, focused and ambitious. Dogmatic and arrogant – benevolent dictator type. Not swayed by flattery or romance, but quietly appreciative of both from time to time.

 SUN SCORPIO, MOON VIRGO: Meticulous, intelligent and dedicated. Suspicious of emotion and close relationships, but once in love it is usually forever.

SUN SCORPIO, MOON PISCES: Altruistic, caring and artistic. Can be sarcastic and occasionally vindictive – especially if crossed in love, when they can avenge themselves with great imagination.

SUN SAGITTARIUS, MOON ARIES: Pioneering, restless and innovative. Impatient and impulsive, and bad with lasting intimacy, although relationships are often passionate while they last.

SUN SAGITTARIUS, MOON TAURUS: Imaginative, practical, motivating and artistic. Inclined to be self-indulgent, lazy and undisciplined, but can pull themselves together when necessary, often producing some very successful work.

SUN SAGITTARIUS, MOON GEMINI: Good with words, proactive and motivated. Impatient – lacking stamina and persistence. Excellent at inspiring others. Good delegators.

SUN SAGITTARIUS, MOON CANCER: Artistic, psychic, intuitive and caring. Can be deluded and unrealistic, with little grasp of day-to-day practicalities. Great daydreamers.

SUN SAGITTARIUS, MOON LEO: Entertaining and extroverted, amusing and gregarious. Often selfish and demanding, especially with their nearest and dearest.

SUN SAGITTARIUS, MOON VIRGO: Organized, thorough and often profound. Dogmatic and pompous, though somewhat afraid of strong emotion, finding heart-to-hearts threatening. Tend to hide behind a mask.

SUN SAGITTARIUS, MOON LIBRA: Forceful, persuasive and analytical. Tend to be fashionable, attractive and stylish – but can be a little impatient and arrogant. Sometimes irritable.

SUN SAGITTARIUS, MOON SCORPIO: An efficient and sometimes inspired mind. Incisive, dogged and profound. Good at lateral thinking. Can be intolerant and peevish.

SUN SAGITTARIUS, MOON SAGITTARIUS: Free-spirited, independent, pioneering and energetic. Impatient with other lifestyles and quick to criticize, but find it easy to forgive and forget.

SUN SAGITTARIUS, MOON CAPRICORN: Bright, persistent and amusing company, with great ambitions. Afraid of emotion and too ready to condemn, with a tendency to pessimism and lack of self-esteem.

SUN SAGITTARIUS, MOON AQUARIUS: Unusual and fascinating, well-read and knowledgeable. Stubborn, eccentric and intractable. May preach tolerance, but can be the most intolerant of people.

SUN SAGITTARIUS, MOON PISCES: Caring, spiritual and soft-hearted. Often unrealistic, with little or no interest in the practicalities of life. Lacking in self-esteem and downtrodden.

SUN CAPRICORN, MOON ARIES: Determined, intelligent, forceful and often ruthlessly ambitious. Callous and cold. Anyone who gets in the way of their climb to the top should watch out.

SUN CAPRICORN, MOON TAURUS: Dependable, artistic and down-to-earth. A good homemaker and manager. Can be obstinate and intolerant, hating change or upheaval.

SUN CAPRICORN, MOON GEMINI: Good with words, and excellent at communicating generally, seeing projects through to the end. Can be glib, superficial and occasionally careless.

SUN CAPRICORN, MOON CANCER: Faithful, family-centered, with shining integrity. A worrier, given to sulking and brooding over what are often imaginary problems.

SUN CAPRICORN, MOON LEO: Tough, purposeful and ambitious, though can sometimes reveal a surprisingly sympathetic streak. Sometimes secretly soft-hearted. Conversely, can be arrogant and cruel.

SUN CAPRICORN, MOON VIRGO: Business-like, serious, dependable and usually very thorough. Can be pompous and sometimes dull company. Old before their time.

SUN CAPRICORN, MOON LIBRA: Good mixer and motivator, though impractical. Innovative thinker and pioneer. Sometimes gullible and a bit childish.

SUN CAPRICORN, MOON SCORPIO: Strong and determined, with a sense of personal destiny. Can be kind and caring, but also sarcastic and too quick to demolish others verbally.

SUN CAPRICORN, MOON SAGITTARIUS: Focused and dedicated, stable, organized and communicative. Need to relax, have more fun and take life a lot easier. Can suffer early burnout.

SUN CAPRICORN, MOON CAPRICORN: Hard workers, with great stamina and powers of endurance. Sympathetic and caring. Uncomfortable with emotion and far too tense. Need to take more time out.

SUN CAPRICORN, MOON AQUARIUS: Efficient, broad-minded and organized, with high standards for themselves and others. Do not suffer fools gladly and can be very intolerant towards those with different lifestyles or views.

SUN CAPRICORN, MOON PISCES: Dedicated, caring and compassionate. Often intuitive with a tendency to have significant dreams. Can be over-sensitive and easily hurt. Should put themselves first occasionally.

SUN AQUARIUS, MOON ARIES: Amusing, energetic and innovative. Often highly motivated, but sometimes rather difficult and arrogant. They can sometimes come over as quirky and a little odd.

SUN AQUARIUS, MOON TAURUS: Dogged and dependable. High fliers who often have a marked artistic streak. Obstinate and grumpy, and inclined to get bogged down in the most boring of details.

SUN AQUARIUS, MOON GEMINI: Quick-witted and intelligent. Good communicators. Can be rather flippant and shallow. Occasionally insensitive to the needs and feelings of others.

SUN AQUARIUS, MOON CANCER: Caring and loving, companionable and amusing. Moody and unpredictable. Good at empathizing with others.

SUN AQUARIUS, MOON LEO: Active and busy, purposeful and frequently highly ambitious. Natural loners who are sometimes socially inept,

though still keen to make a good impression.

SUN AQUARIUS, MOON VIRGO: Scholarly and intelligent. A dogged researcher. Often seen as a bit of an oddball. Rather awkward, old-fashioned and fussy. Loyal to people and causes.

SUN AQUARIUS, MOON LIBRA: Fun, extroverted, attractive and often rather charming. Can be superficial and lacking focus and stamina. Good with people and animals.

SUN AQUARIUS, MOON SCORPIO: Natural leaders, teachers or gurus. Bright and innovative, and take easily to the center stage. Underneath the charisma lurks impatience and arrogance.

SUN AQUARIUS, MOON SAGITTARIUS: Clever, bright, impulsive and enthusiastic. Sometimes overoptimistic and unrealistic. Not good with money or planning for a rainy day.

SUN AQUARIUS, MOON CAPRICORN: Businesslike and naturally protective of their family. Usually very efficient, though too serious and inclined to worry. Need to realize that life is not always hard.

SUN AQUARIUS, MOON AQUARIUS: Idealistic and broad-minded, with unusual ideas, beliefs and even lifestyle. Usually tough on themselves and others. Can lack real warmth.

SUN AQUARIUS, MOON PISCES: Intuitive, spiritual, caring and often very clever, though impractical. They can have a tendency to be too other-worldly and unfocused. They can also be naïve and gullible.

SUN PISCES, MOON ARIES: Intelligent, quick-witted, purposeful and entertaining. Egocentric and occasionally manipulative and emotionally demanding. May even resort to moral blackmail.

SUN PISCES, MOON TAURUS: Musical, harmonious, kind and gregarious. Can be indolent and lacking in motivation and ambition. Easygoing.

SUN PISCES, MOON GEMINI: Quick, bright, spontaneous and amusing. Good company, but tend to be anxious and emotionally insecure. All too often in love with love.

SUN PISCES, MOON CANCER: Caring, sympathetic, sensitive and helpful. Good in a crisis, though usually too dreamy and impractical, leaving decisions to others.

SUN PISCES, MOON LEO: Expansive, encouraging, artistic and compassionate. Often egocentric and arrogant. Petulant if crossed. Depressed by bad luck more than most.

SUN PISCES, MOON VIRGO: Profound, psychic and often very creative. Tend to be nervy, obsessive and somewhat weak-willed. Will seek refuge and peace when life gets too tough.

SUN PISCES, MOON LIBRA: Active, innovative, energetic and enthusiastic. Charismatic and good with people. Can inspire and motivate others, but tend to be unrealistic and lacking in stamina.

SUN PISCES, MOON SCORPIO: Compassionate, profound, psychic and often powerful in their chosen field. Unpredictable and occasionally inclined to depression.

SUN PISCES, MOON SAGITTARIUS: Restless. Great travelers. Often deep and studious, with questing minds. Also unreliable and over-optimistic. Bad planners.

SUN PISCES, MOON CAPRICORN: Intuitive, creative and efficient. Very reliable and solid, with artistic leanings. Tend to be insecure and sometimes lack ambition.

SUN PISCES, MOON AQUARIUS: Open and honest, spiritual and caring. Often have very good ideas. Too otherworldly and inclined to gullibility. Best to keep their feet on the ground.

SUN PISCES, MOON PISCES: Spiritual and mystical, imaginative and intuitive. May have important and powerful dreams. Often lacking in ambition and motivation, and may be somewhat gullible. May suffer from erratic energy levels.

THE MOON IN ARIES

(Ruled by Mars)

The masculine fire of Aries is not extinguished by the Moon's quiet calm. This Moon Sign is all action, energy and impulsiveness. The Arian tendency to rush in where angels fear to tread is enhanced by the Moon's emotionality, so here we have the great movers and shakers of the world.

Moon in Aries people tend to be personally affronted by social injustice. They will rarely pass by a homeless person without giving him something, and they are characteristically inspired to change any situation for the better. They want the world to be a better place right now, and can become very upset when faced with intractable problems and the slow pace of change. Characteristically, these people find it almost impossible to understand opposing views, or even to comprehend that others have a right to express them. They simply cannot see that it is possible to think differently, and so they rarely pause to consider the feelings of others in their headlong rush to get things done – *their* way.

person at work or high-ranking government official. They love tackling problems themselves, and are surprisingly good at it. They can be delegators, though, if somewhat impatient ones.

These people tend to be good with money, too; although from time to time their *joie de vivre* can lead them into unwise spending sprees. They tend to be full of marvelous money-making schemes that may or may not produce results. But even when they fail disastrously, they bounce back with another one.

Lunar Arians are very quick thinking. They have charm, wit and an infectious optimism that may not always be justified. They tend to be unrealistic and to go charging off on madcap schemes that everyone else realizes are doomed. Nobody, though, dares to say so. Lunar Arians see life on an epic scale and rarely notice the irritating details, such as having no capital, or the danger that can lie in the small print.

These people have original minds and can be very creative if given enough freedom to express

Lunar Arians want the world to be a better place right now, and can become very upset when faced with intractable problems and the slow pace of change

Lunar Arians never let the grass grow under their feet. They are not procrastinators. They deal with everything immediately, sometimes without too much thought, but always with great energy and verve. They zoom toward their goals with superb self-motivation and courage. They will stand up to anyone, even the most intimidating

themselves. They hate restriction and their tempers can explode if they are crossed or frustrated in their ambitions. However, a genuine crisis will bring out the best in them. Their natural courage and qualities of leadership will come to the fore, enabling them to save the day.

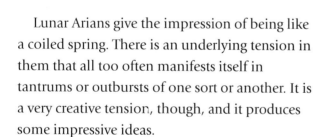

Lunar Arians give the impression of being like a coiled spring. There is an underlying tension in them that all too often manifests itself in tantrums or outbursts of one sort or another. It is a very creative tension, though, and it produces some impressive ideas.

They are never secretive or deceitful, preferring to be loud and outspoken rather than hold back their opinions. They also appreciate this sort of straightforwardness in others. They can be shocked by revelations of plotting, intrigue or deception, and simply do not understand why some people need a secret agenda. Honesty and integrity are central to the character of Lunar Arians.

These people have such unbounded energy and enthusiasm that they have a talent for motivating other less-inspired souls, although they will easily throw caution to the wind. They always have their eyes on the distant horizon, which can be thrilling to others, and their faith in the future and in their own potential can do wonders to bring renewed vigor to a tired project.

Lunar Arians are warm-hearted and more sympathetic and broad-minded than their Sun Sign counterparts. They are tolerant of other colors and creeds, seeing humanity as one large team that needs to pull together to get things done. They are impatient with red tape, prejudice and pessimism.

RELATIONSHIPS

Lunar Arians have no time for whiners. They react best to practical problems, leaving others to deal with the emotional trauma. This can make relationships difficult for this type. Their constant need to get up and go often masks a fear of emotional commitment. They also crave newness and excitement, which is fine in the early stages of romantic pursuit, but it can cause serious rifts later on. It is essential for Lunar Arians to keep the flame of passion alive. Sometimes, however, they may unconsciously seek partners who are steady homebodies in order to compensate for their own fiery temperament. Then, they will expect their home to be a haven from the slings and arrows of fortune, however outrageous.

They are unhappy with competition, which they often take personally, and find equally strong partners impossible to live with. Many choose weaker, more malleable types, often younger and less experienced than themselves. There is a large dose of masculinity in both sexes, which manifests in women as a tendency to dominate their partners and take the initiative sexually. Lunar Arians need a highly charged sex life and will not tolerate a relationship that declines into mere companionship; although they do have a strong need for friendship with a life partner. They are energetic lovers but are rarely too intense. They do enjoy fun and laughter in the bedroom. When things go wrong, however, they are disinclined to seek advice for failing relationships. To them, when it's over, it's over. Lunar Aries types have high standards, sometimes impossibly so. They expect to be given unconditional love and support in all their madcap schemes, while also demanding their

unequivocal independence. Any hint that their partners will permit anything less than total freedom is immediately interpreted as being too demanding. If they feel threatened, their endless fault-finding can become unbearable.

Although Lunar Arians can be happy homemakers, more often than not they leave domesticity to others. They can endure all manner of inconveniences better than most, and often simply do not notice their environment. Many see their home as a base from which they emerge in a blaze of glory to take on the world. Lunar Arians tend to be aloof parents, eager to get the best education they can afford for their offspring, but not so keen to spend quality time with them on a daily basis.

Lunar Arian parents are often hurtfully dismissive of timid or slow children, and should make efforts to see life from their perspective from time to time. Lunar Arians tend to have had problems with their own parents, particularly Arian fathers, who matched their explosive temper and personal ambitions against their children's. Often this erupted into naked rivalry, with the child constantly being compared unfavorably to the father at the same age, their achievements belittled, sometimes scathingly. Sometimes the Arian Moon child is so overawed by their father that they try to emulate him. Every failure to do so is then seen as a tragedy and another nail in the coffin of their own development as mature individuals.

As for their mothers, they may be demanding. These mothers are often too engrossed in their own lives and too busy trying to make their mark to take much notice of their children. Arian Moon children often have childhood experiences that echo those of their mothers, so they spend their whole lives trying to escape from this fate. Yet often great leaders and achievers come out of this tense atmosphere. They may not be too happy at showing their emotions, but they are successful both intellectually and in their careers.

CAREER

If a Lunar Arian is born into a family that is proud of their line of business, which they pass on from generation to generation, it can often be very difficult for this individual to break free of the established pattern. This will almost

inevitably cause great problems within the family if they do.

Lunar Arians tend to be artistic and creative, and even if they fail to fulfill this potential, many communicators and are especially adept with modern technology. They can also make excellent teachers – although their tendency to bully may ruin many a child's school days. Lunar Arians like

Lunar Arians tend to be artistic and creative, and even if they fail to fulfil this potential, many continue to have the burning ambition to learn the piano or take up art

continue to have the burning ambition to learn the piano or take up art, but somehow never get around to it and always wish they had. Even so, with their restless ambition, they need to be the best at everything they do. Producing second-rate paintings or sitting basic piano examinations when they are adults does not appeal to them. If they can't be the best, they don't even want to try.

If they escape the family business, these people seek a career that constantly challenges them. They hate routine or having to defer to someone else, so self-employment is often the answer for them. They can also make good, strong team leaders or fair-minded employers, eager to promote equality in the workforce. But they can be impatient with slow or indecisive workers, and can react angrily to those who challenge their views. Ocassionally, Lunar Arian bosses become real bullies. They simply can't work with people for whom they have no respect. Unfortunately, because they tend to have a massive ego, they usually think that most people fall into that category.

The careers that bolster this ego are the most appealing to Lunar Arians – anything from advertising copy-writing to rising rapidly through the ranks in the army. They tend to be good

to be the center of attention and they will tackle anything that sets them apart as leaders or stars. In the performing arts they do best as dancers.

All Lunar Arians need a firm hand, or they become ridiculously unrealistic. So in any career where a manager or agent is necessary, they should be on their guard against too much flattery or being cushioned from reality. In fact, they prefer straight talking from those who help them run their careers and can become very angry with people who waste time.

HEALTH

On the whole, these people are healthy and energetic, although they are prone to accidents. Traditionally, the Moon governs chronic conditions, which, in the case of Aries, are generally those affecting the ear, nose and throat areas.

THE MOON IN TAURUS

(Ruled by Venus)

*T*he femininity of Venusian Taurus is accentuated here by that of the Moon, which adds extra depth to an already highly-developed sensuality. Traditionally, the Moon is described as being "exalted" in Taurus, which means that Lunar Taureans are emotionally stable and physically strong. These people are happy with their place on Earth, and, even if their lives are difficult, they will endure the vagaries of their lot without any complaint.

Lunar Taureans find great enjoyment in the good things of life, whether it is wining and dining, dancing cheek to cheek in the moonlight or making love. However, they are not naturally assertive, and prefer to go with the flow rather than make things happen. They are conservative and admire the status quo. The placement of the Moon at their birth means that they feel personally threatened by upheavals and can

assertive, but, if their lifestyle and all they hold dear is challenged, they will muster all their considerable strength to preserve it.

RELATIONSHIPS

Moon in Taurus people are among the least promiscuous of all the zodiac. They are solid, dependable types who see relationships as life commitments and are wary of jumping in head first without any thought for the future. They do have occasional lapses, though. They are not nature's bedhoppers and tend to look askance at those who are. But nor do they merely give their hearts: Lunar Taureans see in every serious relationship – and what other

Lunar Taureans find great enjoyment in the good things of life, whether it is wining and dining, dancing cheek to cheek in the moonlight or making love

become very distressed by any kind of change, disturbance or argument. These people are noted not only for their stability in a changing world, but also for their resistance to the new. In some cases, this tendency can be so marked that it almost seems pathological. They will keep faith with a way of life that has long been outmoded. In fact, they are proud to do so and will defend it to the last. Lunar Taureans may not be naturally

sort do they ever have? – the potential for building a family, with all that it entails.

From the first date, they are unconsciously testing their partner for lifelong faithfulness and loyalty. This is why those with the Moon in this position are often described as being jealous and possessive. They are constantly alert for what they see as signs of unsuitability in their future husband or wife and, once married, they are

retreat hurt. They might even brood for years afterward because these people are tenacious about everything, including hanging on to their old emotions – which they tend to bottle up. Their scars go deep, and they may even develop a perverse pride in fretting over a hurt, much later in life.

However, Lunar Taureans will doggedly accept many situations that are less than perfect and stick with them rather than face the consequences of upheaval. Despite their extreme possessiveness, or maybe because of it, they live in uncongenial surroundings and make do with less than fulfilling careers. They can, however, be real pests toward those they live with, constantly demanding that partners uphold the same impossibly high standards as they set themselves.

Socially, Lunar Taureans may be stolid and unimaginative, but they make sensual, erotic lovers and can be a revelation in bed. They love luxurious fabrics, which may make the bed a symphony of silks and satins – even if the rest of the house is decorated in fairly unimaginative, but impeccably good, taste.

It takes a lot for Lunar Taureans to admit that there is a problem with the love of their life. Some never do, even though everyone else has recognized the difficulty for some time. Though always willing to take the rough with the smooth, Lunar Taureans are completely shattered by the breakup of a relationship, particularly if it is a longstanding marriage. They tend to find discussing their feelings extremely difficult, although they can force themselves to seek advice that may help the relationship to work again. They find it very hard to

forever testing the strength of the most important relationship in their lives.

When challenged in love, Lunar Taureans can become very distressed. Having an essentially feminine attitude, they tend not to fight, but

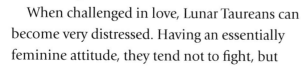

accept the inevitable, and need enormous amounts of love and support from family and friends in messy divorces.

Lunar Taurean women may see themselves as boring, with mundane lives, and seek to counterbalance this by being attracted to exciting rogues. The road to the altar is littered with the corpses of Lunar Taurean dreams, both male and female.

Confidence tricksters, wife batterers and assorted ne'er-do-wells can often make the Lunar Taurean heart flutter as long as they are glamorous, witty and perhaps a little flashy. Dark, saturnine Scorpios, all-too plausible Geminis, slippery Pisceans and rabble-rousing Aquarians can make Lunar Taureans go weak at the knees, forget their natural good taste and discernment, and make complete fools of themselves. They have been warned.

Yet, when they eventually find true love, responsible, reliable and practical Lunar Taureans make excellent providers for their families. They are good homemakers. They always have their insurance and pension plans in order, plus a little tucked away – earning interest – for a rainy day. They may never make a fortune, but even in times of economic stringency they usually manage to do well enough.

These solid citizens can be extremely dull, and many of their more fiery or airy children cause friction by openly rebelling against their conservatism. Lunar Taurean parents long to understand their children, whom they adore in their own, reserved way, but they are genuinely hurt and bewildered when all that they personally hold dear is challenged.

The incoming Age of Aquarius will be tough for most people, with its futuristic technology, social unrest and radical new attitudes, but it will be the ultimate test for Lunar Taureans.

These people are of the Earth and make excellent tillers of the soil, landscapers and gardeners with very high standards. They love looking out across their land and being lords of all they survey. They are also very happy to help others with their own gardens, perhaps in a professional capacity.

The Four of Wands from the Tarot represents country life, repose, concord, good fortune and peace of mind – truly quintessential Taurean aspirations

Lunar Taureans love the open air: trudging through the woods on a crisp autumn afternoon, then home to hot chocolate by the fire is bliss to them. Many aspire to the lifestyle of the landed gentry or aristocratic families, where lots of dogs go along for country pursuits, followed by hearty meals with fine wine. They enjoy hunting, shooting and fishing, which can cause big problems if their relatives or children are into animal rights. Of course, not all Lunar Taureans aspire to this lifestyle, but it is a rare one who, from time to time, fails

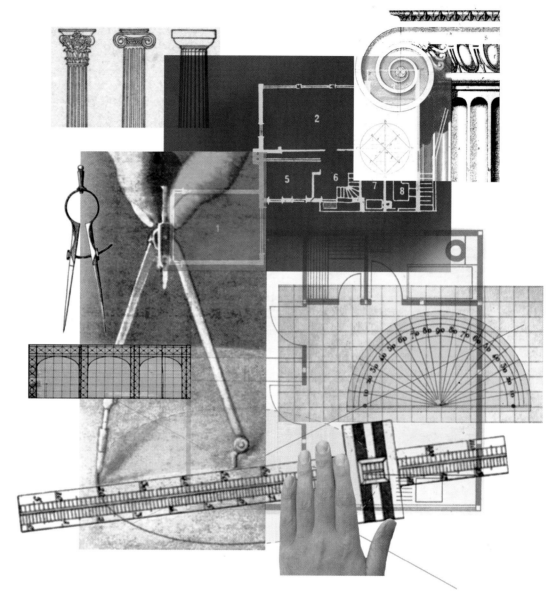

to hanker after life in a large country house surrounded by acres of land.

CAREER

This is a very practical Moon placement, meaning that these people are best at creating solid things, providing food and shelter, making furniture or coping with administrative duties. Anything that requires a good, steady pace and pays well will suit the Lunar Taurean temperament; although many such people will also be attracted to the performing arts. This may find expression in hobbies. It was once said that, being such a feminine position, the caring professions are ideal for Lunar Taureans; although this seems no longer to be the case. After all, it is

unfashionable for many women to be overtly "feminine" these days. Even so, it is unlikely that Lunar Taureans will actively seek to join the army or other similar organizations unless there is a considerable amount of Mars in the rest of their chart.

Lunar Taureans make excellent beauticians, dress designers and craftspeople, because they have an instinctive eye for harmony of line, shape and color. They can also be good architects and appreciate being able to see the fruits of their imagination taking real shape as buildings that will last – the ideal Lunar Taurean achievement!

Many Lunar Taureans have had to give up the idea of realizing their greatest ambitions, often because of restrictive parents or gender-specific conditioning when young. Consequently, some find it hard to motivate themselves in adulthood. They just cannot push themselves forward and seek promotion, often being quite content to sit back and let others win the glittering prizes or take the praise. Lunar Taureans are not given to seeing themselves at the top, which is why so few of them ever reach it. However, in many cases, this is the only reason they fail to become notable achievers. They are hard workers, pay attention to all-important details and are scrupulously honest and fair. Many are extremely talented. However, besides a lack of self-esteem, this is not a lucky Moon position. These people have to work hard to get anywhere in life: they are not likely to be jackpot

lottery winners or to enjoy similar strokes of unexpected luck.

LUNAR TAUREAN CHILDREN

Lunar Taureans often felt they had to keep their thoughts and feelings to themselves as children, and this tendency spills over into adulthood. They can become awkward if pushed into expressing themselves or may suddenly lash out in volcanic explosions of temper. Taureans are known for their stoicism, but also for their bullish rages if pushed to the very edge, and Lunar Taureans are no exception. They feel things deeply, even though they find it almost impossible to say so. Unfortunately, they usually manage to rage at inappropriate moments, bewildering and frightening those around them, especially the youngsters.

HEALTH

Lunar Taureans are generally physically robust, but stress can adversely affect their traditionally weak areas, such as the throat and thyroid, especially in winter. With their sensual love of food, alcohol and all the fine things in life, there is a tendency to put on weight. Fortunately, this can be mitigated by their distaste for poor self-presentation. Lunar Taureans love to have an appealing image, to be slender and chic, so they may well force themselves to work off their overindulgence at the gym.

THE MOON
IN GEMINI

(Ruled by Mercury)

Lunar Geminis are nervy, changeable and witty, and make natural communicators. There is a profound underlying restlessness in this Moon placement, as if they feel their skin doesn't fit. An inner conflict often drives them to achieve great things but can also provoke bursts of extreme irritability and bouts of depression.

people to devastating effect. Both males and females can be "bitchy" and sarcastic, and some revel in the power their superior fluency gives them over others.

The Moon gives added depth to this sign, though. These people can be profound thinkers who – as long as their full interest is engaged – can spend hours grappling with abstract

Lunar Geminis are also natural writers, journalists and radio and television presenters. They were made for the media, and the media was made for them

This Moon Sign cares passionately about promoting themselves and their ego: these people package themselves like a commercial commodity, planning every stage of their climb to the top. They are calculating and shrewd, using their considerable charm as a major weapon against the competition.

A mutable sign, Lunar Geminis are rarely still for very long. They can become bored very easily, although their attention span can differ widely depending on the level of their interest in the subject in question. Some of them find it hard to focus on any topic for any length of time, constantly waxing enthusiastic about the next task, and never finishing the last one.

Words are their natural medium. Lunar Geminis can talk for hours and are never far from a telephone. They tend to be witty, finding humor in puns and wordplay, and may be good at crosswords and anagrams. The negative aspect of this love affair with words is that they can use them as weapons against slower or less articulate

philosophical problems. They make excellent teachers at all educational levels, really caring that their pupils understand the subjects they teach. Lunar Geminis are also natural writers, journalists and radio and television presenters. They were made for the media, and the media was made for them.

Lunar Geminis are very eager to travel – the influence of speedy Mercury – and can often be found in the air travel

Temperance from the Tarot perfectly reflects the Geminian tendency to moderation and restraint. Reversed the card signifies excess and unbalance – the flip side of Gemini

industry or in the car trade. They are also superb salespeople.

Lunar Geminis have very conflicting attitudes to money. They can spend money like water on clothes, cars, aids to grooming and on being seen in all the fashionable places. Yet there is, paradoxically, often an underlying cautious streak that means excess is followed by parsimony.

Not generally as scatter-brained as many Sun Sign Geminis, they appreciate order and logic; although they are not happy taking a back seat, endlessly poring over facts and figures. They derive great pleasure and job satisfaction from being "up front," demonstrating the new ideas to the workforce, representing the company abroad

or taking the microphone at a big sales show.

Lunar Geminis love change and can drive themselves furiously hard in pursuit of their goals. They can be obsessive and workaholic, ignoring all the warning signs as their system becomes overloaded with stress and lack of rest. They constantly push themselves too hard. They can be so eager not to miss any opportunity to better themselves that they reap the sorry harvest of this lifestyle quite abruptly, when their exhausted minds and bodies simply cannot go on any longer. They are not naturally robust, but constantly seek to prove to themselves and others how hard they can work, how little sleep they need and how they can get by without vacations or proper meals.

Lunar Geminis, therefore, need to pace themselves. They should learn calming techniques such as yoga and meditation and should try to take up some exercise to work off all that nervous energy. Swimming is good for them, and so is fast walking or exercising on a trampoline.

They are prone to changeable moods, falling from lofty "highs" to deepest lows. They then retreat from the world and feel that fate has been extremely unkind to let them become so

RELATIONSHIPS

In relationships, Moon Sign Geminis can be irritable, very often feeling trapped and held against their will. Many take a long time to commit themselves emotionally. Some never settle down at all. They prefer to "marry" their careers and make their mark in

Moon Sign Geminis have more depth and sensitivity. They may look trendy, but their interests go well beyond the fashionable

despondent. However, these dark nights of the soul can ultimately be very creative and positive, somehow allowing them to dredge up from the depths of their unconscious minds the elusive answer to their current predicament. Often they pull themselves out of their anguish into a new and exciting world.

Lunar Geminis are very eager to create a memorable first impression. They spend time and money on their image, and they can be startlingly chic and trendy. But while Sun Sign Geminis may go for up-to-date clothes, designer homes, cars, mobile phones and laptop computers, Moon Sign Geminis have more depth and sensitivity. They may look trendy, but their interests go well beyond the fashionable. Sometimes, a Lunar Gemini can be very much in the world though not always totally of it. Some have unusual intellectual hobbies or interests, including unorthodox religious beliefs.

more spectacular fashion than "just" being someone's mom or dad. However, this can be a strange sign – a pleasing and enviable combination of Geminian masculinity and Lunar femininity.

Lunar Geminis are tactile and outgoing. They may appear flirtatious and sexual, but the truth is that many of them prefer to think and talk about sex rather than do it. There is often a lack of real

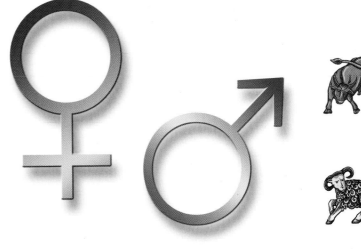

Lunar Geminis can spend money like water on clothes, cars, aids to grooming and on being seen in all the fashionable places

underlying libido and the honest warmth needed for the full expression of physical love. These individuals tend to shy away from putting emotions into words. Sometimes, it is enough for them to know that they are desired. The knowledge alone provides a kind of stable basis for them, both socially and emotionally. They have no real desire to make a relationship out of the first flickerings of attraction. It is easy to flatter a Lunar Gemini simply by flirting.

However, those who do enjoy sex are easily bored with the usual routine and may rapidly progress to something they consider more entertaining, just to spice things up a little bit.

This is a Peter Pan sign, full of children who never grow up, something that can make Lunar Geminis excellent parents but rather tiresome siblings. They move restlessly from one activity to another, thinking up games and bedtime stories until even the most energetic small children get tired. Lunar Geminis are very good at the practical side of parenting, too: they spend money on their offspring, ensuring that they have everything other children have, and more. They also spend quality time with them if they can. However,

many of these people are too busy, working on several projects at once: working late at the office, taking work home, setting up dinner parties, talking on the phone, spending time at the gym and shopping. Often, when they do come home their non-Gemini partner has put the children to bed hours before. Even weekends are such a mad rush that the time can slip by without "quality time" ever arriving.

Lunar Geminis are often so keen to sell themselves and their ideas that they sometimes resort to embroidering the truth because they are inclined to see the truth as a commodity like anything else – to be dressed up or down, depending on the circumstances.

HEALTH

Healthwise, apart from the tendency to overtax their nervous energy, these individuals are traditionally prone to autoimmune diseases and have problems with their lungs, hands and arms. In addition, all that running around may make them prone to accidents.

THE MOON
IN CANCER

(Ruled by the Moon)

Lunar Cancers are plagued by their extreme sensitivity, and so are those around them. They are sympathetic, kind, compassionate people who care deeply about their loved ones, the underdog and everyone else with a genuine hard luck story. They react strongly to any hint of unhappiness, instantly becoming the valiant protector and carer, although often at great cost to their own peace of mind – for Lunar Cancers are obsessive worriers.

Life is a roller coaster of emotions for these people. Responding from the heart, not the head,

for just a moment, their fears will all come true.

Lunar Cancers are sensitive to good or bad atmosphere. Simply by entering a room they can tell what kind of person lives there, or even lived there many years before. Of course, this kind of psychic awareness is a very much a mixed blessing. On the one hand, it enables Lunar Cancers to know, or at least strongly suspect, the truth behind the public mask that most other people show the world. On the other hand, this ability may involve too many unpleasant insights to make for a comfortable social life. Lunar

Lunar Cancers are sympathetic, kind, compassionate people who care deeply about their loved ones, the underdog and everyone else with a genuine hard luck story

is typical of them in most situations. It is said that their moods change as often as the tides. Since they are ruled by the Moon, that idea is especially apt, but some change even more frequently than that. Every new development provokes an emotional reaction, especially in Lunar Cancerian children or those who are not fortunate enough to have strong mental discipline.

Lunar Cancers are great, but unrepentant, worriers. Some seem to make an occupation out of fretting about others. This can often be a rather unattractive trait if carried to extremes. They worry that their loved ones may suffer accidents or that some other fearful fate will befall them. It is almost a superstition: they feel that, in some way, worrying prevents bad things from happening, and if they relax and drop their guard

Cancers are also very much in tune with children and some animals, although their tendency to be sentimental can prevent them from understanding them completely.

Unfortunately, Lunar Cancers can be inveterate sulkers and expect to be cajoled out of their moods. They also have the disconcerting tendency to burst into tears – that is, mostly, but not exclusively, female Lunar Cancers – and throw things around. Fortunately, the outbursts do tend to be short-lived.

When sentiment rules, as it often does here, nostalgia is never far behind. If Sun Sign Cancers hoard every last photograph and memento, then those with the Moon in Cancer are much worse. They have collections of bus tickets and beer coasters going back twenty years, and cannot bear to be parted from them. Deeper still, however, is

their tendency to hoard people, or rather their memories of them. They will not let go, and can wave the fairy wand of wish-fulfilment over reality until it becomes something else entirely. For example, women whose fathers were drunken abusers can really believe they were loving protectors. Men who truly hated their deprived childhood will declare later, hand on heart, that it was the happiest time of their lives. Some Lunar Cancers, however, are eager to create harmony and seek a peaceful atmosphere above all. They can also tend to complain about less-than-perfect surroundings. But as long as there is a degree of emotional stability, they will actually endure a great deal of inconvenience and discomfort.

RELATIONSHIPS

Men and women of this Moon placement have a strong desire to create a nest, and they are willing to roll up their sleeves and tackle the hard work of creating it themselves. They will, however, expect those around them to acknowledge their efforts and be grateful.

Lunar Cancers are great martyrs and will nurture grievances for many years. They may become extremely bitter about some trivial argument that happened in childhood and carry it into adult life. However, they do try to put matters right between warring factions, even if their diplomatic skills are sometimes hampered by their own hypersensitivity.

Lunar Cancers are in touch with their senses and make extremely good lovers. These people really know how to blend a heightened sense of

scenes. But in there somewhere is the capacity to hit out and hurt – or at least give a nasty nip with those overgrown Crab's pincers.

CAREER

Traditionally, Lunar Cancers work best as carers, in hospitals, hospices and with the mentally and physically disabled. They are particularly good as nursery nurses, although their tender loving care is also very effective at the other end of the age spectrum, in geriatric nursing. They are also good counselors, though they need to be thoroughly trained to override their tendency to overempathize with the clients.

Lunar Cancers are not especially ambitious and are best in supporting roles, sometimes literally, for they can be surprisingly good actors –

Lunar Cancers are not especially ambitious and are best in supporting roles, sometimes literally, for they can be surprisingly good actors

the erotic with the expression of true love, which can be an explosive and memorable mix in the bedroom. By nature they are loyal – often to a fault – and so tend to make and keep partners for life, because of their sheer dedication to making the relationship work.

However, unfaithful lovers should take note: they may think they can ride roughshod over poor, clinging Lunar Cancers, but they may be in for an unpleasant surprise. True, any evidence of infidelity will come as a terrible shock to their delicate system, resulting in violently emotional

possibly because their natural reserve can be sublimated by playing at being someone else.

They make excellent teachers and genuinely care for the all-around welfare of their pupils. They are also interested in their subsequent careers and family lives. They have a real sense of contributing to history, even if only in a small way, and often their nostalgic tendency manifests itself in passing a vivid awareness of the past to the children in their class.

They can be practical – using their hands creatively is the perfect way for them to forget their

They really know how to blend a heightened sense of the erotic with the expression of true love

worries – and can find success as decorators, interior designers or carpenters. They love making things for the home and often have hobbies such as tapestry making, pottery or decorative metalworking.

They can easily abandon or suppress their own ambitions in order to support those of their loved ones. They take a real pride in the achievements of others, especially those close to home, but can become huge bores about it – constantly showing photographs of their children to virtual strangers and going on at length about how their husbands or wives have been promoted at work.

However, whether seeking advancement for themselves or basking in the glory of others, Lunar Cancers need financial security. There is nothing devil-may-care about them, nothing of the Sagittarian backpacker or the Geminian tendency to skip quite happily from job to job. Security is imperative for Cancers, both Solar and Lunar. Their emotional happiness often rests on freedom from financial worry.

LUNAR CANCERIAN CHILDREN

Lunar Cancers are often very insecure as children, and may pass this tendency on to the next generation. Often there is a genuine reason for this fear of the future and distrust of the present. Material deprivation or the breakup of their parents' marriage are two examples. However, in many cases it is simply part of the intrinsic baggage of this Lunar placement.

These people believe that they will become social pariahs if they are laid off of a job. In their mind, starvation and destitution are not far behind, so periods of unemployment seem like nothing less than the end of life as they have known it.

Lunar Cancers can be very mean-spirited, both in money terms and – perhaps surprisingly – in emotional terms as well. They can scrimp and save compulsively, even when there really is no urgent need to do so. At such times, they may bewilder and hurt others with their frankly cheap and uninspired gifts. They can also show a marked lack of empathy with those they dislike, and can cut them out of their lives – only to brood over it afterwards. This can upset children greatly, especially those born under more generous-minded signs, who tend to forgive, forget and move on much more easily.

HEALTH

Women with this Lunar placement may suffer more than most with menstrual, menopausal and hormonal problems because of the influence of their ruler, the Moon. Similarly, they may lean toward water retention and should drink at least six large glasses of mineral or filtered water a day in order to keep their water balance healthy. In later life they may react badly to Hormone Replacement Treatment (HRT). Alternative or nutritional therapies could prove more helpful.

Traditionally, this Lunar placement is quite robust physically, although it has a tendency towards breast, chest and stomach problems. However, the extreme emotional sensitivity of these individuals can result in a whole host of psychosomatic ailments such as blinding headaches, stomach upsets, insomnia and a weakened autoimmune system.

Lunar Cancers should seek advice in order to sort out their emotional problems, especially at times of greatest stress, such as bereavement. If they try to soldier on by themselves, their health is in danger of breaking down altogether.

THE MOON
IN LEO

(Ruled by the Sun)

*M*oon Sign Leos are generous, noble, encouraging and optimistic. They are natural leaders who exude energy and drive, and are often protective toward more timid mortals. They have an innate sense of style and love beautiful, chic and successful people. The leaders of the pack, they can genuinely care for those they feel are in some way inferior to them.

They set remarkably high standards for themselves and others, which can lead to all manner of problems. Although endlessly willing to give others the benefit of the doubt, whenever they feel let down, they react with shock, disbelief and dismay. Lunar Leos expect the best but rarely get it. However, what horrifies them the most are their own failings. They tend to have a very elevated image of themselves as the most moral and ethical of people. If the image slips and they experience the less noble emotions – such as jealousy, pessimism, envy, infidelity or even downright dishonesty – they become very depressed and angry at themselves and everyone around them.

Lunar Leos love display. They will always aim to look expensively fashionable, even if their clothes came from a thrift shop, and they like to be surrounded by people with similar style. They

199

can feel mortally offended by those who look dirty or sloppy. They fail to understand people who choose alternative lifestyles, for – being a fixed sign – Lunar Leos are very proud of maintaining the status quo and have little time for rebels or eccentrics.

However, even though they like society itself to be stable and unchanging, they hate routine and sameness in their personal lives. Fired up by their ruler, the Sun, they burst with restless energy,

RELATIONSHIPS

Lunar leos are very romantic and generous and love to wine and dine, going to great lengths to flatter their partner and make them feel very special. In return, they expect loyalty, support and understanding, besides a fair amount of ego-bolstering.

Lunar Leos will go to almost any lengths for those they love or want to protect, but they can

Fired up by their ruler, the Sun, they burst with restless energy, constantly prowling around looking for new experiences and challenges

constantly prowling around looking for new experiences and challenges. Frustration makes them irritable, even aggressive towards others, and they can pounce on tiny mistakes as if they were major blunders.

Leos long for excitement, a longing intensified by the influence of the Moon. They long for the sexual thrill which power gives them, and may seek situations where they can show off their mastery – in relationships, in their careers or in dangerous sports. If there is any chance that a specific course of action will make them powerful, they will follow it – even if it means they have to live very near the edge of danger. Lunar Leos rarely lack courage, although their judgment may be in doubt.

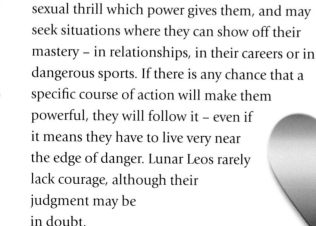

become extremely hurt and angry if their generosity is rejected. To them, ingratitude is a cardinal sin; and they do like to be thanked often and effusively. Sometimes, in fact, their insistence on gratitude can effectively take the shine off the original gift.

They are warm and passionate lovers, and adore the idea of romantic involvement. Sometimes, their own capacity for infidelity takes them by surprise. Their inner restlessness gives them a wandering eye, a hankering after new and exciting experiences and an inner conviction that this is no more than their due. They can put up with a less-than-perfect relationship for a surprisingly long time, often because they feel it is the decent thing to do, but suddenly they will tire of it and begin again with a new partner.

Leos are natural leaders, exuding energy and drive,
and are often protective toward more timid mortals

Lunar Leos can be irritatingly superior and aloof. Many of them believe they have a God-given sovereignty over the rest of humanity and believe they always know best. This can be very annoying, but in an intimate relationship it could prove critical. Few loved ones find this attitude truly attractive, and it can wreck many a promising relationship before it has a chance to begin.

For the same reason, Lunar

CAREER

Despite this, Leos often find young people stimulating company, and become teachers or sports instructors, where their natural qualities of leadership are most appreciated. They are good in a crisis and are often hero-worshipped by the youngsters in their care, who see them as extremely glamorous role models.

Whatever career they choose, Lunar Leos like to be stars. Naturally ambitious, Lunar Leos forge ahead along their particular path to the top, rarely giving the sensibilities of others a thought.

> *Despite this, Leos often find young people stimulating company, and become teachers or sports instructors, where their natural qualities of leadership are most appreciated*

Leos can be overbearing parents and difficult siblings; although their innate charm and generosity will often help restore their popularity. Although they can be irritable with slow or introverted children, or rebellious teenagers, they will – at least in theory – always defend the right of these youngsters to live the way they choose. Lunar Leos are not always at ease in discussions about emotions, which can often upset youngsters who are struggling to explain themselves. Fortunately, Leos usually – if belatedly – know the value of affection.

Lunar Leos can tend to put their children under constant pressure to be great achievers and to repress their natural emotions, which they see as "weak."

Whatever the route, they make excellent employers, and can be surprisingly understanding toward those who work for them.

Lunar Leos love power and can even sublimate their own need for conquest by immersing themselves in a greater enterprise. For this reason, they are excellent career soldiers but are not content with lower ranks. There is, though, another sort of power that fascinates Lunar, though not all Solar, Leos – the world of the paranormal. It is said that many of the great magi, who belonged to the priestly caste of ancient Persia (Iran), were Lunar Leos, and it is easy to see how their power of ritual magic earned respect and a certain amount of awe.

However, magic, apart from stage magic, is

The World from the Tarot represents assurance and worldy success – the very essence of Leos, who stride confidently through life, never doubting that the world and all that's in it is theirs for the taking

rarely a career. It is more of a hobby-cum-religion. Because they love the good things in life, Lunar Leos are attracted by the hotel trade, where they can revel in the bonhomie, although they are considerably less happy working behind the scenes where no one notices them. They are the television chefs with a string of bestselling cookbooks to their names rather than the service station cooks.

Lunar Leos can be all style and little substance, though. Although they think they have stamina and work very hard, this often proves less than true. Their style is very erratic and depends on immediate rewards, which they always expect.

It is said that Lunar Leos are more shy than Sun Sign Leos, but often not by much. They may seem slightly less flashy and be deeper thinkers, but they share the same inner drive and self-regard. A basic personality that revolves around self and the promotion of self means that everything Lunar Leos do is driven by the need for personal fulfillment. Of course, egocentricity can take many forms; and it is not always antisocial since it can be a potent motive in making the world a better place. Many Lunar Leos are zealous charity workers who espouse humanitarian causes with the same energy that their more self-centered co-signs usually reserve for promoting themselves. The Lunar Leo will see the cause as an extension of themselves, and cut swathes through those who stand in their way.

Above all, they love to see action and hate stifling committee work – with its endless discussion and formalities. Grand though they may be, their lunar sensitivity makes them formidable champions of the underdog, and they can move very swiftly if they see injustice being meted out to the socially deprived.

HEALTH

The flamboyant lifestyle of Lunar Leos often has an adverse effect on their waistlines, so they need to work off the excess weight by taking some form of aerobic exercise on a daily basis. Kick boxing is particularly good, though putting on the boxing gloves and doing ten rounds with a punchbag will let off their massive buildup of steam.

In later life Lunar Leos can suffer from heart problems. Unfortunately, they will automatically choose cream-laden sauces and juicy steaks over healthier fare every time. Of course, it would be terribly disappointing for a Leo to have to give up all such treats, so a compromise lifestyle may well be the best solution. They could eat healthily for five or six days every week, then indulge themselves in a social setting at the weekend.

Psychosomatic ailments in Lunar Leos tend to center on back problems, usually when they feel without emotional support.

THE MOON
IN VIRGO

(Ruled by Mercury)

ociable, dutiful, logical and clear-headed, Moon Sign Virgos are the commentators of life. They operate from the shadows, rarely seeking the spotlight like a Leo but analyzing and observing, noting everything and, for the moment, saying little. Yet there is an essential paradox in both Solar and Lunar Virgos. They have all the makings of dullness, and, of course, some of them are. But many of them are very witty and charming, with idiosyncratic and even exciting views about life. Some can be downright eccentric, which certainly contradicts the traditional image of the middle-

and are fond of any kind of word games from Scrabble to anagrams. Whereas a Gemini might spout words just to hear the sound of his or her own voice, a Lunar Virgo would rather be quiet and pick their moment to speak. Then, they can deliver a funny or astute one-liner in quiet, deadpan tones.

Trustworthy and completely reliable, Lunar Virgos are stalwart friends and colleagues, with a naturally strong personal code of ethics. They go to great lengths to keep their word, even if it means suffering as a result. They cannot understand those who break their promises or,

Trustworthy and completely reliable, Lunar Virgos are stalwart friends and colleagues, with a naturally strong personal code of ethics. They go to great lengths to keep their word

of-the-road, somewhat down-to-earth Virgos.

They are by nature self-effacing, although if and when they decide they want to shine, they do so memorably and with great panache. This is rare, though. Most of the time Lunar Virgos are content to take a back seat and concern themselves with the daily minutiae of life. They have and eye for details; for example, travel arrangements must be to the letter.

Mercury, their ruling planet, makes them excellent communicators, although they tend not to be television anchors or top salespeople. Their mode of communication is to present even the most difficult contractual, legal, financial or philosophical concepts in clear, concise terms. They love reducing ideas to the bare essentials,

worse, never intended to keep them in the first place. In many ways, Virgoan standards are even higher than Leo's. Leos can often fool themselves into thinking they are behaving decently, when in fact they are doing no such thing. However, Virgos carefully and coolly analyze their own motives as well as those of other people.

Traditionally, Lunar Virgos are tidy, orderly people with a marked penchant for cubby-holing and categorizing everything. In fact, they may be just as untidy in their surroundings as wild-child Sagittarius, but their thought processes are almost inevitably neat and tidy. In their minds there is a logical flow of ideas from A to Z, and their memories can be phenomenal. They may not be notable stars or leaders, but they are second to none in their ability to think laterally, and can often solve problems through sheer ingenuity.

RELATIONSHIPS

Emotionally, Virgos are often said to be cold fish, but this is rarely the case beyond a superficial level. Their reserve can give the impression that they are passionless, but like still waters, their feelings actually run very deep. It may take them an

unusually long time to commit to a relationship, and even then they will be tentative at first. Once they have declared themselves, they are truly dedicated to lifelong love.

The problem is that Lunar Virgos have an inner conflict where expressing emotion is concerned. They want to be romantic and passionate and, in fact, many of them are accomplished poets. But, somehow, in life itself, it just won't come out right. Some have major problems with emotions and sex, finding the whole business overrated – even though their instincts are much the same as anyone else's. Many actually become celibate, even within relationships. They find that the early sexual passion has fizzled out, never to be rekindled, even though their devotion remains just as strong. Many Lunar Virgos tend to adore from a distance, putting the object of their affections on a pedestal or unconsciously choosing inaccessible people, such as film or rock stars, on whom to lavish their frustrated adoration.

Many Virgos sublimate their sexual energy in

mean-spirited nit-picking. They can become very critical, lashing out with scathing remarks and cutting comments. They can even match Scorpio with their verbal attacks. And when the "No More Mr. Nice Guy" mood is upon them, they rarely regret their outbursts. In many respects they feel, sometimes rightly, that others take their good nature for granted, walk all over their finer feelings, never give them due credit or return favors. It takes just one last straw and the barbed comments burst out – not as explosions of fiery temper as with a Leo, or a headlong charge of anger like Taureans, but usually in a much more controlled

Emotionally, Virgos are often said to be cold fish . . .Their reserve can give the impression that they are passionless, but like still waters, their feelings actually run very deep

work or a more general social round, or both. They are often in great demand as friends because of their ready wit, intelligence and rocklike reliability. However, it can come as something of a shock when their friends discover that they have their failings, too.

Virgos can easily descend from their Olympian heights of good humor and easy fellowship into deep, black depression, prolonged bouts of sulking and nasty,

way. And it is all the more deadly for that.

Like many naturally reserved people, Virgos often feel secretly cheated. They are intelligent enough to realize that others are stealing their thunder, but too introverted and modest to put up a fight for what is theirs by right. They also believe, with uncharacteristic irrationality, that others should somehow realize how they feel, even though even their body language characteristically gives little away.

Lunar Virgos can be good homemakers, preferring solid, lasting homes and furniture to flashy, expensive decor. They can be minimalistic, with a taste for bare white walls and plain furnishings. Conversely, they may live in incredible chaos. Ultimately, as long as they can find what they want, they are happy.

often afraid to express it. Fortunately, they can learn to do so within a loving, stable and faithful relationship.

HEALTH

CAREER

They are not particularly eager to make money, although certain aspects of banking and accounting appeal to their logical nature. They usually have pension plans and insurance coverage arranged even while relatively young. Typically, they will be savers rather than splurgers, but once again, they can surprise with sudden sprees and irresponsible extravagances.

Lunar Virgos are brilliant natural researchers, particularly in the science and technology fields, and are notably skilled with computers. They love all forms of study and information, from the

Lunar Virgos are often obsessed with health – their own and that of others – and make good doctors and efficient nurses. They can also choose careers in the alternative health field and make good homeopaths, naturopaths and nutritionists. They are always trying to push back the boundaries of human knowledge through study and research.

Lunar Virgos tend to worry about the state of their health, both inner and outer. They often take their temperature, check their tongue in the mirror or pop pills for real or imaginary ailments. They can get quite dictatorial on the subject,

Lunar Virgos often take their temperature, check their tongue in the mirror or pop pills for real or imaginary ailments

books in libraries to sifting through e-mail. They also enjoy committee work and the intricacies of office politics. They are superb librarians, archaeologists, theologians, historians, political analysts and systems analysts. Many work in laboratories. They are also good at practical skills, such as driving, computing and even the more mundane filing.

Virgos can be very uncomfortable around children, especially toddlers, who need lots of spontaneous love and affection. They may love them deeply, but at some basic level are

constantly lecturing others on what to eat and what not to eat, regaling everyone with the latest medical research. Their bookshelves are full of diet and vitamin books, although exercise videos may be absent or, at least, underused. Their kitchens will contain jars of vitamin pills and the latest food fads. None of this, however, can avert health problems if they are going to arise anyway. Lunar Virgos can suffer from nervous ailments such as upset stomachs, to which they are particularly prone.

However, they need to find a balance

between excessive worry about their health and a complete lack of interest in it. Perhaps the best course of action is to have regular health checks, maintain a well-balanced diet, avoid doing anything to excess and, above all, try to be happy, which, for them, is more easily said than done.

Happiness for Lunar Virgos is often elusive simply because they think too much about what can go wrong.

THE MOON
IN LIBRA

(Ruled by Venus)

*M*oon Sign Libras are charming, urbane and creative. They seek both harmony and excitement – which can lead to a certain amount of inner tension and contradiction in their behavioral patterns. They also pride themselves on their skills as mediators and diplomats. Libra is a cardinal sign, which adds vibrancy and stamina to the slower, more intuitive characteristics of the Moon in this zodiacal position. Even so, many Lunar Libras find the early stages of a project considerably easier than the latter. Seeing it through to the end can often be truly challenging for them. They are rather lazy and, although they may have more than their fair share of leadership qualities, often prefer to take a back seat and let others take the responsibility.

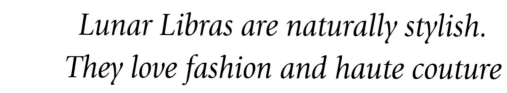

Lunar Libras are naturally stylish.
They love fashion and haute couture

Lunar Libras often find themselves in the role of peacemakers, which they fulfill admirably. They can see all aspects of a problem and are unusually perceptive about its underlying causes. However, they are able to maintain a fair and objective viewpoint. All the same, under that impartial exterior lies the ability to speak passionately on deeply-held views and to hatch plots against those who put obstacles in their path. If the beliefs of Lunar Libran are challenged too strongly, their famed even-handedness will suddenly evaporate.

They become excited by innovative ideas. They may go a long way toward accepting them, but inevitably the time comes when they stop and question them. Many people make the mistake of thinking Libras, both Solar and Lunar, are too gullible. This is not so, as they frequently discover to their cost. There is a strong undercurrent of cynicism and a desire for independence beneath all that Libran charm.

Lunar Libras are naturally stylish. They love fashion and haute couture. When young and impressionable, they may even judge others on their dress sense and superficial image. Many Libras secretly despise those who fail to "make an effort," choosing to have nothing to do with unfashionable or shabbily dressed people.

They love the challenge of travel, and often take off on their own, knowing they will soon make new friends wherever they go. The very thought of new horizons and fresh fields keeps them going when stuck at home or in a routine, and they are usually planning their next vacation or weekend break while still unpacking from their last. They tend to be self-sufficient. They have no problem with being alone, but usually choose to spend more time with others and enjoy parties.

Lunar Libras appreciate glamour and luxury, and can be dedicated home lovers if their environment is calm, tasteful and welcoming. They enjoy entertaining, but will need to set themselves apart from other people from time to time in order to recharge their batteries.

They have very quick minds and can swiftly see straight to the heart of the matter, although it may take them a while to make up their minds about it. The symbol of the Scales, after all, is concerned with weighing up the pros and cons. Libras bore easily and certainly don't put up with fools gladly. Lunar Libras can be very outspoken and sharply critical, despite their open and welcoming smiles.

RELATIONSHIPS

Moon Sign Libras are often in love with love and throw themselves wholeheartedly into the excitement of the chase. They cool off, though, once a relationship is established and everyday reality intrudes. They can be very fussy and even tactless with their loved ones, which is rather uncharacteristic of them. They will criticize them for their bad taste, poor dress sense or even, worst of all, "unacceptable" weight gain. They love to be seen with good-looking people and feel personally insulted if their wives or husbands "let themselves go" or fail to match up to their attractive joint image.

Lunar Libras are adept lovers, though – very tactile and sensual, and can be very uninhibited in bed. They do need gentleness and love and can rapidly become ill at ease in any relationship based on deception or one which exists just for sex alone. They will try to fool themselves, however, that they are happy with the situation.

The Libran search for harmony can go very deep, and anything that may rock the boat can seriously upset their equilibrium.

Although Lunar Libras tend to be hypercritical and fussy, they are not always as difficult to live with as this might suggest. On the contrary, they can be very loving domestic partners. They are excellent in a crisis and can be relied upon to be pushovers, merely that they need to keep their own environment peaceful and free of "bad vibes."

In many ways, Lunar Libras can be disciplinarians, even though they hide behind great urbanity and apparent altruism. They can even be

Even in male Lunar Libras there is a strongly developed gentleness, which can be very attractive to those in need, and can add a caring dimension to most relationships

caring when others are ill; although, if the problem drags on, their sympathy may begin to wane! They love rising to a challenge and can be very practical in their approach to problems – helping with transport, catering, shopping and entertaining the children. Lunar Libras tend to be good with children and animals, although this will vary depending on the rest of their chart. Anyone who is weak or defenseless wins their attention, and they can be formidable champions of the underdog.

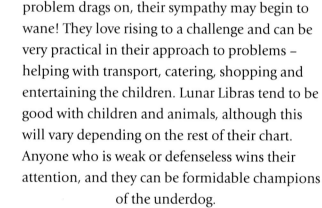

Moon Sign Libras cannot abide a tense atmosphere and will go out of their way to smooth over ruffled feathers in the household, even if it means compromising their own position. However, this certainly does not mean that they are

rather interfering and nosy. They love gossip and rumors, and use the information to spread their influence beyond their immediate circle.

They can often be secret manipulators and exploiters, although this tendency can be mitigated by their compulsively soft hearts. All the same, if they feel that someone deserves it, they will be quite happy to weave a web of intrigue around them.

However, even in male Lunar Libras there is a strongly developed gentleness, which can be very attractive to those in need, and can add a caring dimension to most relationships. Young Lunar Libras characteristically long for the freedom of adulthood, when they feel they can stamp their own personalities on the world and develop their own tastes. They often chafe at the regimentation of school, where scholastic achievement, and not their personal qualities, are the order of the day.

As parents, Lunar Libras are tolerant, open-minded and demonstrative. However, because they

x

hate untidiness and love harmony, they are less inclined to be tolerant of unruly teenagers.

CAREER

This Moon placement encourages careers in some form of negotiation or mediation – perhaps in trade unions or local government, international charities or as a diplomat. A just cause brings out a certain steeliness in Lunar Libras, and their famed humor can successfully defuse many a potentially explosive situation.

They are also good at "fronting" organizations, making excellent public relations officers for large corporations and presenting an admirable image for their employers. In many ways they make excellent representatives. Sometimes, though, their motivation may falter, and they need to be given a strong party line to follow; they are not eager to make major decisions or think on their feet. For that reason, they are not usually senior executive material; although their hard work and personal qualities may take them very close to the top of their chosen career. Besides, their love of luxury will drive them to make as much money as possible – if they can do so without ruining their social life!

They are also artistic, good at selling, marketing, architecture and at ease with technology such as computer graphics and desktop publishing. Modern technology,

in fact, fascinates them so much that they may spend hours entertaining themselves with computers.

Many Lunar Libras are engineers. They also adore speed, and love flying and driving. However, although they enjoy tinkering with engines, the heavy repair work is usually left to someone else.

Few Lunar Libras become workaholics, although they may occasionally come very close to it. They need to work, and can do a great deal in short, sharp bursts – but rarely overdo it for extended periods at a time. Unemployment or the suspicion that their work is not fully appreciated can make them extremely depressed. They feel that how they earn a living is an extension of their own deepest self, which is a serious – and potentially very damaging – misconception.

HEALTH

Lunar Libras, whose lungs are very sensitive, generally suffer from respiratory illness. This means that smoking involves greater risk for them than for most people. Similarly, they should avoid polluted atmospheres and always keep the home and office fresh.

Being acutely aware of disharmony in the environment, they should balance its energies through the application of *feng shui*.

THE MOON
IN SCORPIO

(Ruled by Pluto & Mars)

Moon Sign Scorpios are competitive, intense, sexually inclined and compelling. They seek all sorts of excitement, while at the same time appreciating a stable, calm sort of life. There is usually an element of the contradictory and perverse in these people, which adds to their unfathomability and even to their sex appeal.

This is a potent Moon placement – for good or evil. It is the sign of great reformers, cult leaders and magi, people who inspire others at a very profound level and who rarely do anything without deep personal motivation.

Lunar Scorpios are often very hard to understand because they tend to hide their true feelings. This can go on for years, until some last straw ignites a truly memorable outburst. Scorpios are nervy and intense and hide a great well of sensitivity under their somewhat hard exterior. Everyday problems can be very distressing for them.

Many Scorpios – both Solar and Lunar – have "leaky auras," losing energy from their vital core on a daily basis. They should learn how to retain it through meditation and other spiritual exercises. In fact, most Lunar Scorpios are already interested in such matters, for this is a very psychic placement and many of these people are occultists, psychical researchers or, in some other way, involved with New Age practices or the paranormal.

Traditionally, Lunar Scorpios are drawn to magic. They enjoy the feeling of personal power it gives them, and the thrill of coming into contact with unseen forces. Of course, this is by no means always a good thing. At the very least, they could be wasting their time and deluding themselves. At worst, they could open themselves up to the nasty influence of malign spirits. But, Scorpios are survivors if nothing else, and rarely fall prey to the darker spirits for very long.

This is a potent Moon placement – for good or evil. It is the sign of great reformers, cult leaders and magi, people who inspire others at a very profound level

It is easy for Lunar Scorpios to become depressed and retreat into a world of their own, but that world may be a somewhat dark and threatening place. Many of them are outwardly very gregarious, apparently loving the social round, but occasionally they will need to break off and spend time by themselves to recoup their energies.

The positive side of their psychic awareness is a well-honed intuition about insincere and exploitative people, and the ability to guard against those who have hidden agendas. Lunar Scorpios love slightly dark, dangerous types and can get into trouble very easily because of it. Yet somewhere under all that hankering for a life on the edge is a very robust sense of self-preservation.

These people have the enviable ability to bounce back after personal disaster. Although they may become very depressed and low for long periods, it is rarely forever. They will suddenly rise up from all the gloom again in a new, more positive frame of mind. Many see life as a series of tests of strength, and may even unconsciously manipulate people and events to create the challenges that keep their wits sharp, while at the same time bemoaning their fate.

This placement means that Lunar Scorpios are perhaps more caring than the Solar kind, and they are attached to home and family in an almost Cancerian way. They are keenly aware of the needs of others and can operate very skilfully behind the scenes to ensure they are met. They are also fiercely protective, going to great lengths to help those less fortunate, or simply less aware, than they are. Many see their intuition as a special gift, and waste no time in using it altruistically.

RELATIONSHIPS

The Moon in Water Signs always make for great emotionality. Moon Sign Scorpios have great difficulty when it comes to expressing their feelings. They can be only too eager to unburden themselves to others, but somewhat less willing to be at the receiving end of emotional angst. They can be markedly demanding and possessive, but rapidly distance themselves from those they regard as "clingers."

Sexually, Lunar Scorpios are intense and very active. They have a taste for the unusual, even the dangerous, in the bedroom. However, they also need to be loved and valued as people; and it may be that they will seek to have at least two different relationships running parallel with one another to fulfill their opposing needs.

As with every other aspect of life, Lunar Scorpios like an element of danger in their relationships. They will also provoke inflammatory situations at home – arguments and "scenes" – just to keep the edge of danger nicely sharpened. Even so, they can be surprisingly sympathetic and affectionate, empathizing with the feelings of their loved

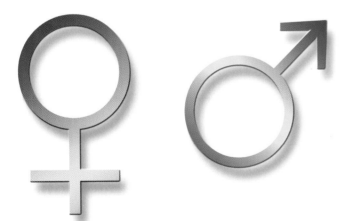

ones; although this will depend on their mood and should never be taken for granted! They are very sensitive and, if approached in the right way, can easily be persuaded to see another's point of view. They are easily hurt if accused of being in any way unjust or uncaring, and will turn over a new leaf immediately – if not permanently. They are eager to reform and become better people.

Many Lunar Scorpios may not have enjoyed their childhood, and may even have felt it was a bit of a battleground. But Scorpios are survivors and will rise like the phoenix from the ashes of even the most arduous or trying situation. However, Scorpios may be left with repressed anger and frustration and should be wary of a tendency, at an unconscious level, to provoke emotional scenes in order to feed their need to be heard. As parents themselves, Lunar Scorpios can be unpredictable and moody. But many of them are loving, dutiful parents whose love of drama and dressing up can provide great entertainment for their children.

CAREER

Lunar Scorpios are naturally good with ideas in concrete form, as in sculpture or architecture. They are excellent engineers or graphic designers, and can be real wizards with computer-generated special effects. They can also be found in the fashion and entertainment industries. Many work in medicine, as surgeons or forensic scientists.

A sign of extremes, Scorpios can experience great ups and downs in a career. Apparent disaster such as downsizing, bankruptcy or disabling illness may strike, only to be followed by another turn of the Wheel of Fortune ushering in a golden

*They will suddenly rise up from all the gloom
again in a new, more positive frame of mind*

time of prosperity, health and happiness. Often this roller coaster fate is unconsciously engineered by the Lunar Scorpio as a test of strength. Scorpios are true believers in fate, and love to pit their wits against it. Although they can, and almost always do, bounce back from the brink of total disaster with staggering regularity, they often take less resilient people down with them – and leave them there. They should realize how unfair it is to involve others in their games of Russian roulette with Destiny.

The Wheel of Fortune represents fortune, success, luck, happiness and opportunity. Despite frequent setbacks, illness and even disaster, the life of a Scorpio – more than any other sign of the zodiac – is characterized by such happy reversals of fortune

Lunar Scorpios can be great worriers about their health but fail to act for some time, letting their symptoms worsen. They must be brave and visit a health professional at the first sign of a problem. Even if they have only imagined that they have some kind of serious ailment, it is far better to be safe than sorry. They simply cannot afford to take chances with their health.

Lunar Scorpios have enormous nervous energy and need to work off their frustrations through healthy exercise. The problem is that this is not an athletic Moon placement, so perhaps they could simply settle for brisk walks and regular visits to the local swimming pool.

HEALTH

Traditionally, women with this Moon placement have exceptionally heavy periods. Both sexes tend to have problems with their reproductive organs. It is a good idea to have regular specialist check-ups and – of course – always to practice safe sex.

THE MOON
IN SAGITTARIUS

(Ruled by Jupiter)

*M*oon Sign Sagittarians are courageous, intellectually inquisitive, studious and very free-spirited. They love their independence, which they guard very jealously, and cannot abide being trapped or regimented. Highly adaptable, Lunar Sagittarians are made for action and are innately gregarious, with a wide circle of admiring friends.

They have clear minds and are able to cut through unnecessary detail to the central issue, communicating its ins and outs to others in easy-to-understand terms. They hate fuss of any sort, preferring things to be clear-cut and direct; they particularly dislike pomposity.

In their love lives, Lunar Sagittarians are eager for new experiences and hate to be tied down, either physically or intellectually. Energetic and optimistic, they really believe that the grass is always greener on the other side. But even when, disappointingly, it turns out not to be so, they readjust their sights and press on.

These are not power-hungry people, nor are

Justice – the card of fairness, rightness and probity. These are essential, motivating characteristics of Lunar Sagittarians, who passionately despise bigotry and injustice

Lunar Sagittarians hate bigotry and prejudice of any sort, and can throw themselves

Moon Sign Sagittarians are, to some degree, less outgoing than their Solar counterparts; but they still possess the same basic desire to like – and be liked by – everyone they meet

they greedy or particularly fond of competition. They cannot be bothered to claw their way to the top. If they have their own space and enough to pay the bills, buy a few books and CDs and travel the world in modest style, they are content enough.

energetically into helping those in trouble. They are firm believers in justice and fair play, but they can also can be oblivious to the feelings of those who stand in their way. Sometimes, though, their best intentions take a rather strident form, alienating the very people they are eager to help.

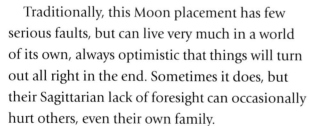

Traditionally, this Moon placement has few serious faults, but can live very much in a world of its own, always optimistic that things will turn out all right in the end. Sometimes it does, but their Sagittarian lack of foresight can occasionally hurt others, even their own family.

Similarly, they can bank – only too literally – on uncertain plans and insubstantial projects, seeing the future as rosy to a ridiculous degree. Even regular dousings with very cold reality often fail to make them see sense.

Moon Sign Sagittarians are, to some degree, less outgoing than their Solar counterparts; but they still possess the same basic desire to like – and be liked by – everyone they meet. However, they tend to withdraw into their own quiet room from time to time and spend many hours reading or daydreaming, just to center themselves. Often, too much of their time is spent in a flurry of activity, so their instinct is to hide away and build up their energies once more. Sometimes they will disappear for many hours at a stretch, perhaps studying intensely or going for long recreational walks.

Lunar Sagittarians can easily become carried away by the sound of their own voice and forget the sensitivities of others. Many are too blunt and most can be very tactless. Yet, in general, they are kind, compassionate people who never intend to hurt those around them.

They are good in a crisis – almost enjoying them sometimes – and can be extremely practical

their partners have feelings and needs of their own. Too often, Sagittarians merely pay lip service to this concept.

On a day-to-day basis they are easy to live with. They are tidy and clean about the house and quite willing to do their share of the chores, even if

These people make energetic and inspiring teachers, although they will often rebel against too strict a regime

if they have to be. Although they can be rather lazy about the house, once they start the work they actually like putting up shelves and fixing the gutter. Restlessness aside, once they settle down in their own home, they will take pride in it, and decorate and furnish it in a solid, tasteful, unpretentious style.

RELATIONSHIPS

Lunar Sagittarians may find problems with close relationships. They tend to make a distinction between sexual passion and the gentler sort of unconditional love – although their partners may not see it in quite the same way. Obviously, this is not the recipe for long-lasting love, and many Lunar Sagittarians have several relationships going at once. In a one-to-one situation, they may feel their partners are trying to trap them or take away their independence.

Lunar Sagittarians are often more attracted to the idea of sexual encounters than to the act itself. The problem is that

they do need reminding from time to time. They will not accept nagging or dogmatic demands, however, and emotional blackmail is anathema to them.

Lunar Sagittarians can have filthy tempers. All that inner fire and energy can suddenly explode in a volcanic eruption of fury and a spate of highly colorful abuse. It can come as a real shock to those at the receiving end. However, the fire usually fizzles out and is forgotten, at least by Sagittarians – although others may remain shaken for some time afterwards.

They often talk big, persuading themselves and others that they are high-fliers, but do nothing to make their dreams become reality. Their innate charm (which can be excessive) is their biggest asset. At its most negatively aspected, this Moon placement creates fantasists. However, their tall tales are not deliberate manipulations – they often believe them themselves.

Lunar Sagittarians can have filthy tempers. All that inner fire and energy can suddenly explode in a volcanic eruption of fury

As parents, Lunar Sagittarians love their children, but find it hard to be good disciplinarians or help them keep their feet on the ground. Both Lunar and Solar Sagittarians tend to be like overgrown children themselves, which at least makes for some interesting games but not much guidance. They are not very good with the boring or downright unpleasant aspects of parenthood and can be rather forgetful about mealtimes and other routine demands of daily life.

CAREER

These people make energetic and inspiring teachers, although they will often rebel against too strict a regime in much the same way as their pupils.

They enjoy working in the entertainment industry, although many with this Moon placement may be too shy to work in front of the microphone or camera, preferring to stay behind the scenes. Many make excellent tour guides or seasonal workers and are usually happiest when self-employed or signing up for short contracts. They like to feel in control of their working lives and able to get up and go at a moment's notice. Many Lunar Sagittarians are excellent television researchers, moving from program to program as each series ends, enjoying the change of pace and subject.

Any kind of selling is attractive to this type, but the hurly-burly of market trading is not for them. They prefer to work in comfortable, classy surroundings with interesting people, and dislike chaotic working conditions.

Overoptimism can lead them to make some very unwise career moves and, possibly, tempt them into gambling more than is advisable. The

problem is that few Lunar Sagittarians ever truly learn from their mistakes.

HEALTH

Lunar Sagittarians use up a great deal of energy in the simple conduct of their daily lives. But they need some form of structured exercise, such as team games, to keep them mentally and physically on track. They are good swimmers and also tend to be adept at surfing.

Traditionally, Lunar Sagittarians suffer from problems connected with their legs and hips, although this may be a symptom of general wear and tear. Being so active, they are constantly putting a strain on various parts of their bodies, and the legs bear much of it.

Other problem areas include the veins, and varicose veins can be a real bugbear in later life. So as not to encourage this painful condition, they should train themselves not to cross legs or ankles when sitting and to eat plenty of fiber to prevent overfull intestines putting pressure on the veins.

Sagittarians should get into the habit of taking regular naps during the day to keep up their energy, and should avoid sugar and caffeine, which throw their blood sugar levels out of balance.

227

THE MOON
IN CAPRICORN

(Ruled by Saturn)

Moon Sign Capricorns are serious, dependable and controlled. Very practical people, they do not shirk responsibility and have great foresight and powers of endurance. Sensitive and refined by nature, they may seem slightly old-fashioned and out of place in the modern world, but they can adapt surprisingly well to new situations.

They tend to be reserved and somewhat shy when young, but gradually develop an outward sophistication. This, though, is often merely a device for keeping the outside world at arm's length. They have beautiful manners and great respect for the old traditions of country and home.

Lunar Capricorns tend to plan their future when others are still more interested in

shoulders – and the chance to develop spiritually well beyond the usual opportunities granted to most people. Significantly, it is usually a flighty Gemini or a ludicrously overoptimistic Sagittarius who accuses them of being so unexciting, so perhaps that criticism should be taken with a pinch of salt.

RELATIONSHIPS

Under their wise, cautious image, Lunar Capricorns hide a great deal of sensitivity – more so than their Sun Sign counterparts. However, they learn early in life to keep their feelings under control – perhaps to obscure them with their bright and charming manner. They are very uncomfortable with any kind of

Many Lunar Capricorns endure totally incompatible relationships simply because it would not, in their eyes, be honorable to break them off

playground games, and can seem rather serious and studious. Their solemn ruler Saturn bestows very mixed blessings: they are expected to take life seriously right from the cradle.

Capricorns, both Solar and Lunar, have acquired an unfair reputation as boring and pessimistic people plagued with bad luck and all sorts of restrictions. In fact, this is not the case. Saturn gives them a great deal of wisdom – which can bestow somewhat old heads on young

emotional scene, though deep down inside they may be crying out in sympathy. Outwardly they can appear cold, but this is rarely – truly – the case at all.

They are slow to give their hearts, even in friendship, but once committed to a relationship will honor it through thick and thin. Many Lunar Capricorns endure totally incompatible relationships simply because it would not, in their eyes, be honorable to break them off.

Because they are inhibited and overcontrolled, they usually find sex and demonstrations of affection very difficult to cope with. Love and sex are inextricably entwined for these people, and marriage is for life.

They need patience and understanding to bring out the best in them sexually, but they can be great romantics under that aloof exterior and respond enthusiastically to a more experienced partner.

Being an Earth Sign, they love romantic walks in the country and the scent of flowers, and will rarely miss an anniversary or birthday – although these cautious types don't like surprise parties.

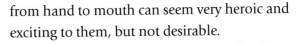

Once they have found their life partner, they are happy to settle down, since now they have acquired a safe environment in which they can truly express themselves. It is important to them to have security, both emotional and financial, and the thought of having it taken away from them is too much to bear. They worry about financial collapse, even if it is the least likely disaster to befall them, and hardly dare admit that they sometimes wonder how they could cope with divorce or the death of their loved one.

However, the opposite side of this obsessive worrying means that they understand the need which others also possess to be centered and safe, and are wonderful providers and protectors. Where Lunar Cancers can be seen as the archetypal mothers, Lunar Capricorns are classic fathers. Women with this Lunar placement will also have a great urge to defend their nearest and dearest against the world.

However, they do need their own protectors against the insensitivity of the outside world. Their ideal partner is a strong, warm and understanding person with an independent mind and a well-established career. They don't understand rebels or those who choose a more bohemian lifestyle, although they may entertain a sneaking admiration for them. Anyone who lives from hand to mouth can seem very heroic and exciting to them, but not desirable.

As parents, Lunar Capricorns can often be too severe when handling sensitive or unorthodox children. Somewhat repressed themselves, they need to be encouraged to let go and have fun. Often this skips a generation, making them somewhat stiff parents but wonderful and adored grandparents. They like children to be orderly and disciplined, which may sometimes seem like a contradiction in terms, but they love their offspring dearly – even if they fail to empathize with them.

Lunar Capricorns hurt easily, and nurse the scars of secret humiliations for years, often forever. They bottle up their feelings, believing that "it's not allowed" to cry at funerals or punch the air with joy in moments of triumph.

Decency, self-control and hard work are their watchwords. Many Lunar Capricorns have a delightfully dry sense of humor, often at their own expense, and can reveal surprising insights and great depth of thought.

Lunar Capricorns enjoy relaxing. They love taking even short breaks, varying the location and types of vacation with a sense of adventure. However, even if they claim they have no problem with solo vacations, this is rarely true. Most do not cope well alone, and need a bright and energetic companion to lift their spirits and share their adventures.

CAREER

Moon Sign Capricorns are disciplined and reliable, and they need to work hard to feel valued as people. They are particularly affected by setbacks, disappointments and bad news of any kind, and can see lay-offs and unemployment as

Lunar Capricorns can become very fussy and irritable. They hate sloppiness of any sort, and have a natural regard for routine and order – although the armed forces suit their solar counterparts rather more. These people are basically too easily humiliated to enjoy the boisterous tumult of the military life, although the regimentation has many attractions for them.

They like to see the results of their labors and are good at what others consider tedious office work. It is important to Lunar Capricorns to feel they make a concrete contribution. With minds so well equipped to deal with detail, they make adept engineers and architects – although perhaps not the most imaginative around. They like tradition and stability in whatever they do.

Lunar Capricorns hate being rushed. The unruly chaos of a busy newspaper office or live television studio is not for them. They appreciate being able to settle down to their tasks in their own time, working through them slowly and methodically, then checking and double-checking their own work. Many Lunar Capricorns are

The Tower from the Tarot, which signifies disaster waiting around the corner, has particular significance for Lunar Capricorns, who – unlike Scorpios, who bounce back effortlessly from catastrophe – are more than usually adversely affected by setbacks and disappointments. In fact, they may never truly recover

Lunar Capricorns hate being rushed. The unruly chaos of a busy newspaper office or live television studio is not for them. They appreciate being able to settle down to their tasks in their own time

true catastrophes. If such situations arise, they may never fully recover in their deepest psyches, even if they go on to achieve great things in their future careers. Business and the financial world are attractive to them, and they often enjoy jobs in insurance or accounting.

happiest when working with a partner in their own company, and will enjoy working out the tax returns and maintaining the books.

However, it is not a good idea to treat the loyal, efficient Lunar Capricorn like a doormat. As with all Earth Signs, it takes a great deal to make them

angry, but once they are, stand well back. When Capricorns blow, they can be coldly furious, dredging up old scores and being bitterly sarcastic and downright nasty. The hurt of decades can finally surface in a shower of insults and innuendo that may or may not be connected with the issue in question. Even with their great respect for authority, this venom can be aimed at their superiors in the workplace. Of course, they will bitterly regret any such outburst and will very probably offer to resign. Such an offer will probably not be accepted because many Lunar Capricorns are simply too good at their jobs.

HEALTH

Lunar Capricorns live long lives and are fairly robust. They can suffer from skin disorders, rheumatism and stress ailments such as upset stomachs and headaches. Bottling up emotions can have serious repercussions for their health, especially in later life, taking the form of heart problems and even some types of cancer.

It is important for Lunar Capricorns to learn to express their feelings and work off their tension through some form of exercise. This is especially true because they can dwell on things that have gone wrong in life, blaming themselves and feeling shame where others would only see bad luck.

Although they usually manage to keep quite trim and are not given to excesses in food and drink, many have no interest in their diets and can exist for years on substandard food. They should educate themselves about healthy eating, and begin a regime that includes fruit and vegetables, and plenty of vitamins.

Their loved ones would do well to encourage them to enjoy mealtimes a little more, which will do wonders for their overall health.

THE MOON
IN AQUARIUS

(Ruled by Uranus & Saturn)

oon Sign Aquarians are cool, broad-minded, humanitarian and optimistic. They are idealists with high personal standards, exemplars of integrity and honesty, and their strongly developed sense of independence means that they rarely become a burden to others, either financially or emotionally.

They are unusual in their tastes, embracing a wide social spectrum where their friends are concerned. They have no time for any form of prejudice or bigotry. However, Lunar Aquarians are often emotionally detached. They can give the impression of not really caring deep down about

individuals, although their commitment to large groups such as charities or environmental organizations is second to none.

Progressive and optimistic, they embrace the future with enthusiasm. They can be slow to learn the lessons of history, though – often a major mistake. They also have a tendency to be too eager to abandon old ways of doing things, and the traditions that have become hallowed by age, and they can be very insensitive to those who still uphold them.

Lunar Aquarians are extremely gregarious and may seem very open and universally friendly. There is a steely watchfulness about them, though, and that can be disconcerting. It is as if

they are constantly holding back some secret part of themselves while being eager to give the impression of total openness. What you see is not necessarily all you get with this Moon placement.

They hate to appear weak or needy, and will suffer in silence rather than ask for help. They feel that they are the guardians of society and should be the ones who look after the rest of us, rather than the other way around. In many ways, there is a quiet arrogance about Lunar Aquarians which can become very irritating. It is an almost subliminal aloofness that speaks volumes about their inner attitude. Not surprisingly, Lunar Aquarians rarely lack self-esteem.

This strong sense of inner worth can lead to some spectacular risk-taking; although few possess the often childish overoptimism of a Sagittarius or the blithe boastfulness of a Gemini. Lunar Aquarians tend to take calculated risks virtually every day of their lives, acting from an inner core of belief in their own destiny and the essential rightness of their actions.

Taken to extremes, this Lunar placement encourages a rather cool, unemotional attitude toward other people that is masked by a tendency to interfere and intrude. This is the sign of the bossy charity worker who organizes everyone, regardless of their actual needs.

Energetic and highly motivated, these people love to be in control, whether in their home life or at work. Many of them extend their sphere of influence into hobby groups or charities and will work long hours on their behalf, although they are rarely content to take a minor role.

On the whole, however, Lunar Aquarians are easygoing, congenial folk who attract a wide range of friends and lovers. Sexually, they can be romantic, passionate and – being a Fixed sign – very loyal, even to partners who repeatedly let them down. Some Lunar Aquarians have such an impossible dream of their ideal love that they spend their entire lives alone, waiting in vain for them to come along. Even then, though, they will not be particularly unhappy. Aquarians, both Solar and Lunar, rarely sulk or brood, being far too busy with a hundred and one plans and schemes.

When they finally give their hearts, though, they do so willingly and are happy to settle down – although their home may be somewhat eccentric in some way.

President Kennedy in 1963. The more personal planets they have in Aquarius, the more pronounced this tendency will be.

Most Lunar Aquarians, however, have a certain emotional objectivity which prevents them from

It is essential for Lunar Aquarians to find a life partner who shares the same interests. Aquarians desperately need to find their own niche in life and stay there

They don't mind chaos as long as it is their sort of chaos! Some barely notice their surroundings and need a partner who is more centered and meticulous about the mundane chores of daily life. Others, however, are orderly and proud of their homes, imposing their own taste very quickly on a shared home and being happy to help with the housework, the decorating and the financial upkeep.

Many Lunar Aquarians have no regard whatsoever for orthodoxy or tradition. They tend to espouse bizarre beliefs and alternative lifestyles, and can be rather gullible about the more unusual New Age fads. Their homes tend to sparkle with large collections of crystals, wind chimes and Aboriginal and Native American artifacts. Their bookshelves are crammed with tomes on extreme political, religious, mystical or sociological beliefs.

They may be fruitarian, vegetarian or, possibly, vegan. They tend to believe conspiracy theories – especially those alleging governmental involvement in famous assassinations, such as that of

going too far, and a well-developed logic that enables them to see through some of the wilder theories. There is a feeling that many Aquarians embrace eccentric ideas or belief systems simply because they feel they are the way of the future. This seems logical to them, for they never want to miss out on the latest ideas or the next big opportunity for social and self-development.

RELATIONSHIPS

It is essential for Lunar Aquarians to find a life partner who shares the same interests. Aquarians desperately need to find their own niche in life and stay there, and anyone who is uncomfortable with that or has completely different views will not last the course. Some Lunar Aquarians enter into a relationship with high hopes

of it making the world a better place – only to discover later on that their loved one has no interest in that, but has other concerns. However, being essentially loyal and devoted, Lunar Aquarians will make every effort to block out the truth of the situation, because they don't enjoy having to begin again with someone else. They hate underhanded dealings and dislike the idea of illicit affairs, even though their hearts and the demands of their sexuality may point them in that direction.

The irony is that Lunar Aquarians can easily become bored within a relationship, despite their protestations of lifelong love, and may simply fall into other relationships without making any particular effort. Although they have no intention of hurting anyone, their essential self-centered-ness can harden their hearts when they are faced with a romantic breakup. Aquarians operate from the premise that they know what is best and have the only valid interpretation of events; others had better do things their way or get out.

On the whole, however, these people are kind and compassionate parents who encourage their children to express themselves, bring their friends home and turn a blind eye to the inevitable mess.

Lunar Aquarians tend to have big egos no matter how soft, gentle and understanding they may seem. For once, the Moon has the effect of diminishing emotionality, and this can help create some very cool customers indeed.

AQUARIAN CHILDREN

As children they are unusual, self-possessed and probably of above-average intelligence. They have a practical streak, which makes them natural leaders and organizers from an early age, although paradoxically they can be rather shy in some social situations. They are independent children with strongly-developed opinions, and they show remarkable self-discipline. They are funny and have an easy charm, but are also stubborn and intolerant of the opinions of others.

They can be delightful parents themselves, appreciating the problems of childhood and the teenage years, and showing great sympathy toward youngsters who are disabled or different in any way. However, they may be overeager to impose their view of the world on their offspring who may dare to think differently.

CAREER

The patient and devoted Lunar Aquarians are suited to careers in education, perhaps with children with special needs. They love the principle of learning and are often attracted to higher education, perhaps becoming a university lecturer or graduate research student.

Being a Fixed Sign, Lunar Aquarians are naturally determined and see projects through to the finish. They have no time for empty talk or procrastination. This innate self-discipline makes them ideal team leaders; and although they can be inept and reluctant delegators, they do well working for themselves. Lunar Aquarians can be very irritable with those whose work is not up to the same high standard as their own, treating them with withering sarcasm.

HEALTH

Traditionally, where health is concerned, the legs and ankles are problem areas, manifesting themselves as ailments connected with veins and ulcers. Lunar Aquarians tend to suffer from food intolerances and allergies – from seasonal hay fever to violent reactions to dust mites, chemicals and household pets. It is a good idea for them to have themselves checked for food intolerances or allergies with a reputable nutritionist.

They are rarely overweight – in fact, Lunar Aquarians tend to despise obesity. However, they can easily adopt a diet that is far too restricted for good health. Perhaps they should realize that food is not always a major political or moral issue, and that meals can be relaxed, fun occasions.

THE MOON IN PISCES

(Ruled by Neptune & Jupiter)

oon Sign Pisceans are emotional, kind, creative and psychic. They instinctively reach out to others, and may even sacrifice their own well-being in order to help and support those around them. Soft-hearted and vulnerable, this Moon placement cannot bear disharmony or "bad vibes," and works hard to eliminate all upsets – real, potential or imagined!

These are very artistic people who enjoy poetry, dancing and painting. They can be surprisingly ambitious in these fields, even though they are naturally disinclined to push themselves forward in most other areas of life. They have a profound awareness of balance and harmony, and their creative work tends to reflect a striving for peace. They hate ugliness in any form. Living in an unpleasant environment can make them feel quite ill.

Lunar Pisceans are the psychics of the zodiac, picking up information about people and places at a profound, often inexplicable, level. They instinctively know that life is more complex than is suggested by the evidence of our five senses and, with their well-honed spiritual antennae, feel the curious ebb and flow of unseen energies.

Many of them are committed to religious or mystical belief systems and ponder deeply over the great questions of life and death. They may read widely about the afterlife and reincarnation and have a strong personal belief in a continued existence after bodily death.

This colors their whole attitude toward life, and gives them a firm base on which to build their personal development.

Cancer comes close. They constantly fret about their nearest and dearest. But they also spend valuable time worrying about the state of the

These people love their friends almost as much as they love family, and would go to the ends of the Earth for them if they felt it was necessary

In fact, this underlying conviction is a very good thing. Lunar Pisceans tend to be tossed this way and that by the demands of others, and they rarely stand up for themselves or insist on their own rights. Naturally supportive and caring, they can easily sublimate their own needs and desires by looking after others. This can escalate to a very unhealthy degree: many become uncomplaining, downtrodden martyrs who harbor secret resentments for years.

Traditionally, Lunar Pisceans are extremely moody, unpredictable, irritable and often sulky. In reality they are so sensitive and easily hurt that they are often merely taking time out to recover. An unguarded or unwise word, even a mild joke at their expense, will go deep and continue to rankle in their sensitive souls for a long time.

Other people come first to a Lunar Piscean, which is not always a good thing. They can be rather bossy and smothering, interfering in the lives of others when they would do better to leave well enough alone. Often they see all ills as their problem, and are constantly weighed down with the sorrows of the world.

Lunar Pisceans are also the olympian worriers of the zodiac – not even the most motherly

world, seeing global warming and the possibility of collision with meteors as not only imminent, but also intensely personal problems. Unfortunately, by their very nature these particular problems are intractable, adding to the burden of Lunar Piscean worry.

RELATIONSHIPS

These people love their friends almost as much as they love family, and would go to the ends of the Earth for them if they felt it was necessary. They are loyal and supportive, rarely letting relationships grow cold through lack of contact, and are usually extremely dependable in a crisis. For their friends there will always be a shoulder to cry on, a hot meal and a sofa to sleep on. And this is despite the fact that Lunar Pisceans types often find that people take advantage of their good nature, using and exploiting their soft-heartedness with no regard for their needs.

Many of them are committed to religious or mystical belief systems and ponder deeply over the great questions of life and death

243

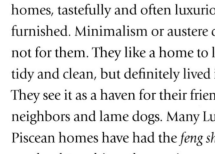

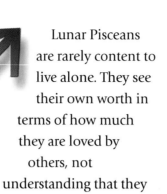

Lunar Pisceans are rarely content to live alone. They see their own worth in terms of how much they are loved by others, not understanding that they themselves need to love just as much, if not more. But if the reality of love never quite matches up to their romantic expectations, they are happy to make believe, living in a world of illusion – perhaps even seriously deluding themselves. The presence of their co-ruler Neptune encourages escapism, which can become a serious threat to their mental well-being. A safe way of channeling this trait is in creative pursuits, where imagination can take a concrete form without any danger to the psyche.

They are intensely loyal to their life partners and may be happy to put their own ambitions on hold while their partners struggle to get to the top. This is not always desirable, though, and can eventually make for a tense home atmosphere of resentment and rivalry.

Sexually, Lunar Pisceans are eager, sensuous and imaginative. They enjoy erotic caresses and know how to wed deep feelings of love with shows of intense passion, all to the great delight of their partners.

Lunar Pisceans usually have lovely, comfortable homes, tastefully and often luxuriously furnished. Minimalism or austere chic is not for them. They like a home to look tidy and clean, but definitely lived in. They see it as a haven for their friends, neighbors and lame dogs. Many Lunar Piscean homes have had the *feng shui* overhaul to achieve the maximum harmony possible, and the resulting relaxed, welcoming atmosphere is balm to the soul of everyone who enters.

These people detest being ridiculed or humiliated. Their self-esteem is low enough as it is, but criticism reduces it even further, and they are vulnerable for a very long time afterward. Even well-meant constructive criticism is a deeply personal slight, a rejection of their whole selves. Their feelings are easily hurt, which is why some people with this Moon placement hide behind a tough exterior. Seeming hard, even indifferent to everything that fate can throw at them, conceals the hurt inside.

LUNAR PISCEAN CHILDREN

Pisceans often fear rejection – especially in the context of intimate relationships. Young Lunar Pisceans tend not to have a happy time, and often have difficulty facing the grim facts of life when confronted with them at an early age. If a parent or sibling should become gravely ill or die, the resulting insecurity lays down a pattern of desperation and desire to be loved that typifies this sign in later life.

Sometimes fragile children, they seek compensation for life's hard knocks by becoming teacher's pet, burying their heads in books or in an elaborate fantasy world. Daydreaming can become a way of life for unhappy Lunar Pisceans.

With their own children, they are loving and warm, but may communicate their own sense of worthlessness to them. They need to build up their children's self-esteem and confidence, a process that may help with their own self-image.

Their tendency to be fussy and over-protective can be counter-productive, however, alienating the people they love and for whom they want only the best.

CAREER

Glamorous and creative work appeals to Lunar Pisceans more than mundane routine in offices, shops or factories. They are good with their hands and make excellent dress designers, florists and craftspeople of all kinds. They also make imaginative cooks and excel at preparing more unusual and exotic foreign dishes. Because they are fond of detail, they can be very well-suited to the complex worlds of computer graphics and engineering.

Many people with this Moon placement are natural dancers, or can earn a decent living as professionals or teachers. Most Pisceans, either Solar or Lunar, love music in all its forms and are happy to surround themselves with it, both at work and home. Some may play an instrument professionally.

An increasing number of Lunar Pisceans are attempting to earn a living by harnessing their psychic powers, perhaps as mediums, channelers or tarot card readers. Most have a passionate interest in the paranormal, mystical and unexplained, and can often be found freezing on night-long "ghost watches" at haunted houses, or on the tops of hills

searching the skies for UFOs. They feel part of the great unseen cosmic dance and want to understand it.

These are meaningful dreamers, whose lives are full of astonishing coincidences. They are very superstitious and tend to interpret weird events as omens. Having a strongly developed intuition, they can be very successful clairvoyants.

However, there is a certain danger in becoming too obsessed with the unseen world and not properly connecting to this one. Problems can arise, too, from Pisceans deluding themselves about the extent of their powers. Where possible, budding psychics should have disciplined training of the kind available in development circles for mediums.

HEALTH

Since they are so hypersensitive, Lunar Pisceans should take care not to overtax their rather limited strength and lay themselves open to unwanted influences that can drain their vital energy. They need to get plenty of fresh air and exercise and eat properly at regular intervals. They could top up blood sugar levels by nibbling at dried fruit every hour or so, and should avoid caffeine and sugar, which actually depletes energy after the initial "rush."

Traditionally, they tend to suffer from blood disorders, respiratory problems and heart trouble, in later life. They also face a host of psycho-somatic ailments and allergies. This is not a physically robust sign, and those born under it should learn to take great care of themselves.

MOON CHARTS

In the charts below, the position of the Moon is shown at midnight on alternate days. To find your Moon Sign, find the day of your birthday or the day before if you were born on an even-numbered day. The sign given for that day is your Moon Sign, and the figure next to it indicates the number of degrees of that sign (the maximum number of degrees for any one sign is 29). The number of degrees indicates the greater or lesser extent to which you are influenced by that sign. Unless you were born on or just after midnight, you will have to add half a degree per hour to find the number of degrees for your sign.

If your counting takes you beyond 29 degrees, then you move on to the next sign. For example, if you were born just after midnight on June 19, 1961, then your sign would be 1Vi (one degree of Virgo as given in chart for 1961 on page 249). If you were born at 10:00a.m., then you would add five degrees (half a degree for each hour after midnight), which gives you 6Vi – six degrees of Virgo. If you were born at midnight on June 20, 1961, then add 12 degrees, which gives you 13Vi. If you were born at 8:00a.m. on June 20, you would add 16 degrees, which gives you 17Vi.

If you were born on May 17, 1962 at or just after midnight, your sign would be 25Li (25 degrees of Libra as given in the chart for 1962 on page 249). If you were born at noon on the 17th, then you would add six degrees, which completes the cycle for Libra (25 plus four gives the maximum number of degrees of 29) and pushes you two degrees into the next sign, giving you 2Sc – two degrees of Scorpio. If you were born eight hours later at 8:00p.m. on the 17th, you would add a further four degrees to arrive at 6Sc – six degrees of Scorpio. Adding a further half degree for every subsequent hour up to midnight on the 19th would bring you to 20Sc, which, as you can see, is the figure already given for this day in the chart for 1962.

These figure are based on Greenwich Mean Time/Universal Time (UT). If you were born in another time zone, then take into account the number of hours that it is ahead of, or behind, UT, and add or subtract another half degree per hour difference from UT. For example, New York is five hours ahead of UT, so anyone born in New York should add another 2.5 degrees. Someone born in Bangalore, India, should subtract 2.5 degrees because Bangalore is five hours behind UT. Finally, for an absolutely accurate placement, it is best to consult an astrologer and provide him or her with precise details of the time and place of your birth.

1930

	Jan	Feb	Mar	Apr	May	Jun	Jul	Aug	Sep	Oct	Nov	Dec
1	20Cp	5Pi	14Pi	1Ta	7Ge	0Le	10Vi	1Sc	19Sg	22Cp	6Pi	8Ar
3	14Aq	19Pi	9Ar	27Ta	5Cn	29Le	8Li	27Sc	13Cp	16Aq	0Ar	2Ta
5	8Pi	24Ar	4Ta	25Ge	4Le	27Vi	4Sc	22Sg	7Aq	10Pi	24Ar	29Ta
7	2Ar	20Ta	0Ge	23Cn	2Vi	24Li	0Sg	16Cp	1Pi	4Ar	20Ta	26Ge
9	28Ar	18Ge	28Ge	22Le	0Li	20Sc	25Sg	10Aq	25Pi	28Ar	17Ge	25Cn
11	25Ta	18Cn	27Cn	20Vi	28Li	16Sg	19Cp	4Pi	19Ar	24Ta	14Cn	24Le
13	24Ge	18Le	18Le	19Li	24Sc	11Cp	13Aq	28Pi	14Ta	20Ge	13Le	22Vi
15	25Cn	18Vi	18Vi	16Sc	20Sg	5Aq	7Pi	22Ar	10Ge	18Cn	11Vi	20Li
17	25Le	17Li	17Li	12Sg	14Cp	28Aq	1Ar	17Ta	7Cn	16Le	9Li	17Sc
19	24Vi	13Sc	21Sc	7Cp	8Aq	22Pi	25Ar	14Ge	6Le	15Vi	7Sc	13Sg
21	22Li	8Sg	16Sg	1Aq	2Pi	17Ar	21Ta	12Cn	6Vi	14Li	5Sg	9Cp
23	17Sc	2Cp	11Cp	24Aq	26Pi	11Ta	19Ge	12Le	6Li	13Sc	1Cp	4Aq
25	12Sg	26Cp	4Aq	19Pi	22Ar	11Ge	19Cn	13Vi	5Sc	10Sg	26Cp	28Aq
27	6Cp	20Aq	28Aq	14Ar	18Ta	10Cn	19Le	12Li	2Sg	6Cp	20Aq	21Pi
29	29Cp		23Pi	10Ta	17Ge	10Le	19Vi	10Sc	28Sg	0Aq	14Pi	15Ar
31	23Aq		18Ar		16Cn		18Li	6Sg		24Aq		10Ta

1931

	Jan	Feb	Mar	Apr	May	Jun	Jul	Aug	Sep	Oct	Nov	Dec
1	23Ta	13Cn	21Cn	14Vi	23Li	14Sg	19Cp	5Pi	19Ar	22Ta	9Cn	16Le
3	20Ge	12Le	20Le	14Li	22Sc	11Cp	15Aq	29Pi	13Ta	16Ge	5Le	13Vi
5	19Cn	13Vi	21Vi	14Sc	20Sg	8Aq	9Pi	23Ar	7Ge	12Cn	3Vi	12Li
7	19Le	12Li	21Li	12Sg	16Cp	1Pi	3Ar	17Ta	3Cn	9Le	2Li	11Sc
9	18Vi	10Sc	20Sc	8Cp	11Aq	25Pi	26Ar	12Ge	1Le	8Vi	2Sc	10Sg
11	17Li	7Sg	18Sg	3Aq	5Pi	18Ar	21Ta	9Cn	0Vi	8Li	2Sg	8Cp
13	14Sc	2Cp	12Cp	27Aq	29Pi	13Ta	17Ge	7Le	0Li	9Sc	0Cp	5Aq
15	10Sg	27Cp	6Aq	20Pi	22Ar	9Ge	14Cn	7Vi	0Sc	8Sg	27Cp	0Pi
17	5Cp	21Aq	0Pi	14Ar	17Ta	5Cn	13Le	6Li	29Sc	5Cp	22Aq	24Pi
19	0Aq	15Pi	23Pi	8Ta	13Ge	3Le	12Vi	5Sc	26Sg	1Aq	16Pi	18Ar
21	24Aq	8Ar	17Ar	3Ge	9Cn	2Vi	11Li	3Sg	22Cp	26Aq	10Ar	12Ta
23	18Pi	2Ta	11Ta	29Ge	7Le	0Li	9Sc	0Cp	17Aq	20Pi	4Ta	6Ge
25	11Ar	27Ta	6Ge	26Cn	5Vi	28Li	6Sg	25Cp	11Pi	13Ar	28Ta	2Cn
27	6Ta	23Ge	2Cn	24Le	3Li	26Sc	3Cp	20Aq	4Ar	7Ta	23Ge	29Cn
29	1Ge		0Le	23Vi	2Sc	23Sg	28Cp	14Pi	28Ar	1Ge	19Cn	26Le
31	28Ge		29Le		0Sg		23Aq	7Ar		26Ge		24Vi

1932

	Jan	Feb	Mar	Apr	May	Jun	Jul	Aug	Sep	Oct	Nov	Dec
1	8Li	1Sg	26Sg	15Aq	18Pi	2Ta	5Ge	21Cn	10Vi	18Li	12Sg	20Cp
3	6Sc	29Sg	22Cp	9Pi	12Ar	26Ta	29Ge	17Le	9Li	18Sc	11Cp	17Aq
5	5Sg	25Cp	17Aq	3Ar	6Ta	21Ge	25Cn	15Vi	8Sc	17Sg	8Aq	13Pi
7	3Cp	21Aq	12Pi	27Ar	29Ta	16Ge	21Le	13Li	7Sg	15Cp	4Pi	8Ar
9	0Aq	16Pi	6Ar	20Ta	24Ge	11Le	18Vi	11Sc	5Cp	12Aq	29Pi	2Ta
11	25Aq	10Ar	0Ta	14Ge	18Cn	8Vi	16Li	10Sg	2Aq	7Pi	23Ar	25Ta
13	20Pi	3Ta	24Ta	9Cn	14Le	6Li	15Sc	8Cp	28Aq	2Ar	17Ta	19Ge
15	14Ar	27Ta	18Ge	5Le	11Vi	4Sc	14Sg	5Aq	23Pi	26Ar	10Ge	13Cn
17	7Ta	22Ge	13Cn	2Vi	10Li	4Sg	12Cp	2Pi	17Ar	20Ta	4Cn	8Le
19	2Ge	18Cn	10Le	1Li	10Sc	3Cp	10Aq	27Pi	11Ta	13Ge	29Cn	4Vi
21	27Ge	16Le	8Vi	2Sc	10Sg	2Aq	6Pi	21Ar	5Ge	8Cn	25Le	0Li
23	24Cn	15Vi	8Li	2Sg	10Cp	28Aq	1Ar	15Ta	29Ge	2Le	21Vi	28Li
25	22Le	15Li	9Sc	1Cp	7Aq	23Pi	25Ar	9Ge	24Cn	28Le	19Li	28Sc
27	20Vi	14Sc	8Sg	28Cp	3Pi	17Ar	19Ta	3Cn	20Le	25Vi	19Sc	27Sg
29	19Li	12Sg	6Cp	24Aq	27Pi	11Ta	13Ge	29Cn	18Vi	26Li	20Sg	27Cp
31	17Sc		2Aq		21Ar		8Cn	26Le		27Sc		25Aq

1933

	Jan	Feb	Mar	Apr	May	Jun	Jul	Aug	Sep	Oct	Nov	Dec
1	9Pi	24Ar	2Ta	16Ge	18Cn	4Vi	9Li	2Sg	25Cp	3Pi	2Ar	26Ta
3	4Ar	18Ta	26Ta	10Cn	12Le	0Li	7Sc	1Cp	24Aq	0Ar	17Ta	20Ge
5	28Ar	12Ge	20Ge	4Le	8Vi	28Li	7Sg	1Aq	22Pi	26Ar	12Ge	14Cn
7	22Ta	6Cn	14Cn	0Vi	5Li	28Sc	7Cp	29Aq	18Ar	21Ta	5Cn	7Le
9	16Ge	1Le	9Le	27Vi	4Sc	29Sg	7Aq	27Pi	13Ar	15Ge	29Cn	2Vi
11	10Cn	27Le	5Vi	26Li	5Sg	28Cp	5Pi	23Ar	8Ge	9Cn	23Le	27Vi
13	5Le	24Vi	3Li	25Sc	5Cp	27Aq	2Ar	18Ta	1Cn	3Le	18Vi	23Li
15	1Vi	21Li	2Sc	25Sg	4Aq	23Pi	27Ar	11Ge	25Cn	28Le	15Li	22Sc
17	27Vi	20Sc	1Sg	24Cp	1Pi	18Ar	21Ta	5Cn	20Le	24Vi	14Sc	22Sg
19	25Li	18Sg	29Sg	21Aq	27Pi	12Ta	15Ge	29Cn	16Vi	21Li	14Sg	23Cp
21	23Sc	16Cp	27Aq	17Pi	21Ar	6Ge	9Cn	23Le	11Li	20Sc	13Cp	20Pi
23	22Sg	14Aq	24Aq	12Ar	15Ta	0Cn	3Le	20Vi	11Sc	20Sg	13Aq	20Pi
25	21Cp	11Pi	20Pi	6Ta	9Ge	24Cn	28Le	17Li	9Sg	18Cp	10Pi	16Ar
27	19Aq	7Ar	15Ar	0Ge	3Cn	18Le	23Vi	14Sc	8Cp	16Aq	6Ar	11Ta
29	16Pi		10Ta	24Ge	27Cn	13Vi	20Li	12Sg	6Aq	13Pi	2Ta	5Ge
31	12Ar		4Ge		21Le		17Sc	11Cp		9Ar		29Ge

1934

	Jan	Feb	Mar	Apr	May	Jun	Jul	Aug	Sep	Oct	Nov	Dec
1	11Cn	25Le	4Vi	22Li	29Sc	22Cp	1Pi	22Ar	9Ge	12Cn	25Le	27Vi
3	4Le	20Vi	29Vi	19Sc	28Sg	21Aq	29Pi	18Ta	4Cn	6Le	19Vi	22Li
5	28Le	16Li	26Li	17Sg	26Cp	19Pi	26Ar	13Ge	27Cn	29Le	14Li	19Sc
7	23Vi	12Sc	23Sc	16Cp	25Aq	16Ar	21Ta	7Cn	21Le	24Vi	11Sc	17Sg
9	19Li	10Sg	20Sg	14Aq	22Pi	12Ta	16Ge	0Le	15Vi	19Li	8Sg	16Cp
11	16Sc	9Cp	19Cp	12Pi	19Ar	7Ge	10Cn	24Le	10Li	15Sc	7Cp	15Aq
13	15Sg	9Aq	18Aq	9Ar	15Ta	1Cn	3Le	18Vi	5Sc	12Sg	5Aq	14Pi
15	16Cp	8Pi	17Pi	6Ta	10Ge	25CN	27Le	13Li	2Sg	10Cp	3Pi	12Ar
17	16Aq	7Ar	14Ar	2Ge	4Cn	18Le	21Vi	8Sc	29Sg	8Aq	1Ar	8Ta
19	15Pi	3Ta	11Ta	26Ge	28Cn	12Vi	16Li	5Sg	28Cp	7Pi	29Ar	4Ge
21	12Ar	28Ta	6Ge	20Cn	22Le	7Li	12Sc	3Cp	27Aq	5Ar	25Ta	29Ge
23	8Ta	22Ge	0Cn	14Le	16Vi	3Sc	10Sg	3Aq	26Pi	3Ta	21Ge	24Cn
25	2Ge	16Cn	24Cn	8Vi	12Li	1Sg	9Cp	3Pi	25Ar	0Ge	16Cn	17Le
27	26Ge	10Le	18Le	4Li	9Sc	1Cp	10Aq	3Ar	22Ta	26Ge	9Le	11Vi
29	20Cn		13Vi	1Sc	8Sg	1Aq	10Pi	1Ta	18Ge	20Cn	3Vi	5Li
31	13Le		8Li		7Cp		8Ar	27Ta		13Le		0Sc

1935

	Jan	Feb	Mar	Apr	May	Jun	Jul	Aug	Sep	Oct	Nov	Dec
1	13Sc	3Cp	12Cp	5Pi	14Ar	5Ge	10Cn	25Le	9Li	13Sc	0Cp	7Aq
3	11Sg	3Aq	11Aq	5Ar	12Ta	1Cn	4Le	19Vi	3Sc	8Sg	27Cp	5Pi
5	10Cp	3Pi	11Pi	4Ta	10Ge	26Cn	28Le	12Li	28Sc	3Cp	25Aq	4Ar
7	10Aq	3Ar	12Ar	2Ge	6Cn	20Le	22Vi	7Sc	24Sg	0Aq	23Pi	2Ta
9	10Pi	2Ta	10Ta	28Ge	1Le	14Vi	16Li	2Sg	21Cp	29Aq	23Ar	1Ge
11	8Ar	28Ta	7Ge	23Cn	24Le	8Li	11Sc	29Sg	21Aq	20Pi	22Ta	28Ge
13	5Ta	23Ge	2Cn	16Le	18Vi	3Sc	7Sg	27Cp	21Pi	0Ta	21Ge	25Cn
15	1Ge	17Cn	26Cn	10Vi	12Li	29Sc	5Cp	27Aq	21Ar	29Ta	17Cn	20Le
17	26Ge	11Le	20Le	4Li	8Sc	26Sg	4Aq	28Pi	20Ta	26Ge	12Le	14Vi
19	20Cn	5Vi	13Vi	29Li	4Sg	25Cp	4Pi	27Ar	17Ge	22Cn	6Vi	7Li
21	14Le	28Vi	8Li	25Sc	1Cp	24Aq	3Ar	25Ta	13Cn	16Le	0Li	2Sc
23	8Vi	23Li	2Sc	21Sg	29Cp	22Pi	1Ta	21Ge	7Le	9Vi	24Li	26Sc
25	2Li	18Sc	28Sc	18Cp	27Aq	20Ar	28Ta	16Cn	1Vi	3Li	18Sc	23Sg
27	26Li	14Sg	24Sg	16Aq	25Pi	18Ta	24Ge	10Le	25Vi	27Li	14Sg	20Cp
29	22Sc		21Cp	15Pi	24Ar	14Ge	19Cn	4Vi	18Li	22Sc	10Cp	18Aq
31	19Sg		20Aq		21Ta		13Le	27Vi		17Sg		16Pi

1936

	Jan	Feb	Mar	Apr	May	Jun	Jul	Aug	Sep	Oct	Nov	Dec
1	1Ar	23Ta	17Ge	5Le	8Vi	22Li	25Sc	11Cp	1Pi	9Ar	3Ge	10Cn
3	29Ar	20Ge	13Cn	29Le	2Li	16Sc	20Sg	8Aq	0Ar	9Ta	2Cn	8Le
5	27Ta	16Cn	8Le	23Vi	26Li	11Sg	16Cp	6Pi	0Ta	9Ge	29Cn	3Vi
7	24Ge	11Le	2Vi	17Li	20Sc	6Cp	13Aq	5Ar	29Ta	7Cn	25Le	28Vi
9	20Cn	6Vi	26Vi	11Sc	14Sg	3Aq	11Pi	4Ta	27Ge	3Le	19Vi	22Li
11	15Le	0Li	20Li	5Sg	10Cp	0Pi	9Ar	2Ge	23Cn	28Le	13Li	16Sc
13	10Vi	23Li	14Sc	0Cp	6Aq	28Pi	7Ta	0Cn	18Le	22Vi	7Sc	9Sg
15	3Li	17Sc	8Sg	26Cp	3Pi	27Ar	6Ge	26Cn	13Vi	16Li	1Sg	4Cp
17	27Li	12Sg	3Cp	23Aq	2Ar	26Ta	3Cn	22Le	7Li	10Sc	25Sg	29Cp
19	22Sc	8Cp	0Aq	22Pi	2Ta	24Ge	0Le	17Vi	1Sc	4Sg	19Cp	25Aq
21	17Sg	6Aq	29Aq	23Ar	1Ge	22Cn	26Le	11Li	25Sc	28Sg	15Aq	22Pi
23	14Cp	6Pi	29Pi	23Ta	0Cn	18Le	21Vi	5Sc	19Sg	23Cp	12Pi	20Ar
25	13Aq	6Ar	0Ta	22Ge	27Cn	13Vi	15Li	28Sc	14Cp	19Aq	11Ar	19Ta
27	12Pi	6Ta	29Ta	19Cn	22Le	7Li	8Sc	23Sg	10Aq	17Pi	10Ta	19Ge
29	11Ar	4Ge	27Ge	14Le	17Vi	1Sc	3Sg	19Cp	9Pi	17Ar	11Ge	18Cn
31	10Ta		23Cn		11Li		28Sg	16Aq		18Ta		15Le

1937

	Jan	Feb	Mar	Apr	May	Jun	Jul	Aug	Sep	Oct	Nov	Dec
1	29Le	14Li	22Li	6Sg	8Cp	25Aq	1Ar	24Ta	17Cn	25Le	13Li	17Sc
3	24Vi	8Sc	16Sc	29Sg	3Aq	21Pi	29Ar	23Ge	15Le	21Vi	8Sc	10Sg
5	18Li	1Sg	9Sg	24Cp	28Aq	19Ar	28Ta	21Cn	12Vi	17Li	2Sg	4Cp
7	12Sc	26Sg	3Cp	20Aq	26Pi	19Ta	28Ge	20Le	8Li	11Sc	25Sg	28Cp
9	6Sg	21Cp	29Cp	18Pi	25Ar	19Ge	27Cn	17Vi	3Sc	5Sg	19Cp	22Aq
11	0Cp	17Aq	26Aq	17Ar	26Ta	19Cn	25Le	13Li	27Sc	29Sg	13Aq	17Pi
13	25Cp	15Pi	24Pi	17Ta	26Ge	17Le	22Vi	7Sc	21Sg	23Cp	9Pi	14Ar
15	22Aq	14Ar	23Ar	17Ge	25Cn	14Vi	17Li	1Sg	15Cp	18Aq	6Ar	13Ta
17	19Pi	12Ta	23Ta	15Cn	22Le	9Li	11Sc	25Sg	10Aq	14Pi	5Ta	13Ge
19	17Ar	10Ge	21Ge	12Le	17Vi	3Sc	5Sg	19Cp	6Pi	12Ar	5Ge	13Cn
21	15Ta	8Cn	19Cn	8Vi	12Li	26Sc	29Sg	14Ar	4Ar	12Ta	5Cn	13Le
23	14Ge	5Le	15Le	3Li	6Sc	20Sg	23Cp	11Pi	3Ta	11Ge	4Le	11Vi
25	12Cn	2Vi	11Vi	29Sc	29Sc	14Cp	18Aq	9Ar	1Ge	10Cn	2Vi	7Li
27	10Le	27Vi	6Li	23Sg	23Sg	9Aq	15Pi	7Ta	0Cn	8Le	28Vi	2Sc
29	6Vi		0Sc	17Cp	17Cp	5Pi	12Ar	5Ge	28Cn	5Vi	23Li	25Sc
31	2Li		24Sc	12Aq	12Aq		10Ta	3Cn		1Li		19Sg

1938

	Jan	Feb	Mar	Apr	May	Jun	Jul	Aug	Sep	Oct	Nov	Dec
1	1Cp	16Aq	25Aq	13Ar	20Ta	13Cn	22Le	13Li	29Sc	1Cp	15Aq	17Pi
3	25Cp	11Pi	21Pi	11Ta	19Ge	13Le	20Vi	9Sc	23Sg	25Cp	9Pi	12Ar
5	19Aq	7Ar	17Ar	9Ge	18Cn	11Vi	17Li	3Sg	17Cp	19Aq	5Ar	9Ta
7	14Pi	4Ta	15Ta	8Cn	17Le	7Li	12Sc	27Sg	11Aq	14Pi	1Ta	8Ge
9	10Ar	2Ge	13Ge	6Le	14Vi	3Sc	6Sg	20Cp	5Pi	10Ar	29Ta	8Cn
11	8Ta	0Cn	11Cn	4Vi	10Li	27Sc	0Cp	14Aq	1Ar	6Ta	28Ge	7Le
13	6Ge	0Le	9Le	1Li	6Sc	21Sg	24Cp	9Pi	27Ar	4Ge	27Cn	6Vi
15	6Cn	29Le	8Vi	27Li	0Sg	15Cp	17Aq	4Ar	24Ta	2Cn	26Le	4Li
17	6Le	27Vi	5Li	22Sc	24Sg	8Aq	12Pi	0Ta	21Ge	0Le	23Vi	0Sc
19	5Vi	23Li	1Sc	16Sg	18Cp	3Pi	7Ar	27Ta	20Cn	29Le	20Li	25Sc
21	3Li	18Sc	26Sc	10Cp	12Aq	28Pi	3Ta	25Ge	19Le	27Vi	16Sc	20Sg
23	28Li	12Sg	20Sg	3Aq	6Pi	24Ar	1Ge	24Cn	18Vi	24Li	11Sg	14Cp
25	22Sc	6Cp	14Cp	28Aq	2Ar	22Ta	0Cn	24Le	16Li	20Sc	5Cp	7Aq
27	16Sg	0Aq	8Aq	24Pi	29Ar	22Ge	1Le	23Vi	12Sc	15Sg	29Cp	1Pi
29	9Cp		3Pi	21Ar	28Ta	22Cn	1Vi	21Li	7Sg	9Cp	23Aq	25Pi
31	4Aq		29Pi		28Ge		29Vi	17Sc		3Aq		20Ar

1939

	Jan	Feb	Mar	Apr	May	Jun	Jul	Aug	Sep	Oct	Nov	Dec
1	3Ta	24Ge	3Cn	27Le	5Li	26Sc	0Cp	15Aq	0Ar	3Ta	22Ge	0Le
3	1Ge	24Cn	2Le	26Vi	3Sc	21Sg	25Cp	9Pi	24Ar	29Ta	19Cn	28Le
5	1Cn	24Le	2Vi	25Li	0Sg	16Cp	18Aq	3Ar	19Ta	25Ge	17Le	26Vi
7	1Le	24Vi	2Li	22Sc	26Sg	10Aq	12Pi	27Ar	15Ge	22Cn	16Vi	24Li
9	1Vi	23Li	1Sc	18Sg	20Cp	4Pi	6Ar	22Ta	12Cn	21Le	14Li	22Sc
11	0Li	19Sc	27Sc	12Cp	14Aq	28Pi	1Ta	19Ge	12Le	21Vi	13Sc	19Sg
13	27Li	14Sg	22Sg	6Aq	8Pi	23Ar	27Ta	18Cn	12Vi	20Li	10Sg	15Cp
15	22Sc	8Cp	16Cp	0Pi	2Ar	19Ta	25Ge	18Le	12Li	19Sc	7Cp	9Aq
17	17Sg	1Aq	10Aq	24Pi	28Ar	17Ge	25Cn	19Vi	11Sc	16Sg	2Aq	3Pi
19	11Cp	25Aq	4Pi	19Ar	24Ta	16Cn	25Le	18Li	8Sg	11Cp	26Aq	27Pi
21	4Aq	19Pi	28Pi	15Ta	22Ge	16Le	25Vi	16Sc	3Cp	6Aq	19Pi	21Ar
23	28Aq	14Ar	23Ar	12Ge	21Cn	15Vi	23Li	12Sg	27Cp	29Sq	13Ar	16Ta
25	22Pi	9Ta	19Ta	10Cn	20Le	12Li	19Sc	6Cp	21Aq	23Pi	8Ta	13Ge
27	17Ar	5Ge	16Ge	8Le	18Vi	9Sc	15Sg	0Aq	15Pi	18Ar	4Ge	11Cn
29	12Ta		13Cn	7Vi	16Li	5Sg	9Cp	24Aq	9Ar	13Ta	2Cn	10Le
31	9Ge		12Le		12Sc		3Aq	18Pi		9Ge		9Vi

1940

	Jan	Feb	Mar	Apr	May	Jun	Jul	Aug	Sep	Oct	Nov	Dec
1	23Vi	15Sc	8Sg	26Cp	29Aq	12Ar	14Ta	1Cn	22Le	0Li	23Sc	0Cp
3	21Li	12Sg	4Cp	20Aq	22Pi	6Ta	10Ge	29Cn	21Vi	0Sc	22Sg	28Cp
5	18Sc	7Cp	29Cp	14Pi	16Ar	1Ge	6Cn	28Le	21Li	0Sg	20Cp	24Aq
7	15Sg	2Aq	23Aq	7Ar	10Ta	27Ge	4Le	27Vi	20Sc	28Sg	15Aq	18Pi
9	10Cp	26Aq	17Pi	1Ta	5Ge	24Cn	3Vi	26Li	18Sg	24Cp	10Pi	12Ar
11	5Aq	20Pi	10Ar	26Ta	1Cn	22Le	1Li	24Sc	14Cp	19Aq	3Ar	5Ta
13	29Aq	13Ar	4Ta	21Ge	28Cn	20Vi	29Li	21Sg	9Aq	13Pi	27Ar	29Ta
15	23Pi	7Ta	29Ta	17Cn	25Le	19Li	27Sc	17Cp	4Pi	6Ar	21Ta	25Ge
17	17Ar	2Ge	24Ge	15Le	24Vi	17Sc	24Sg	13Aq	28Pi	0Ta	15Ge	21Cn
19	11Ta	28Ge	21Cn	14Vi	23Li	15Sg	21Cp	7Pi	21Ar	24Ta	11Cn	17Le
21	7Ge	27Cn	20Le	14Li	22Sc	12Cp	16Aq	1Ar	15Ta	18Ge	7Le	15Vi
23	4Cn	27Le	20Vi	13Sc	20Sg	8Aq	11Pi	24Ar	9Ge	14Cn	4Vi	13Li
25	4Le	27Vi	20Li	12Sg	17Cp	3Pi	4Ar	18Ta	4Cn	10Le	2Li	11Sc
27	4Vi	27Li	20Sc	9Cp	12Aq	26Pi	28Ar	13Ge	1Le	8Vi	2Sc	10Sg
29	3Li	25Sc	17Sg	4Aq	7Pi	20Ar	22Ta	9Cn	0Vi	8Li	1Sg	8Cp
31	2Sc		13Cp		0Ar		18Ge	7Le		8Sc		6Aq

1941

	Jan	Feb	Mar	Apr	May	Jun	Jul	Aug	Sep	Oct	Nov	Dec
1	19Aq	3Ar	12Ar	25Ta	29Ge	16Le	23Vi	16Sc	9Cp	16Aq	4Ar	7Ta
3	14Pi	27Ar	5Ta	19Ge	23Cn	13Vi	21Li	14Sg	6Aq	12Pi	28Ar	0Ge
5	8Ar	21Ta	29Ta	14Cn	19Le	11Li	20Sc	13Cp	3Pi	7Ar	22Ta	24Ge
7	1Ta	15Ge	23Ge	10Le	17Vi	10Sc	19Sg	11Aq	28Pi	1Ta	15Ge	18Cn
9	25Ta	11Cn	19Cn	8Vi	16Li	10Sg	18Cp	7Pi	23Ar	25Ta	9Cn	13Le
11	20Ge	8Le	16Le	8Li	16Sc	10Cp	16Aq	2Ar	17Ta	19Ge	4Le	9Vi
13	16Cn	6Vi	15Vi	8Sc	17Sg	8Aq	12Pi	27Ar	10Ge	13Cn	29Le	5Li
15	13Le	5Li	15Li	8Sg	16Cp	4Pi	7Ar	21Ta	5Cn	8Le	26Vi	4Sc
17	11Vi	4Sc	14Sc	7Cp	13Aq	29Pi	1Ta	14Ge	0Le	4Vi	25Li	4Sg
19	9Li	3Sg	13Sg	4Aq	8Pi	23Ar	24Ta	9Cn	26Le	3Li	26Sc	4Cp
21	8Sc	0Cp	11Cp	29Aq	2Ar	16Ta	19Ge	5Le	25Vi	2Sc	26Sg	4Aq
23	6Sg	27Cp	7Aq	23Pi	26Ar	10Ge	14Cn	2Vi	24Li	3Sg	26Cp	1Pi
25	4Cp	23Aq	2Pi	17Ar	19Ta	5Cn	9Le	0Li	23Sc	2Cp	23Aq	27Pi
27	1Aq	17Pi	26Pi	11Ta	13Ge	0Le	6Vi	28Li	22Sg	0Aq	18Pi	22Ar
29	27Aq		20Ar	4Ge	8Cn	26Le	4Li	27Sc	20Cp	26Aq	13Ar	15Ta
31	21Pi		14Ta		3Le		2Sc	25Sg		22Pi		9Ge

1942

	Jan	Feb	Mar	Apr	May	Jun	Jul	Aug	Sep	Oct	Nov	Dec
1	21Ge	7Le	15Le	3Li	11Sc	5Cp	13Aq	3Ar	19Ta	21Ge	5Le	7Vi
3	15Cn	2Vi	11Vi	2Sc	11Sg	4Aq	11Pi	29Ar	13Ge	15Cn	29Le	2Li
5	10Le	29Vi	9Li	1Sg	10Cp	2Pi	7Ar	23Ta	7Cn	9Le	24Vi	29Li
7	6Vi	26Li	7Sc	0Cp	9Aq	28Pi	2Ta	17Ge	1Le	4Vi	22Li	29Sc
9	2Li	24Sc	5Sg	28Cp	6Pi	23Ar	26Ta	11Cn	26Le	0Li	20Sc	29Sg
11	29Li	23Sg	4Cp	25Aq	1Ar	17Ta	20Ge	5Le	21Vi	27Li	20Sg	29Cp
13	28Sc	21Cp	2Aq	22Pi	26Ar	11Ge	14Cn	29Le	18Li	26Sc	19Cp	28Aq
15	28Sg	20Aq	29Aq	17Ar	20Ta	5Cn	8Le	25Vi	16Sc	25Sg	18Aq	25Pi
17	27Cp	17Pi	25Pi	12Ta	14Ge	29Cn	3Vi	21Li	14Sg	23Cp	15Pi	21Ar
19	26Aq	13Ar	21Ar	6Ge	8Cn	23Le	28Vi	19Sc	12Cp	21Aq	11Ar	16Ta
21	22Pi	8Ta	15Ta	29Ge	2Le	18Vi	24Li	17Sg	10Aq	18Pi	7Ta	10Ge
23	18Ar	2Ge	9Ge	23Cn	26Le	15Li	22Sc	16Cp	8Pi	15Ar	1Ge	4Cn
25	12Ta	25Ge	3Cn	18Le	22Vi	13Sc	22Sg	15Aq	6Ar	10Ta	25Ge	28Cn
27	6Ge	20Cn	27Cn	14Vi	20Li	13Sg	22Cp	14Pi	2Ta	5Ge	19Cn	21Le
29	29Ge		23Le	11Li	19Sc	13Cp	21Aq	11Ar	27Ta	29Ge	13Le	16Vi
31	24Cn		19Vi		20Sg		19Pi	7Ta		23Cn		11Li

1943

	Jan	Feb	Mar	Apr	May	Jun	Jul	Aug	Sep	Oct	Nov	Dec
1	24Li	15Sg	25Sg	19Aq	27Pi	17Ta	21Ge	6Le	20Vi	24Li	14Sg	22Cp
3	22Sc	15Cp	24Cp	17Pi	24Ar	12Ge	15Cn	29Le	15Li	20Sc	11Cp	20Aq
5	22Sg	15Aq	23Aq	15Ar	20Ta	6Cn	9Le	23Vi	10Sc	17Sg	9Aq	18Pi
7	22Cp	15Pi	23Pi	12Ta	16Ge	0Le	2Vi	18Li	6Sg	14Cp	8Pi	16Ar
9	22Aq	13Ar	21Ar	8Ge	10Cn	24Le	26Vi	13Sc	4Cp	13Aq	6Ar	13Ta
11	21Pi	9Ta	17Ta	2Cn	4Le	18Vi	21Li	10Sg	3Aq	12Pi	4Ta	10Ge
13	18Ar	4Ge	12Ge	26Cn	27Le	13Li	18Sc	9Cp	3Pi	11Ar	1Ge	5Cn
15	13Ta	28Ge	6Cn	19Le	22Vi	9Sc	16Sg	9Aq	2Ar	9Ta	27Ge	29Cn
17	7Ge	21Cn	0Le	144Vi	18Li	8Sg	16Cp	9Pi	1Ta	6Ge	21Cn	23Le
19	1Cn	15Le	24Le	9Li	15Sc	7Cp	16Aq	9Ar	28Ta	1Cn	15Le	17Vi
21	25Cn	10Vi	18Vi	6Sc	14Sg	7Aq	16Pi	6Ta	23Ge	25Cn	9Vi	11Li
23	18Le	5Li	14Li	4Sg	13Cp	6Pi	14Ar	2Ge	17Cn	19Le	3Li	6Sc
25	13Vi	0Sc	11Sc	3Cp	12Aq	4Ar	10Ta	27Ge	11Le	13Vi	28Li	3Sg
27	7Li	27Sc	8Sg	1Aq	10Pi	1Ta	6Ge	21Cn	5Vi	8Li	25Sc	2Cp
29	3Sc		6Cp	29Aq	7Ar	26Ta	0Cn	14Le	29Vi	3Sc	23Sg	1Aq
31	1Sg		4Aq		4Ta		24Cn	8Vi		0Sg		1Pi

1944

	Jan	Feb	Mar	Apr	May	Jun	Jul	Aug	Sep	Oct	Nov	Dec
1	15Pi	7Ta	29Ta	16Cn	18Le	2Li	4Sc	21Sg	12Aq	20Pi	14Ta	21Ge
3	13Ar	3Ge	25Ge	10Le	12Vi	26Li	0Sg	19Cp	12Pi	21Ar	13Ge	18Cn
5	10Ta	28Ge	19Cn	4Vi	6Li	22Sc	27Sg	19Aq	12Ar	21Ta	10Cn	13Le
7	6Ge	22Cn	13Le	27Vi	0Sc	18Sg	25Cp	19Pi	12Ta	18Ge	5Le	7Vi
9	1Cn	16Le	7Vi	22Li	26Sc	16Cp	24Aq	18Ar	10Ge	15Cn	0Vi	1Li
11	26Cn	10Vi	1Li	17Sc	22Sg	14Aq	23Pi	16Ta	5Cn	9Le	23Vi	25Li
13	19Le	4Li	25Li	12Sg	20Cp	13Pi	22Ar	13Ge	0Le	3Vi	17Li	20Sc
15	13Vi	28Li	20Sc	9Cp	17Aq	11Ar	19Ta	8Cn	24Le	27Vi	11Sc	15Sg
17	7Li	23Sc	15Sg	7Aq	16Pi	9Ta	16Ge	3Le	18Vi	20Li	6Sg	12Cp
19	1Sc	19Sg	13Cp	5Pi	14Ar	6Ge	11Cn	27Le	11Li	15Sc	2Cp	9Aq
21	27Sc	18Cp	11Aq	5Ar	13Ta	2Cn	6Le	21Vi	5Sc	9Sg	29Cp	7Pi
23	25Sg	17Aq	11Pi	4Ta	11Ge	28Cn	0Vi	14Li	0Sg	5Cp	26Aq	5Ar
25	24Cp	18Pi	11Ar	2Ge	7Cn	22Le	24Vi	8Sc	25Sg	2Aq	24Pi	3Ta
27	25Aq	18Ar	10Ta	29Ge	2Le	16Vi	18Li	3Sg	22Cp	0Pi	23Ar	2Ge
29	24Pi	16Ta	8Ge	24Cn	26Le	10Li	12Sc	29Sg	20Aq	29Pi	22Ta	29Ge
31	23Ar		4Cn		20Vi		8Sg	27Cp		29Ar		26Cn

1945

	Jan	Feb	Mar	Apr	May	Jun	Jul	Aug	Sep	Oct	Nov	Dec
1	8Le	23Vi	2Li	16Sc	19Sg	7Aq	15Pi	9Ta	1Cn	8Le	24Vi	27Li
3	3Vi	17Li	25Li	10Sg	14Cp	4Pi	13Ar	7Ge	28Cn	3Vi	18Li	21Sc
5	27Vi	11Sc	19Sc	5Cp	10Aq	3Ar	12Ta	4Cn	23Le	27Vi	12Sc	15Sg
7	21Li	5Sg	13Sg	1Aq	8Pi	2Ta	11Ge	1Le	18Vi	21Li	6Sg	9Cp
9	15Sc	1Cp	9Cp	29Aq	7Ar	1Ge	9Cn	27Le	13Li	15Sc	0Cp	4Aq
11	10Sg	28Cp	6Aq	28Pi	7Ta	0Cn	6Le	22Vi	7Sc	9Sg	24Cp	0Pi
13	7Cp	27Aq	5Pi	29Ar	7Ge	28Cn	2Vi	16Li	0Sg	3Cp	20Aq	27Pi
15	4Aq	27Pi	6Ar	29Ta	6Cn	24Le	26Vi	10Sc	24Sg	28Cp	17Pi	26Ar
17	3Pi	26Ar	6Ta	28Ge	3Le	18Vi	20Li	4Sg	19Cp	25Aq	16Ar	25Ta
19	2Ar	25Ta	5Ge	24Cn	28Le	12Li	14Sc	29Sg	16Aq	23Pi	17Ta	25Ge
21	0Ta	22Ge	2Cn	19Le	22Vi	6Sc	8Sg	25Cp	15Pi	23Ar	17Ge	24Cn
23	28Ta	18Cn	28Cn	14Vi	16Li	0Sg	4Cp	22Aq	15Ar	24Ta	16Cn	21Le
25	25Ge	13Le	22Le	7Li	10Sc	25Sg	0Aq	21Pi	15Ta	23Ge	13Le	17Vi
27	21Cn	7Vi	16Vi	1Sc	4Sg	21Cp	27Aq	21Ar	14Ge	21Cn	9Vi	12Li
29	17Le		10Li	25Sc	29Sg	18Aq	26Pi	20Ta	12Cn	17Le	3Li	6Sc
31	11Vi		4Sc		24Cp		24Ar	18Ge		12Vi		29Sc

1946

	Jan	Feb	Mar	Apr	May	Jun	Jul	Aug	Sep	Oct	Nov	Dec
1	11Sg	27Cp	5Aq	24Pi	2Ta	25Ge	3Le	23Vi	9Sc	11Sg	24Cp	27Aq
3	6Cp	23Aq	2Pi	23Ar	2Ge	25Cn	1Vi	19Li	3Sg	4Cp	19Aq	23Pi
5	1Aq	20Pi	0Ar	23Ta	2Cn	23Le	28Vi	13Sc	26Sg	28Cp	15Pi	20Ar
7	27Aq	18Ar	29Ar	22Ge	0Le	19Vi	23Li	7Sg	20Cp	23Aq	12Ar	19Ta
9	24Pi	17Ta	28Ta	20Cn	27Le	14Li	17Sc	0Cp	15Aq	20Pi	11Ta	19Ge
11	22Ar	15Ge	26Ge	17Le	22Vi	8Sc	10Sg	25Cp	12Pi	18Ar	11Ge	20Cn
13	20Ta	13Cn	23Cn	13Vi	17Li	2Sg	4Cp	20Aq	9Ar	18Ta	11Cn	19Le
15	19Ge	10Le	20Le	8Li	11Sc	25Sg	28Cp	16Pi	8Ta	17Ge	10Le	16Vi
17	18Cn	7Vi	16Vi	2Sc	5Sc	19Cp	23Aq	13Ar	6Ge	15Cn	7Vi	12Li
19	16Le	3Li	11Li	26Sc	28Sg	14Aq	20Pi	11Ta	4Cn	13Le	3Li	7Sc
21	12Vi	27Li	5Sc	19Sg	22Cp	9Pi	16Ar	9Ge	2Le	10Vi	27Li	1Sg
23	8Li	21Sc	29Sc	13Cp	17Aq	6Ar	14Ta	8Cn	0Vi	6Li	22Sc	24Sg
25	2Sc	15Sg	23Sg	8Aq	13Pi	4Ta	13Ge	6Le	26Vi	1Sc	15Sg	18Cp
27	25Sc	9Cp	17Cp	4Pi	11Ar	4Ge	13Cn	4Vi	22Li	25Sc	9Cp	12Aq
29	19Sg		12Aq	2Ar	10Ta	4Cn	12Le	1Li	17Sc	19Sg	3Aq	6Pi
31	14Cp		10Pi		10Ge		10Vi	27Li		12Cp		2Ar

1947

	Jan	Feb	Mar	Apr	May	Jun	Jul	Aug	Sep	Oct	Nov	Dec
1	15Ar	7Ge	17Ge	10Le	19Vi	8Sc	11Sg	26Cp	11Pi	15Ar	5Ge	13Cn
3	13Ta	6Cn	16Cn	9Vi	15Li	2Sg	5Cp	20Aq	6Ar	12Ta	3Cn	13Le
5	12Ge	6Le	15Le	6Li	11Sc	26Sg	29Cp	14Pi	2Ta	9Ge	2Le	11Vi
7	13Cn	5Vi	13Vi	2Sc	6Sg	20Cp	22Aq	9Ar	28Ta	7Cn	0Vi	8Li
9	13Le	3Li	11Li	27Sc	0Cp	14Aq	17Pi	5Ta	26Ge	5Le	28Vi	5Sc
11	11Vi	29Li	7Sc	22Sg	23Cp	8Pi	12Ar	2Ge	25Cn	4Vi	25Li	0Sg
13	8Li	24Sc	2Sg	15Cp	17Aq	3Ar	8Ta	0Cn	24Le	2Li	21Sc	25Sg
15	3Sc	18Sg	26Sg	9Aq	12Pi	0Ta	7Ge	0Le	23Vi	0Sc	16Sg	19Cp
17	28Sc	11Cp	19Cp	4Pi	8Ar	28Ta	6Cn	0Vi	22Li	26Sc	11Cp	13Aq
19	21Sg	5Aq	13Aq	0Ar	5Ta	28Ge	7Le	29Vi	18Sc	21Sg	5Aq	6Pi
21	15Cp	0Pi	9Pi	27Ar	5Ge	28Cn	7Vi	27Li	13Sg	15Cp	28Aq	1Ar
23	9Aq	26Pi	5Ar	26Ta	4Cn	28Le	5Li	23Sc	7Cp	9Aq	23Pi	26Ar
25	3Pi	22Ar	2Ta	24Ge	4Le	26Vi	1Sc	17Sg	1Aq	3Pi	18Ar	23Ta
27	29Pi	19Ar	0Ge	23Cn	2Vi	22Li	26Sc	11Cp	25Aq	28Pi	15Ta	22Ge
29	25Ar		28Ge	21Le	29Vi	17Sc	20Sg	4Aq	19Pi	24Ar	14Ge	22Cn
31	23Ta		26Cn		25Li		14Cp	28Aq		21Ta		22Le

1948

	Jan	Feb	Mar	Apr	May	Jun	Jul	Aug	Sep	Oct	Nov	Dec
1	7Vi	28Li	20Sc	6Cp	8Aq	21Pi	24Ar	11Ge	3Le	12Vi	5Sc	11Sg
3	5Li	24Sc	15Sg	0Aq	2Pi	16Ar	20Ta	10Cn	3Vi	12Li	3Sg	8Cp
5	2Sc	19Sg	10Cp	24Aq	26Pi	12Ta	17Ge	9Le	4Li	11Sc	0Cp	3Aq
7	27Sc	13Cp	3Aq	18Pi	21Ar	9Ge	16Cn	10Vi	3Sc	9Sg	25Cp	27Aq
9	22Sg	6Aq	27Aq	12Ar	16Ta	7Cn	16Le	10Li	0Sg	5Cp	19Aq	21Pi
11	16Cp	0Pi	21Pi	8Ta	14Ge	6Le	15Vi	8Sc	26Sg	29Cp	13Pi	15Ar
13	9Aq	24Pi	16Ar	4Ge	11Cn	5Vi	14Li	4Sg	20Cp	23Aq	7Ar	9Ta
15	3Pi	19Ar	11Ta	1Cn	10Le	3Li	11Sc	29Sg	14Aq	17Pi	1Ta	5Ge
17	27Pi	14Ta	7Ge	29Cn	8Vi	1Sc	7Sg	23Cp	8Pi	11Ar	27Ta	2Cn
19	22Ar	10Ge	4Cn	27Le	6Li	27Sc	2Cp	17Aq	2Ar	5Ta	23Ge	1Le
21	18Ta	8Cn	3Le	26Vi	4Sc	23Sg	26Cp	11Pi	26Ar	0Ge	21Cn	29Le
23	15Ge	8Le	2Vi	25Li	1Sg	18Cp	20Aq	5Ar	21Ta	27Ge	18Le	28Vi
25	15Cn	9Vi	2Li	23Sc	27Sg	12Aq	14Pi	29Ar	16Ge	24Cn	17Vi	26Li
27	16Le	9Li	1Sc	19Sg	22Cp	6Pi	8Ar	24Ta	13Cn	22Le	15Li	23Sc
29	16Vi	7Sc	28Sc	14Cp	16Aq	0Ar	2Ta	20Ge	12Le	21Vi	13Sc	20Sg
31	15Li		24Sg		10Pi		28Ta	18Cn		20Li		16Cp

1949

	Jan	Feb	Mar	Apr	May	Jun	Jul	Aug	Sep	Oct	Nov	Dec
1	28Cp	13Pi	22Pi	6Ta	10Ge	29Cn	7Vi	1Sc	23Sg	29Cp	15Pi	17Ar
3	23Aq	7Ar	15Ar	1Ge	6Cn	27Le	6Li	29Sc	19Cp	24Aq	9Ar	11Ta
5	17Pi	1Ta	9Ta	26Ge	2Le	25Vi	4Sc	26Sg	14Aq	18Pi	2Ta	5Ge
7	11Ar	25Ta	4Ge	22Cn	0Vi	23Li	2Sg	22Cp	9Pi	12Ar	26Ta	0Cn
9	5Ta	21Ge	29Ge	20Le	29Vi	22Sc	29Sg	18Aq	3Ar	5Ta	20Ge	25Cn
11	0Ge	19Cn	27Cn	20Vi	28Li	20Sg	26Cp	12Pi	26Ar	29Ta	16Cn	22Le
13	27Ge	18Le	26Le	20Li	28Sc	18Cp	22Aq	6Ar	20Ta	23Ge	12Le	19Vi
15	25Cn	18Vi	27Vi	20Sc	26Sg	14Aq	16Pi	0Ta	14Ge	19Cn	9Vi	17Li
17	25Le	18li	27Li	18Sg	23Cp	8Pi	10Ar	24Ta	10Cn	16Le	8Li	16Sc
19	24Vi	17Sc	26Sc	15Cp	18Aq	2Ar	4Ta	19Ge	7Le	14Vi	7Sc	16Sg
21	23Li	13Sg	23Sg	10Aq	12Pi	26Ar	28Ta	15Cn	6Vi	14Li	7Sg	14Cp
23	20Sc	9Cp	19Cp	4Pi	6Ar	20Ta	24Ge	13Le	6Li	14Sc	6Cp	12Aq
25	16Sg	4Aq	13Aq	28Pi	0Ta	15Ge	21Cn	13Vi	6Sc	14Sg	4Aq	7Pi
27	12Cp	28Aq	7Pi	21Ar	24Ta	12Cn	19Le	12Li	5Sg	12Cp	29Aq	1Ar
29	7Aq		1Ar	15Ta	19Ge	9Le	18Vi	11Sc	3Cp	8Aq	23Pi	25Ar
31	1Pi		24Ar		16Cn		17Li	9Sg		3Pi		19Ta

1950

	Jan	Feb	Mar	Apr	May	Jun	Jul	Aug	Sep	Oct	Nov	Dec
1	1Ge	17Cn	25Cn	14Vi	22Li	16Sg	24Cp	13Pi	28Ar	0Ge	14Cn	18Le
3	26Ge	14Le	22Le	14Li	23Sc	16Cp	22Aq	8Ar	22Ta	24Ge	9Le	14Vi
5	22Cn	12Vi	21Vi	14Sc	23Sg	14Aq	18Pi	2Ta	16Ge	18Cn	5Vi	11Li
7	19Le	11Li	20Li	14Sg	21Cp	10Pi	12Ar	26Ta	10Cn	14Le	2Li	10Sc
9	16Vi	9Sc	20Sc	12Cp	18Aq	4Ar	6Ar	20Ge	6Le	10Vi	2Sc	10Sg
11	14Li	7Sg	18Sg	9Aq	13Pi	28Ar	0Ge	15Cn	2Vi	9Li	2Sg	11Cp
13	12Sc	5Cp	15Cp	4Pi	7Ar	22Ta	24Ge	11Le	0Li	9Sc	2Cp	10Aq
15	11Sg	2Aq	11Aq	28Pi	1Ta	15Ge	19Cn	7Vi	29Li	8Sg	1Aq	7Pi
17	9Cp	28Aq	7Pi	22Ar	25Ta	10Cn	15Le	5Li	28Sc	7Cp	28Aq	3Ar
19	6Aq	23Pi	1Ar	16Ta	19Ge	5Le	11Vi	3Sc	27Sg	5Aq	24Pi	27Ar
21	2Pi	17Ar	25Ar	9Ge	13Cn	1Vi	8Li	2Sg	24Cp	1Pi	18Ar	21Ta
23	27Pi	11Ta	19Ta	4Cn	8Le	28Vi	6Sc	0Cp	21Aq	26Pi	12Ta	14Ge
25	21Ar	4Ge	13Ge	28Cn	4Vi	26Li	5Sg	28Cp	17Pi	21Ar	6Ge	8Cn
27	15Ta	29Ge	7Cn	25Le	2Li	25Sc	4Cp	25Aq	12Ar	15Ta	29Ge	3Le
29	9Ge		3Le	23Vi	1Sc	25Sg	2Aq	21Pi	6Ta	9Ge	23Cn	28Le
31	4Cn		0Vi		1Sg		0Pi	16Ar		2Cn		23Vi

1951

	Jan	Feb	Mar	Apr	May	Jun	Jul	Aug	Sep	Oct	Nov	Dec
1	7Li	29Sc	10Sg	3Aq	10Pi	28Ar	2Ge	16Cb	1Vi	6Li	26Sc	5Cp
3	4Sc	28Sg	8Cp	0Pi	6Ar	22Ta	25Ge	10Le	27Vi	3Sc	25Sg	5Aq
5	3Sg	27Cp	6Aq	27Pi	1Ta	16Ge	19Cn	5Vi	23Li	1Sg	24Cp	3Pi
7	4Cp	26Aq	4Pi	22Ar	26Ta	10Cn	13Le	0Li	20Sc	29Sg	22Aq	0Ar
9	3Aq	23Pi	1Ar	17Ta	20Ge	4Le	7Vi	26Li	18Sg	28Cp	20Pi	26Ar
11	2Pi	19Ar	27Ar	11Ge	13Cn	28Le	3Li	23Sc	17Cp	26Aq	16Ar	21Ta
13	28Pi	13Ta	21Ta	5Cn	7Le	23Vi	29Li	22Sg	16Aq	23Pi	12Ta	15Ge
15	23Ar	7Ge	15Ge	29Cn	2Vi	20Li	28Sc	22Cp	14Pi	20Ar	7Ge	9Cn
17	17Ta	1Cn	9Cn	24Le	28Vi	19Sc	27Sg	21Aq	12Ar	16Ta	1Cn	3Le
19	11Ge	25Cn	3Le	20Vi	26Li	19Sg	28Cp	20Pi	8Ta	11Ge	24Cn	27Le
21	5Cn	21Le	29Le	18Li	25Sc	19Cp	27Aq	17Ar	3Ge	5Cn	18Le	21Vi
23	29Cn	17Vi	25Vi	17Sc	26Sg	19Aq	25Pi	12Ta	27Ge	28Cn	13Vi	16Li
25	24Le	14Li	23Li	16Sg	25Cp	17Pi	22Ar	7Ge	20Cn	22Le	8Li	14Sc
27	20Vi	11Sc	22Sc	16Cp	24Aq	13Ar	16Ta	1Cn	15Le	17Vi	6Sc	13Sg
29	17Li		21Sg	14Aq	20Pi	8Ta	10Ge	24Cn	9Vi	14Li	5Sg	13Cp
31	15Sc		19Cp		16Ar		4Cn	19Le		12Sc		14Aq

1952

	Jan	Feb	Mar	Apr	May	Jun	Jul	Aug	Sep	Oct	Nov	Dec
1	28Aq	19Ar	10Ta	26Ge	27Cn	11Vi	14Li	2Sg	24Cp	3Pi	25Ar	2Ge
3	26Pi	15Ta	5Ge	20Cn	21Le	6Li	10Sc	0Cp	24Aq	2Ar	23Ta	28Ge
5	23Ar	9Ge	0Cn	13Le	15Vi	2Sc	8Sg	0Aq	24Pi	1Ta	20Ge	23Cn
7	18Ta	3Cn	23Cn	7Vi	10Li	29Sc	7Cp	1Pi	23Ar	29Ta	15Cn	17Le
9	12Ge	27Cn	17Le	2Li	7Sc	28Sg	7Aq	0Ar	21Ta	25Ge	9Le	10Vi
11	6Cn	21Le	11Vi	28Li	5Sg	28Cp	7Pi	29Ar	16Ge	19Cn	3Vi	4Li
13	0Le	15Vi	6Li	25Sc	4Cp	27Aq	5Ar	25Ta	11Cn	13Le	26Vi	29Li
15	24Le	9Li	2Sc	23Sg	2Aq	25Pi	2Ta	20Ge	5Le	7Vi	21Li	26Sc
17	18Vi	5Sc	29Sc	21Cp	1Pi	22Ar	28Ta	14Cn	28Le	1Li	17Sc	23Sg
19	12Li	2Sg	26Sg	20Aq	28Pi	18Ta	23Ge	8Le	22Vi	26Li	15Sg	22Cp
21	9Sc	0Cp	25Cp	18Pi	25Ar	14Ge	17Cn	1Vi	17Li	22Sc	13Cp	21Aq
23	6Sg	0Aq	24Aq	16Ar	22Ta	8Cn	11Le	25Vi	12Sc	18Sg	11Aq	20Pi
25	6Cp	29Aq	23Pi	13Ta	17Ge	2Le	4Vi	20Li	8Sg	16Cp	9Pi	18Ar
27	6Aq	29Pi	21Ar	9Ge	12Cn	26Le	28Vi	15Sc	5Cp	14Aq	7Ar	15Ta
29	6Pi	27Ar	18Ta	4Cn	5Le	19Vi	23Li	11Sg	3Aq	12Pi	5Ta	11Ge
31	5Ar		13Ge		29Le		18Sc	9Cp		11Ar		6Cn

1953

	Jan	Feb	Mar	Apr	May	Jun	Jul	Aug	Sep	Oct	Nov	Dec
1	19Cn	3Vi	12Vi	27Li	1Sg	21Cp	29Aq	23Ar	15Ge	20Cn	5Vi	7Li
3	13Le	27Vi	6Li	22Sc	27Sg	19Aq	28Pi	21Ta	10Cn	14Le	29Vi	1Sc
5	7Vi	21Li	0Sc	17Sg	24Cp	17Pi	26Ar	18Ge	5Le	8Vi	22Li	25Sc
7	0Li	15Sc	25Sc	14Cp	22Aq	15Ar	24Ta	13Cn	29Le	2Li	17Sc	21Sg
9	24Li	11Sg	20Sg	12Aq	21Pi	14Ta	21Ge	8Le	23Vi	26Li	11Sg	17Cp
11	20Sc	9Cp	18Cp	11Pi	20Ar	11Ge	17Cn	2Vi	17Li	20Sc	7Cp	14Aq
13	17Sg	9Aq	17Aq	11Ar	19Ta	8Cn	12Le	26Vi	10Sc	14Sg	3Aq	11Pi
15	16Cp	9Pi	17Pi	10Ta	17Ge	3Le	6Vi	20Li	5Sg	10Cp	1Pi	10Ar
17	16Aq	9Ar	17Ar	8Ge	13Cn	28Le	29Vi	14Sc	0Cp	7Aq	29Pi	8Ta
19	15Pi	8Ta	16Ta	5Cn	8Le	21Vi	23Li	9Sg	27Cp	5Pi	29Ar	7Ge
21	14Ar	5Ge	14Ge	0Le	2Vi	15Li	18Sc	5Cp	26Aq	5Ar	28Ta	5Cn
23	12Ta	0Cn	9Cn	24Le	25Vi	10Sc	14Sg	3Aq	27Pi	5Ta	27Ge	1Le
25	8Ge	24Cn	3Le	17Vi	19Li	6Sg	11Cp	3Pi	27Ar	5Ge	24Cn	27Le
27	3Cn	18Le	27Le	11Li	14Sc	3Cp	10Aq	3E	27Ta	3Cn	19Le	21Vi
29	27Cn		21Vi	6Sc	10Sg	1Aq	9Pi	3Ta	24Ge	29Cn	13Vi	15Li
31	21Le		15Li		7Cp		9Ar	1Ge		23Le		9Sc

1954

	Jan	Feb	Mar	Apr	May	Jun	Jul	Aug	Sep	Oct	Nov	Dec
1	21Sc	7Cp	15Cp	5Pi	13Ar	7Ge	14Cn	3Vi	18Li	20Sc	5Cp	9Aq
3	16Sg	4Aq	12Aq	5Ar	14Ta	6Cn	12Le	28Vi	12Sc	14Sg	29Cp	5Pi
5	12Cp	3Pi	12Pi	5Ta	14Ge	4Le	7Vi	22Li	6Sg	8Cp	25Aq	2Ar
7	10Aq	2Ar	12Ar	5Ge	12Cn	29Le	2Li	16Sc	0Cp	3Aq	23Pi	1Ta
9	8Pi	1Ta	11Ta	3Cn	8Le	24Vi	26Li	10Sg	25Cp	1Pi	23Ar	1Ge
11	6Ar	0Ge	10Ge	29Cn	3Vi	18Li	20Sc	5Cp	22Aq	0Ar	23Ta	1Cn
13	5Ta	27Ge	7Cn	24Le	27Vi	12Sc	14Sg	1Aq	21Pi	0Ta	23Ge	0Le
15	3Ge	23Cn	3Le	19Vi	21Li	6Sg	9Cp	28Aq	21Ar	0Ge	22Cn	27Le
17	0Cn	18Le	27Le	12Li	15Sc	1Cp	5Aq	27Pi	21Ta	29Ge	19Le	23Vi
19	27Cn	13Vi	22Vi	6Sc	9Sg	26Cp	3Pi	26Ar	19Ge	26Cn	14Vi	17Li
21	22Le	7Li	15Li	0Sg	4Cp	22Aq	1Ar	24Ta	16Cn	22Le	9Li	11Sc
23	17Vi	1Sc	9Sc	24Sg	29Cp	20Pi	29Ar	22Ge	12Le	17Vi	2Sc	5Sg
25	11Li	24Sc	3Sg	19Cp	25Aq	18Ar	27Ta	19Cn	8Vi	11Li	26Sc	29Sg
27	4Sc	19Sg	27Sg	16Aq	23Pi	17Ta	26Ge	16Le	2Li	5Sc	20Sg	23Cp
29	29Sc		23Cp	14Pi	22Ar	16Ge	23Cn	11Vi	27Li	29Sc	14Cp	19Aq
31	24Sg		20Aq		22Ta		20Le	6Li		23Sg		15Pi

1955

	Jan	Feb	Mar	Apr	May	Jun	Jul	Aug	Sep	Oct	Nov	Dec
1	28Pi	21Ta	2Ge	25Cn	2Vi	19Li	22Sc	6Cp	21Aq	26Pi	18Ta	26Ge
3	26Ar	20Ge	0Cn	22Le	27Vi	13Sc	15Sg	0Aq	17Pi	24Ar	17Ge	26Cn
5	25Ta	18Cn	28Cn	18Vi	22Li	7Sg	9Cp	25Aq	15Ar	23Ta	16Cn	24Le
7	25Ge	16Le	25Le	13Li	16Sc	0Cp	3Aq	21Pi	13Ta	22Ge	14Le	21Vi
9	24Cn	13Vi	21Vi	7Sc	10Sg	24Cp	28Aq	18Ar	11Ge	20Cn	11Vi	17Li
11	22Le	9Li	17Li	1Sg	3Cp	19Aq	24Pi	16Ta	9Cn	17Le	7Li	12Sc
13	18Vi	3Sc	11Sc	25Sg	27Cp	14Pi	21Ar	14Ge	7Le	15Vi	2Sc	6Sg
15	13Li	27Sc	5Sg	19Cp	22Aq	11Ar	19Ta	13Cn	5Vi	11Li	27Sc	29Sg
17	7Sc	21Sg	28Sg	13Aq	18Pi	10Ta	19Ge	12Le	2Li	6Sc	21Sg	23Cp
19	1Sg	15Cp	23Cp	10Pi	17Ar	10Ge	18Cn	10Vi	28Li	0Sg	14Cp	17Aq
21	25Sg	11Aq	18Aq	8Ar	16Ta	10Cn	18Le	7Li	22Sc	24Sg	8Aq	11Pi
23	20Cp	7Pi	16Pi	8Ta	17Ge	9Le	16Vi	2Sc	16Sg	18Cp	3Pi	7Ar
25	15Aq	5Ar	15Ar	8Ge	16Cn	7Vi	12Li	27Sc	10Cp	12Aq	29Pi	4Ta
27	12Pi	4Ta	14Ta	7Cn	15Le	3Li	6Sc	20Sg	4Aq	7Pi	26Ar	3Ge
29	9Ar		13Ge	5Le	11Vi	28Li	0Sg	14Cp	29Aq	4Ar	26Ta	4Cn
31	7Ta		11Cn		7Li		24Sg	9Aq		3Ta		4Le

1956

	Jan	Feb	Mar	Apr	May	Jun	Jul	Aug	Sep	Oct	Nov	Dec
1	19Le	9Li	0Sc	15Sg	17Cp	1Pi	4Ar	23Ta	15Cn	24Le	17Li	23Sc
3	17Vi	5Sc	25Sc	9Cp	11Aq	26Pi	0Ta	21Ge	15Le	23Vi	14Sc	18Sg
5	14Li	29Sc	19Sg	3Aq	5Pi	22Ar	28Ta	21Cn	15Vi	22Li	10Sg	12Cp
7	9Sc	23Sg	13Cp	27Aq	1Ar	20Ta	27Ge	21Le	14Li	19Sc	4Cp	6Aq
9	3Sg	17Cp	7Aq	23Pi	28Ar	19Ge	28Cn	21Vi	11Sc	14Sg	28Cp	0Pi
11	26Sg	11Aq	1Pi	19Ar	26Ta	19Cn	28Le	19Li	6Sg	9Cp	22Aq	24Pi
13	20Cp	5Pi	27Pi	17Ta	25Ge	19Le	27Vi	15Sc	1Cp	2Aq	16Pi	19Ar
15	14Aq	1Ar	24Ar	15Ge	24Cn	17Vi	24Li	10Sg	24Cp	26Aq	11Ar	16Ta
17	8Pi	27Ar	21Ta	14Cn	23Le	14Li	19Sc	4Cp	18Aq	21Pi	8Ta	14Ge
19	4Ar	24Ta	19Ge	12Le	20Vi	9Sc	13Sg	28Cp	12Pi	16Ar	6Ge	13Cn
21	0Ta	22Ge	17Cn	10Vi	17Li	4Sg	7Cp	22Aq	8Ar	13Ta	4Cn	13Le
23	28Ta	21Cn	15Le	7Li	13Sc	28Sg	1Aq	16Pi	3Ta	10Ge	3Le	12Vi
25	27Ge	20Le	14Vi	3Sc	7Sg	22Cp	25Aq	11Ar	0Ge	8Cn	2Vi	10Li
27	27Cn	19Vi	12Li	29Sc	1Cp	16Aq	19Pi	6Ta	27Ge	6Le	29Vi	6Sc
29	27Le	17Li	8Sc	23Sg	25Cp	10Pi	14Ar	3Ge	25Cn	5Vi	26Li	2Sg
31	26Vi		3Sg		19Aq		10Ta	1Cn		3Li		27Sg

1957

	Jan	Feb	Mar	Apr	May	Jun	Jul	Aug	Sep	Oct	Nov	Dec
1	9Cp	23Aq	2Pi	17Ar	22Ta	12Cn	21Le	15Li	5Sg	10Cp	25Aq	27Pi
3	3Aq	17Pi	26Pi	13Ta	19Ge	11Le	20Vi	13Sc	1Cp	5Aq	19Pi	20Ar
5	27Aq	11Ar	21Ar	9Ge	16Cn	10Vi	19Li	9Sg	26Cp	28Aq	12Ar	15Ta
7	20Pi	6Ta	16Ta	5Cn	14Le	8Li	16Sc	4Cp	20Aq	22Pi	7Ta	11Ge
9	15Ar	2Ge	12Ge	3Le	13Vi	5Sc	12Sg	28Cp	13Pi	16Ar	2Ge	8Cn
11	10Ta	0Cn	9Cn	2Vi	11Li	2Sg	7Cp	23Aq	7Ar	10Ta	28Ge	6Le
13	7Ge	29Cn	8Le	2Li	9Sc	28Sg	2Aq	16Pi	1Ta	5Ge	25Cn	4Vi
15	6Cn	0Vi	8Vi	1Sc	7Sg	23Cp	26Aq	10Ar	26Ta	1Cn	23Le	2Li
17	7Le	0Li	8Li	29Sc	3Cp	17Aq	20Pi	4Ta	21Ge	28Cn	21Vi	0Sc
19	7Vi	29Li	7Sc	25Sg	27Cp	11Pi	13Ar	29Ta	19Cn	27Le	20Li	28Sc
21	6Li	26Sc	4Sg	20Cp	21Aq	5Ar	8Ta	26Ge	18Le	26Vi	19Sc	25Sg
23	3Sc	21Sg	29Sg	13Aq	15Pi	0Ta	4Ge	24Cn	18Vi	26Li	17Sg	21Cp
25	29Sc	15Cp	23Cp	7Pi	9Ar	26Ta	1Cn	24Le	18Li	25Sc	13Cp	16Aq
27	24Sg	9Aq	17Aq	1Ar	4Ta	23Ge	1Le	25Vi	17Sc	23Sg	9Aq	11Pi
29	18Cp		11Pi	26Ar	1Ge	22Cn	1Vi	24Li	14Sg	18Cp	3Pi	4Ar
31	12Aq		5Ar		28Ge		1Li	22Sc		13Aq		28Ar

1958

	Jan	Feb	Mar	Apr	May	Jun	Jul	Aug	Sep	Oct	Nov	Dec
1	10Ta	27Ge	5Cn	26Le	4Li	28Sc	5Cp	23Aq	8Ar	10Ta	25Ge	0Le
3	6Ge	25Cn	3Le	26Vi	4Sc	26Sg	2Aq	18Pi	2Ta	4Ge	20Cn	27Le
5	3Cn	24Le	2Vi	26Li	4Sg	24Cp	27Aq	12Ar	25Ta	28Ge	17Le	24Vi
7	1Le	24Vi	3Li	26Sc	2Cp	19Aq	22Pi	5Ta	20Ge	24Cn	14Vi	23Li
9	0Vi	24Li	3Sc	24Sg	29Cp	14Pi	16Ar	29Ta	16Cn	21Le	14Li	22Sc
11	29Vi	21Sc	1Sg	20Cp	24Aq	8Ar	9Ta	24Ge	13Le	20Vi	14Sc	22Sg
13	27Li	18Sg	28Sg	15Aq	18Pi	1Ta	4Ge	21Cn	12Vi	21Li	14Sg	20Cp
15	25Sc	14Cp	24Cp	9Pi	11Ar	26Ta	29Ge	19Le	12Li	21Sc	13Cp	18Aq
17	21Sg	9Aq	18Aq	3Ar	5Ta	21Ge	26Cn	18Vi	12Sc	20Sg	9Aq	13Pi
19	17Cp	3Pi	12Pi	26Ar	29Ta	17Cn	24Le	18Li	11Sg	17Cp	5Pi	7Ar
21	12Aq	27Pi	6Ar	20Ta	24Ge	14Le	23Vi	16Sc	8Cp	13Aq	29Pi	1Ta
23	7Pi	21Ar	29Ar	15Ge	20Cn	12Vi	21Li	14Sg	4Aq	8Pi	22Ar	24Ta
25	0Ar	14Ta	23Ta	10Cn	17Le	10Li	19Sc	11Cp	29Aq	2Ar	16Ta	19Ge
27	24Ar	9Ge	18Ge	7Le	15Vi	9Sc	17Sg	7Aq	23Pi	26Ar	10Ge	14Cn
29	18Ta		14Cn	5Vi	14Li	7Sg	14Cp	2Pi	17Ar	19Ta	5Cn	10Le
31	14Ge		11Le		13Sc		10Aq	26Pi		13Ge		7Vi

1959

	Jan	Feb	Mar	Apr	May	Jun	Jul	Aug	Sep	Oct	Nov	Dec
1	21Vi	14Sc	24Sc	17Cp	23Aq	9Ar	12Ta	26Ge	12Le	17Vi	8Sc	17Sg
3	18Li	12Sg	23Sg	13Aq	18Pi	3Ta	5Ge	20Cn	8Vi	15Li	8Sg	17Cp
5	17Sc	10Cp	20Cp	9Pi	12Ar	27Ta	29Ge	16Le	6Li	14Sc	8Cp	16Aq
7	16Sg	7Aq	16Aq	3Ar	6Ta	21Ge	24Cn	13Vi	4Sc	14Sg	6Aq	13Pi
9	14Cp	3Pi	12Pi	27Ar	0Ge	15Cn	20Le	10Li	3Sg	12Cp	3Pi	8Ar
11	12Aq	29Pi	7Ar	21Ta	24Ge	10Le	16Vi	8Sc	1Cp	10Aq	28Pi	2Ta
13	8Pi	23Ar	1Ta	15Ge	18Cn	6Vi	13Li	6Sg	29Cp	6Pi	23Ar	26Ta
15	3Ar	16Ta	24Ta	9Cn	13Le	3Li	11Sc	5Cp	26Aq	1Ar	17Ta	20Ge
17	27Ar	10Ge	18Ge	4Le	9Vi	1Sc	10Sg	3Aq	22Pi	26Ar	11Ge	13Cn
19	20Ta	5Cn	13Cn	0Vi	7Li	1Sg	9Cp	1Pi	18Ar	20Ta	4Cn	8Le
21	15Ge	1Le	9Le	29Vi	7Sc	1Cp	8Aq	27Pi	12Ta	14Ge	28Cn	2Vi
23	10Cn	28Le	6Vi	29Li	7Sg	0Aq	6Pi	22Ar	6Ge	8Cn	23Le	28Vi
25	6Le	27Vi	5Li	29Sc	7Cp	28Aq	2Ar	16Ta	0Cn	2Le	19Vi	25Li
27	3Vi	26Li	5Sc	29Sg	6Aq	24Pi	26Ar	10Ge	24Cn	27Le	17Li	24Sc
29	1Li		5Sg	27Cp	2Pi	18Ar	20Ta	4Cn	20Le	24Vi	16Sc	25Sg
31	29Li		3Cp		27Pi		14Ge	29Cn		23Li		25Cp

1960

	Jan	Feb	Mar	Apr	May	Jun	Jul	Aug	Sep	Oct	Nov	Dec
1	10Aq	29Pi	20Ar	5Ge	7Cn	21Le	25Vi	14Sc	7Cp	16Aq	8Ar	13Ta
3	8Pi	25Ar	15Ta	29Ge	1Le	16Vi	21Li	13Sg	6Aq	15Pi	4Ta	8Ge
5	4Ar	19Ta	9Ge	22Cn	25Le	12Li	19Sc	12Cp	6Pi	12Ar	0Ge	3Cn
7	29Ar	13Ge	3Cn	17Le	20Vi	10Sc	18Sg	12Aq	4Ar	9Ta	24Ge	26Cn
9	23Ta	7Cn	27Cn	12Vi	18Li	10Sg	19Cp	12Pi	1Ta	4Ge	18Cn	20Le
11	16Ge	1Le	22Le	9Li	17Sc	10Cp	19Aq	10Ar	26Ta	28Ge	12Le	14Vi
13	10Cn	26Le	18Vi	8Sc	16Sg	10Aq	18Pi	6Ta	20Ge	22Cn	6Vi	9Li
15	5Le	22Vi	15Li	7Sg	16Cp	9Pi	14Ar	0Ge	14Cn	16Le	1Li	6Sc
17	29Le	19Li	13Sc	6Cp	15Aq	5Ar	9Ta	24Ge	8Le	11Vi	28Li	4Sg
19	25Vi	16Sc	11Sg	4Aq	12Pi	0Ta	4Ge	18Cn	3Vi	6Li	26Sc	4Cp
21	22Li	14Sg	9Cp	2Pi	8Ar	25Ta	27Ge	12Le	28Vi	3Sc	26Sg	5Aq
23	19Sc	13Cp	8Aq	28Pi	3Ta	19Ge	21Cn	6Vi	24Li	2Sg	25Cp	4Pi
25	18Sg	12Aq	5Pi	24Ar	28Ta	12Cn	15Le	2Li	22Sc	0Cp	24Aq	1Ar
27	18Cp	10Pi	2Ar	19Ta	22Ge	6Le	9Vi	28Li	20Sg	29Cp	21Pi	28Ar
29	18Aq	7Ar	28Ar	13Ge	15Cn	0Vi	5Li	25Sc	18Cp	27Aq	18Ar	23Ta
31	16Pi		23Ta		9Le		1Sc	23Sg		24Pi		17Ge

1961

	Jan	Feb	Mar	Apr	May	Jun	Jul	Aug	Sep	Oct	Nov	Dec
1	29Ge	14Le	22Le	8Li	13Sc	4Cp	13Aq	6Ar	26Ta	0Cn	15Le	16Vi
3	23Cn	8Vi	17Vi	4Sc	10Sg	3Aq	12Pi	4Ta	22Ge	25Cn	8Vi	10Li
5	17Le	2Li	11Li	0Sg	9Cp	2Pi	10Ar	0Ge	16Cn	18Le	2Li	5Sc
7	11Vi	27Li	7Sc	28Sg	7Aq	0Ar	7Ta	25Ge	10Le	12Vi	27Li	2Sg
9	5Li	23Sc	3Sg	26Cp	5Pi	27Ar	3Ge	19Cn	3Vi	6Li	23Sc	29Sg
11	1Sc	21Sg	1Cp	24Aq	3Ar	23Ta	28Ge	13Le	27Vi	1Sc	20Sg	28Cp
13	28Sc	21Cp	0Aq	23Pi	0Ta	19Ge	22Cn	6Vi	22Li	27Sc	17Cp	26Aq
15	27Sg	21Aq	29Aq	21Ar	27Ta	13Cn	16Le	0Li	17Sc	23Sg	15Aq	24Pi
17	28Cp	21Pi	29Pi	19Ta	23Ge	7Le	9Vi	24Li	13Sg	20Cp	13Pi	22Ar
19	28Aq	19Ar	27Ar	15Ge	17Cn	1Vi	3Li	20Sc	10Cp	19Aq	12Ar	20Ta
21	27Pi	16Ta	24Ta	9Cn	11Le	25Vi	28Li	17Sg	9Aq	18Pi	10Ta	16Ge
23	24Ar	11Ge	19Ge	3Le	5Vi	19Li	24Sc	15Cp	8Pi	17Ar	7Ge	12Cn
25	20Ta	5Cn	13Cn	27Le	29Vi	16Sc	22Sg	15Aq	8Ar	15Ta	4Cn	6Le
27	14Ge	29Cn	7Le	21Vi	24Li	14Sg	22Cp	15Pi	7Ta	13Ge	28Cn	0Vi
29	8Cn		1Vi	16Li	21Sc	13Cp	22Aq	15Ar	5Ge	8Cn	22Le	24Vi
31	2Le		25Vi		20Sg		22Pi	13Ta		3Le		18Li

1962

	Jan	Feb	Mar	Apr	May	Jun	Jul	Aug	Sep	Oct	Nov	Dec
1	0Sc	17Sg	26Sg	17Aq	26Pi	19Ta	26Ge	13Le	28Vi	1Sc	16Sg	22Cp
3	26Sc	15Cp	24Cp	16Pi	25Ar	17Ge	22Cn	8Vi	22Li	25Sc	12Cp	18Aq
5	23Sg	15Aq	23Aq	17Ar	25Ta	14Cn	17Le	1Li	16Sc	19Sg	8Aq	16Pi
7	22Cp	15Pi	23Pi	16Ta	23Ge	9Le	11Vi	25Li	10Sg	15Cp	5Pi	14Ar
9	22Aq	15Ar	24Ar	14Ge	19Cn	3Vi	5Li	19Sc	6Cp	12Aq	5Ar	14Ta
11	21Pi	13Ta	22Ta	11Cn	13Le	27Vi	29Li	14Sg	3Aq	11Pi	5Ta	13Ge
13	19Ar	10Ge	19Ge	5Le	7Vi	21Li	24Sc	11Cp	3Pi	11Ar	5Ge	11Cn
15	16Ta	5Cn	14Cn	29Le	1Li	16Sc	20Sg	10Aq	3Ar	12Ta	3Cn	7Le
17	13Ge	29Cn	9Le	23Vi	25Li	11Sg	17Cp	9Pi	3Ta	11Ge	0Le	3Vi
19	8Cn	23Le	2Vi	17Li	20Sc	8Cp	16Aq	9Ar	2Ge	8Cn	25Le	27Vi
21	3Le	17Vi	26Vi	11Sc	16Sg	6Aq	15Pi	8Ta	29Ge	4Le	19Vi	20Li
23	27Le	11Li	20Li	6Sg	12Cp	4Pi	14Ar	6Ge	25Cn	28Le	12Li	14Sc
25	20Vi	5Sc	14Sc	2Cp	10Aq	3Ar	12Ta	2Cn	19Le	22Vi	6Sc	9Sg
27	14Li	0Sg	9Sg	29Cp	7Pi	1Ta	9Ge	28Cn	13Vi	16Li	1Sg	5Cp
29	8Sc		5Cp	27Aq	6Ar	29Ta	5Cn	22Le	7Li	10Sc	26Sg	1Aq
31	4Sg		3Aq		5Ta		1Le	16Vi		4Sg		29Aq

1963

	Jan	Feb	Mar	Apr	May	Jun	Jul	Aug	Sep	Oct	Nov	Dec
1	13Pi	6Ta	17Ta	8Cn	14Le	29Vi	2Sc	16Sg	1Aq	7Pi	29Ar	8Ge
3	11Ar	4Ge	15Ge	4Le	9Vi	23Li	25Sc	10Cp	29Aq	6Ar	0Ge	8Cn
5	9Ta	1Cn	12Cn	29Le	3Li	17Sc	20Sg	6Aq	27Pi	6Ta	29Ge	6Le
7	8Ge	28Cn	7Le	24Vi	26Li	11Sg	15Cp	4Pi	26Ar	6Ge	28Cn	3Vi
9	5Cn	23Le	2Vi	18Li	20Sc	6Cp	11Aq	2Ar	25Ta	4Cn	24Le	28Vi
11	2Le	18Vi	27Vi	11Sc	14Sg	1Aq	7Pi	0Ta	24Ge	1Le	19Vi	23Li
13	28Le	12Li	21Li	5Sg	9Cp	27Aq	5Ar	29Ta	21Cn	27Le	14Li	16Sc
15	22Vi	6Sc	14Sc	29Sg	4Aq	24Pi	4Ta	27Ge	17Le	22Vi	7Sc	10Sg
17	16Li	0Sg	8Sg	24Cp	0Pi	23Ar	2Ge	24Cn	13Vi	17Li	1Sg	4Cp
19	10Sc	25Sg	3Cp	21Aq	28Pi	22Ta	1Cn	21Le	8Li	11Sc	25Sg	28Cp
21	4Sg	21Cp	29Cp	19Pi	28Ar	22Ge	29Cn	17Vi	2Sc	4Sg	19Cp	23Aq
23	0Cp	19Aq	26Aq	19Ar	28Ta	20Cn	26Le	12Li	26Sc	28Sg	14Aq	20Pi
25	27Cp	18Pi	26Pi	20Ta	28Ge	18Le	21Vi	6Sc	19Sg	22Cp	10Pi	17Ar
27	24Aq	17Ar	26Ar	20Ge	26Cn	13Vi	16Li	29Sc	14Cp	18Aq	8Ar	16Ta
29	23Pi		26Ta	18Cn	22Le	8Li	10Sc	23Sg	9Aq	15Pi	7Ta	16Ge
31	22Ar		25Ge		17Vi		3Sg	18Cp		14Ar		15Cn

1964

	Jan	Feb	Mar	Apr	May	Jun	Jul	Aug	Sep	Oct	Nov	Dec
1	0Le	19Vi	10Li	25Sc	27Sg	11Aq	16Pi	6Ta	29Ge	8Le	29Vi	4Sc
3	28Le	15Li	5Sc	18Sg	20Cp	6Pi	12Ar	5Ge	28Cn	6Vi	25Li	29Sc
5	24Vi	9Sc	29Sc	12Cp	15Aq	3Ar	10Ta	4Cn	26Le	3Li	20Sc	23Sg
7	19Li	3Sg	22Sg	7Aq	11Pi	1Ta	10Ge	3Le	24Vi	29Li	14Sg	16Cp
9	13Sc	26Sg	16Cp	2Pi	8Ar	1Ge	10Cn	2Vi	21Li	24Sc	8Cp	10Aq
11	7Sg	21Cp	11Aq	0Ar	7Ta	1Cn	9Le	0Li	16Sc	18Sg	1Aq	4Pi
13	0Cp	16Aq	8Pi	29Ar	8Ge	1Le	8Vi	26Li	10Sg	12Cp	26Aq	29Pi
15	25Cp	13Pi	6Ar	29Ta	8Cn	29Le	5Li	20Sc	4Cp	5Aq	21Pi	26Ar
17	20Aq	10Ar	5Ta	28Ge	6Le	26Vi	0Sc	14Sg	28Cp	0Pi	18Ar	25Ta
19	17Pi	8Ta	3Ge	26Cn	3Vi	21Li	24Sc	8Cp	22Aq	27Pi	17Ta	25Ge
21	14Ar	7Ge	2Cn	23Le	29Vi	15Sc	17Sg	2Aq	18Pi	25Ar	17Ge	25Cn
23	12Ta	5Cn	29Cn	19Vi	24Li	9Sg	11Cp	27Aq	16Ar	23Ta	17Cn	25Le
25	10Ge	3Le	26Le	15Li	18Sc	2Cp	5Aq	23Pi	14Ta	23Ge	16Le	23Vi
27	9Cn	0Vi	23Vi	9Sc	12Sg	26Cp	0Pi	20Ar	12Ge	21Cn	13Vi	19Li
29	8Le	27Vi	18Li	3Sg	5Cp	21Aq	26Pi	17Ta	10Cn	19Le	9Li	14Sc
31	6Vi		13Sc		29Cp		23Ar	15Ge		16Vi		8Sg

1965

	Jan	Feb	Mar	Apr	May	Jun	Jul	Aug	Sep	Oct	Nov	Dec
1	20Sg	4Aq	12Aq	28Pi	3Ta	25Ge	4Le	27Vi	17Sc	20Sg	4Aq	6Pi
3	13Cp	28Aq	7Pi	25Ar	2Ge	25Cn	4Vi	25Li	12Sg	14Cp	28Aq	0Ar
5	7Aq	23Pi	2Ar	22Ta	0Cn	24Le	2Li	21Sc	6Cp	8Aq	22Pi	25Ar
7	1Pi	18Ar	29Ar	20Ge	29Cn	22Vi	29Li	15Sg	0Aq	2Pi	17Ar	22Ta
9	26Pi	15Ta	25Ta	18Cn	27Le	19Li	24Sc	9Cp	24Aq	26Pi	14Ta	20Ge
11	22Ar	13Ge	23Ge	16Le	25Vi	14Sc	18Sg	3Aq	18Pi	22Ar	11Ge	19Cn
13	19Ta	12Cn	21Cn	15Vi	22Li	9Sg	12Cp	27Aq	13Ar	18Ta	9Cn	18Le
15	18Ge	11Le	20Le	12Li	18Sc	3Cp	6Aq	21Pi	8Ta	15Ge	7Le	17Vi
17	18Cn	11Vi	19Vi	9Sc	13Sg	27Cp	0Pi	16Ar	4Ge	13Cn	6Vi	15Li
19	18Le	10Li	17Li	4Sg	7Cp	21Aq	24Pi	11Ta	2Cn	11Le	4Li	11Sc
21	18Vi	6Sc	14Sc	29Sg	1Aq	15Pi	19Ar	8Ge	0Le	10Vi	1Sc	7Sg
23	15Li	1Sg	9Sg	23Cp	24Aq	10Ar	15Ta	6Cn	0Vi	8Li	28Sc	2Cp
25	10Sc	25Sg	3Cp	16Aq	19Pi	6Ta	13Ge	6Le	29Vi	6Sc	23Sg	26Cp
27	5Sg	19Cp	27Cp	11Pi	14Ar	4Ge	12Cn	6Vi	28Li	3Sg	18Cp	20Aq
29	28Sg		21Aq	6Ar	12Ta	4Cn	12Le	6Li	25Sc	28Sg	12Aq	14Pi
31	22Cp		15Pi		10Ge		13Vi	4Sc		22Cp		8Ar

1966

	Jan	Feb	Mar	Apr	May	Jun	Jul	Aug	Sep	Oct	Nov	Dec
1	20Ar	8Ge	17Ge	8Le	18Vi	10Sc	17Sg	4Aq	18Pi	21Ar	7Ge	13Cn
3	16Ta	6Cn	14Cn	8Vi	17Li	8Sg	12Cp	28Aq	12Ar	15Ta	3Cn	10Le
5	13Ge	6Le	14Le	8Li	15Sc	4Cp	7Aq	21Pi	6Ta	10Ge	0Le	8Vi
7	13Cn	6Vi	14Vi	7Sc	13Sg	29Cp	1Pi	15Ar	1Ge	6Cn	28Le	7Li
9	13Le	6Li	15Li	5Sg	8Cp	23Aq	25Pi	9Ta	26Ge	3Le	27Vi	5Sc
11	13Vi	5Sc	13Sc	1Cp	3Aq	17Pi	19Ar	5Ge	24Cn	2Vi	26Li	3Sg
13	11Li	1Sg	10Sg	25Cp	27Aq	11Ar	13Ta	1Cn	24Le	2Li	25Sc	1Cp
15	8Sc	26Sg	5Cp	19Aq	21Pi	6Ta	10Ge	0Le	24Vi	2Sc	23Sg	27Cp
17	4Sg	20Cp	29Cp	13Pi	15Ar	1Ge	7Cn	0Vi	24Li	1Sg	19Cp	22Aq
19	29Sg	14Aq	22Aq	7Ar	10Ta	29Ge	7Le	1Li	23Sc	28Sg	14Aq	16Pi
21	23Cp	7Pi	16Pi	2Ta	6Ge	27Cn	6Vi	0Sc	20Sg	24Cp	9Pi	10Ar
23	17Aq	1Ar	10Ar	27Ta	4Cn	26Le	6Li	27Sc	15Cp	18Aq	2Ar	4Ta
25	10Pi	25Ar	5Ta	23Ge	1Le	25Vi	4Sc	23Sg	10Aq	12Pi	26Ar	29Ta
27	4Ar	20Ta	0Ge	21Cn	0Vi	23Li	1Sg	18Cp	4Pi	6Ar	21Ta	25Ge
29	29Ar		26Ge	19Le	28Vi	20Sc	26Sg	13Aq	27Pi	0Ta	16Ge	23Cn
31	24Ta		24Cn		26Li		21Cp	7Pi		25Ta		21Le

1967

	Jan	Feb	Mar	Apr	May	Jun	Jul	Aug	Sep	Oct	Nov	Dec
1	5Vi	28Li	8Sc	29Sg	4Aq	20Pi	21Ar	5Ge	22Cn	27Le	20Li	28Sc
3	4Li	26Sc	6Sg	25Cp	29Aq	13Ar	15Ta	0Cn	19Le	27Vi	20Sc	28Sg
5	2Sc	23Sg	3Cp	20ASq	23Pi	7Ta	9Ge	27Cn	18Vi	27Li	20Sg	27Cp
7	29Sc	19Cp	28Cp	14Pi	17Ar	1Ge	5Cn	25Le	18Li	27Sc	18Cp	23Aq
9	26Sg	14Aq	23Aq	8Ar	10Ta	26Ge	2Le	24Vi	17Sc	25Sg	15Aq	19Pi
11	23Cp	8Pi	17Pi	2Ta	5Ge	22Cn	29Le	23Li	15Sg	23Cp	10Pi	13Ar
13	18Aq	2Ar	11Ar	25Ta	29Ge	19Le	28Vi	21Sc	13Cp	18Aq	4Ar	6Ta
15	12Pi	26Ar	4Ta	20Ge	25Cn	17Vi	26Li	19Sg	9Aq	13Pi	28Ar	0Ge
17	6Ar	20Ta	28Ta	15Cn	22Le	15Li	24Sc	16Cp	4Pi	7Ar	21Ta	24Ge
19	0Ta	14Ge	23Ge	12Le	20Vi	14Sc	22Sg	12Sq	28Pi	1Ta	15Ge	19Cn
21	24Ta	11Cn	19Cn	11Vi	19Li	12Sg	19Cp	7Pi	22Ar	24Ta	10Cn	15Le
23	20Ge	9Le	17Le	10Li	19Sc	11Cp	16Aq	2Ar	16Ta	18Ge	5Le	12Vi
25	17Cn	9Vi	17Vi	11Sc	18Sg	8Aq	11Pi	25Ar	9Ge	13Cn	1Vi	9Li
27	16Le	9Li	17Li	10Sg	16Cp	3Pi	5Ar	19Ta	4Cn	8Le	29Vi	8Sc
29	15Vi		17Sc	8Cp	13Aq	28Pi	29Ar	13Ge	0Le	6Vi	28Li	7Sg
31	14Li		16Sg		8Pi		23Ta	8Cn		5Li		6Cp

1968

	Jan	Feb	Mar	Apr	May	Jun	Jul	Aug	Sep	Oct	Nov	Dec
1	20Cp	9Pi	0Ar	14Ta	17Ge	2Le	7Vi	28Li	22Sg	1Aq	21Pi	25Ar
3	18Aq	4Ar	24Ar	8Ge	11Cn	27Le	4Li	26Sc	20Cp	28Aq	16Ar	19Ta
5	14Pi	28Ar	18Ta	2Cn	5Le	24Vi	2Sc	25Sg	18Aq	24Pi	10Ta	13Ge
7	9Ar	22Ta	12Ge	27Cn	1Vi	22Li	1Sg	24Cp	15Pi	19Ar	4Ge	7Cn
9	2Ta	16Ge	6Cn	23Le	29Vi	21Sc	1Cp	23Aq	11Ar	14Ta	28Ge	0Le
11	26Ta	11Cn	1Le	20Vi	28Li	22Sg	0Aq	20Pi	6Ta	8Ge	22Cn	25Le
13	20Ge	7Le	28Le	20Li	28Sc	22Cp	28Aq	15Ar	0Ge	1Cn	16Le	20Vi
15	15Cn	4Vi	27Vi	20Sc	29Sg	20Aq	25Pi	10Ta	23Ge	25Cn	11Vi	17Li
17	12Le	2Li	26Li	20Sg	28Cp	17Pi	20Ar	4Ge	17Cn	20Le	9Li	16Sc
19	8Vi	1Sc	25Sc	18Cp	25Aq	11Ar	14Ta	27Ge	12Le	17Vi	7Sc	16Sg
21	6Li	29Sc	24Sg	15Aq	20Pi	5Ta	7Ge	22Cn	9Vi	15Li	8Sg	16Cp
23	4Sc	27Sg	22Cp	11Pi	14Ar	29Ta	1Cn	17Le	7Li	14Sc	8Cp	16Aq
25	2Sg	25Cp	18Aq	5Ar	8Ta	23Ge	26Cn	14Vi	5Sc	14Sg	7Aq	14Pi
27	1Cp	21Aq	14Pi	29Ar	2Ge	17Cn	21Le	11Li	4Sg	13Cp	5Pi	10Ar
29	29Cp	17Pi	8Ar	23Ta	26Ge	12Le	18Vi	9Sc	3Cp	11Aq	0Ar	4Ta
31	26Aq		3Ta		20Cn		14Li	7Sg		8Pi		28Ta

1969

	Jan	Feb	Mar	Apr	May	Jun	Jul	Aug	Sep	Oct	Nov	Dec
1	10Ge	24Cn	2Le	18Vi	24Li	16Sg	25Cp	18Pi	7Ta	10Ge	24Cn	25Le
3	4Cn	19Le	27Le	15Li	23Sc	16Cp	25Aq	15Ar	2Ge	4Cn	18Le	20Vi
5	28Cn	14Vi	23Vi	13Sc	22Sg	16Aq	23Pi	11Ta	26Ge	28Cn	12Vi	15Li
7	22Le	10Li	20Li	12Sg	21Cp	14Pi	20Ar	5Ge	20Cn	22Le	7Li	12Sc
9	17Vi	7Sc	17Sc	11Cp	20Aq	10Ar	15Ta	0Cn	14Le	16Vi	4Sc	11Sg
11	13Li	5Sg	15Sg	9Aq	17Pi	5Ta	9Ge	23Cn	8Vi	12Li	2Sg	11Cp
13	10Sc	3Cp	14Cp	6Pi	13Ar	0Ge	3Cn	17Le	3Li	9Sc	1Cp	10Aq
15	9Sg	3Aq	12Aq	3Ar	8Ta	24Ge	26Cn	11Vi	29Li	7Sg	0Aq	9Pi
17	9Cp	2Pi	10Pi	29Ar	3Ge	17Cn	20Le	6Li	26Sc	5Cp	28Aq	6Ar
19	9Aq	0Ar	8Ar	24Ta	27Ge	11Le	14Vi	2Sc	24Sg	3Aq	26Pi	2Ta
21	8Pi	26Ar	4Ta	18Ge	21Cn	5Vi	9Li	29Sc	23Cp	2Pi	22Ar	28Ta
23	5Ar	21Ta	28Ta	12Cn	14Le	0Li	6Sc	28Sg	21Aq	29Pi	18Ta	22Ge
25	0Ta	15Ge	22Ge	6Le	9Vi	26Li	4Sg	27Cp	20Pi	26Ar	14Ge	16Cn
27	25Ta	8Cn	16Cn	1Vi	4Li	25Sc	3Cp	27Aq	18Ar	23Ta	8Cn	10Le
29	18Ge		10Le	26Vi	2Sc	25Sg	4Aq	26Pi	15Ta	18Ge	2Le	4Vi
31	12Cn		5Vi		1Sg		3Pi	24Ar	27Ta	12Cn		28Vi

1970

	Jan	Feb	Mar	Apr	May	Jun	Jul	Aug	Sep	Oct	Nov	Dec
1	10Li	28Sc	8Sg	1Aq	10Pi	2Ta	8Ge	24Cn	9Vi	11Li	28Sc	5Cp
3	6Sc	27Sg	6Cp	29Aq	8Ar	28Ta	3Cn	18Le	2Li	6Sc	25Sg	3Aq
5	4Sg	27Cp	5Aq	29Pi	6Ta	24Ge	27Cn	11Vi	26Li	1Sg	22Cp	1Pi
7	4Cp	27Aq	5Pi	27Ar	3Ge	19Cn	21Le	5Li	21Sc	28Sg	20Aq	29Pi
9	4Aq	27Pi	5Ar	25Ta	28Ge	13Le	15Vi	0Sc	18Sg	25Cp	18Pi	27Ar
11	4Pi	25Ar	3Ta	20Ge	23Cn	6Vi	9Li	25Sc	15Cp	24Aq	17Ar	25Ta
13	3Ar	21Ta	0Ge	15Cn	17Le	0Li	3Sc	22Sg	15Aq	23Pi	16Ta	22Ge
15	29Ar	16Ge	25Ge	9Le	10Vi	25Li	0Sg	21Cp	15Pi	23Ar	13Ge	17Cn
17	25Ta	10Cn	19Cn	2Vi	5Li	22Sc	28Sg	21Aq	15Ar	22Ta	9Cn	12Le
19	19Ge	4Le	12Le	27Vi	0Sc	20Sg	28Cp	22Pi	13Ta	19Ge	4Le	6Vi
21	13Cn	28Le	6Vi	22Li	27Sc	19Cp	28Aq	21Ar	11Ge	14Cn	28Le	29Vi
23	7Le	22Vi	1Li	18Sc	25Sg	18Aq	27Pi	18Ta	6Cn	8Le	22Vi	24Li
25	1Vi	16Li	26Li	15Sg	24Cp	17Pi	25Ar	14Ge	0Le	2Vi	16Li	19Sc
27	25Vi	12Sc	22Sc	13Cp	22Aq	15Ar	22Ta	9Cn	24Le	26Vi	11Sc	16Sg
29	19Li		19Sg	11Aq	21Pi	12Ta	18Ge	3Le	17Vi	20Li	7Sg	14Cp
31	15Sc		16Cp		18Ar		12Cn	27Le		15Sc		13Aq

1971

	Jan	Feb	Mar	Apr	May	Jun	Jul	Aug	Sep	Oct	Nov	Dec
1	27Aq	20Ar	0Ta	20Ge	25Cn	9Vi	11Li	25Sc	12Cp	18Aq	11Ar	19Ta
3	26Pi	18Ta	28Ta	16Cn	19Le	3Li	5Sc	20Sg	10Aq	17Pi	11Ta	19Ge
5	24Ar	15Ge	24Ge	11Le	13Vi	27Li	0Sg	17Cp	9Pi	18Ar	11Ge	17Cn
7	21Ta	10Cn	10Cn	4Vi	6Li	21Sc	26Sg	16Aq	9Ar	18Ta	9Cn	13Le
9	18Ge	5Le	14Le	28Vi	0Sc	17Sg	23Cp	15Pi	9Ta	16Ge	5Le	8Vi
11	13Cn	29Le	7Vi	22Li	25Sc	14Cp	21Aq	14Ar	7Ge	14Cn	0Vi	2Li
13	8Le	22Vi	1Li	16Sc	21Sg	11Aq	20Pi	13Ta	4Cn	9Le	24Vi	26Li
15	2Vi	16Li	25Li	11Sg	17Cp	9Pi	18Ar	11Ge	0Le	3Vi	18Li	20Sc
17	26Vi	10Sc	19Sc	7Cp	14Aq	7Ar	16Ta	7Cn	24Le	27Vi	12Sc	15Sg
19	19Li	5Sg	14Sg	4Aq	12Pi	6Ta	14Ge	3Le	18Vi	21Li	6Sg	10Cp
21	14Sc	1Cp	10Cp	2Pi	11Ar	4Ge	11Cn	27Le	12Li	15Sc	1Cp	6Aq
23	10Sg	0Aq	8Aq	1Ar	10Ta	1Cn	6Le	21Vi	6Sc	9Sg	26Cp	3Pi
25	7Cp	29Aq	8Pi	1Ta	9Ge	28Cn	1Vi	15Li	0Sg	4Cp	23Aq	1Ar
27	7Aq	0Ar	8Ar	1Ge	7Cn	23Le	25Vi	9Sc	24Sg	29Cp	21Pi	0Ta
29	6Pi		8Ta	29Ge	3Le	17Vi	19Li	3Sg	20Cp	27Aq	20Ar	29Ta
31	6Ar		7Ge		27Le		13Sc	28Sg		26Pi		27Ge

1972

	Jan	Feb	Mar	Apr	May	Jun	Jul	Aug	Sep	Oct	Nov	Dec
1	11Cn	29Le	20Vi	5Sc	7Sg	23Cp	29Aq	21Ar	14Ge	23Cn	12Vi	16Li
3	8Le	24Vi	14Li	28Sc	1Cp	19Aq	26Pi	19Ta	12Cn	19Le	6Li	10Sc
5	4Vi	18Li	8Sc	22Sg	26Cp	15Pi	24Ar	18Ge	9Le	15Vi	1Sc	3Sg
7	28Vi	12Sc	2Sg	17Cp	22Aq	14Ar	23Ta	16Cn	5Vi	10Li	24Sc	27Sg
9	22Li	6Sg	26Sg	13Aq	20Pi	13Ta	22Ge	13Le	1Li	4Sc	18Sg	21Cp
11	16Sc	1Cp	21Cp	11Pi	19Ar	13Ge	21Cn	10Vi	25Li	28Sc	12Cp	16Aq
13	10Sg	27Cp	18Aq	10Ar	19Ta	12Cn	18Le	5Li	19Sc	21Sg	6Aq	11Pi
15	6Cp	25Aq	17Pi	11Ta	20Ge	10Le	14Vi	29Li	13Sg	15Cp	2Pi	8Ar
17	2Aq	24Pi	17Ar	11Ge	18Cn	6Vi	9Li	23Sc	7Cp	10Aq	29Pi	7Ta
19	0Pi	23Ar	17Ta	9Cn	15Le	1Li	3Sc	17Sg	2Aq	7Pi	28Ar	7Ge
21	28Pi	22Ta	16Ge	6Le	10Vi	25Li	27Sc	12Cp	29Aq	5Ar	29Ta	7Cn
23	26Ar	19Ge	13Cn	1Vi	5Li	29Sc	21Sg	7Aq	27Pi	5Ta	29Ge	6Le
25	25Ta	16Cn	9Le	26Vi	29Li	13Sg	16Cp	4Pi	27Ar	6Ge	28Cn	4Vi
27	23Ge	12Le	4Vi	20Li	22Sc	7Cp	12Aq	3Ar	26Ta	5Cn	25Le	0Li
29	20Cn	7Vi	29Vi	13Sc	16Sg	3Aq	9Pi	1Ta	25Ge	3Le	21Vi	24Li
31	16Le		23Li		11Cp		7Ar	0Ge		29Le		18Sc

1973

	Jan	Feb	Mar	Apr	May	Jun	Jul	Aug	Sep	Oct	Nov	Dec
1	0Sg	14Cp	22Cp	8Pi	14Ar	7Ge	16Cn	8VI	27Li	0Sg	13Cp	15Aq
3	24Sg	9Aq	17Aq	6Ar	14Ta	7Cn	15Le	6Li	22Sc	24Sg	7Aq	9Pi
5	18Cp	5Pi	14Pi	5Ta	14Ge	7Le	14Vi	1Sc	16Sg	17Cp	1Pi	5Ar
7	13Aq	1Ar	11Ar	4Ge	13Cn	5Vi	10Li	26Sc	9Cp	11Aq	27Pi	2Ta
9	8Pi	29Ar	10Ta	3Cn	11Le	1Li	5Sc	19Sg	3Aq	6Pi	24Ar	1Ge
11	5Ar	27Ta	8Ge	1Le	8Vi	26Li	29Sc	13Cp	28Aq	3Ar	23Ta	1Cn
13	2Ta	25Ge	6Cn	28Le	4Li	20Sc	23Sg	7Aq	24Pi	0Ta	23Ge	2Le
15	1Ge	24Cn	4Le	24Vi	29Li	14Sg	16Cp	2Pi	21Ar	29Ta	22Cn	0Vi
17	0Cn	22Le	1Vi	20Li	23Sc	8Cp	10Aq	28Pi	19Ta	27Ge	20Le	28Vi
19	0Le	20Vi	28Vi	14Sc	17Sg	1Aq	5Pi	24Ar	17Ge	26Cn	18Vi	24Li
21	28Le	16Li	24Li	8Sg	11Cp	26Aq	1Ar	22Ta	15Cn	24Le	14Li	19Sc
23	25Vi	10Sc	18Sc	2Cp	4Aq	21Pi	27Ar	20Ge	13Le	21Vi	9Sc	13Sg
25	20Li	4Sg	12Sg	26Cp	29Aq	18Ar	25Ta	19Cn	11Vi	17Li	4Sg	7Cp
27	15Sc	28Sg	6Cp	20Aq	25Pi	16Ta	24Ge	18Le	9Li	13Sc	28Sg	0Aq
29	8Sg		0Aq	16Pi	23Ar	16Ge	24Cn	16Vi	5Sc	8Sg	22Cp	24Aq
31	2Cp		25Aq		22Ta		24Le	14Li		2Cp		18Pi

1974

	Jan	Feb	Mar	Apr	May	Jun	Jul	Aug	Sep	Oct	Nov	Dec
1	1Ar	20Ta	0Ge	23Cn	2Vi	23Li	29Sc	14Cp	29Aq	2Ar	19Ta	26Ge
3	27Ar	18Ge	28Ge	21Le	0Li	19Sc	23Sg	8Aq	23Pi	27Ar	16Ge	24Cn
5	25Ta	17Cn	27Cn	20Vi	27Li	14Sg	17Cp	2Pi	18Ar	23Ta	14Cn	23Le
7	24Ge	18Le	26Le	18Li	23Sc	9Cp	11Aq	26Pi	13Ta	20Ge	12Le	22Vi
9	25Cn	17Vi	25Vi	15Sc	18Sg	2Aq	5Pi	20Ar	9Ge	17Cn	11Vi	19Li
11	25Le	16Li	23Li	10Sg	12Cp	26Aq	29Pi	16Ta	7Cn	16Le	9Li	16Sc
13	24Vi	12Sc	20Sc	5Cp	6Aq	20Pi	24Ar	13Ge	6Le	15Vi	7Sc	12Sg
15	20Li	7Sg	15Sg	28Cp	0Pi	15Ar	20Ta	12Cn	6Vi	14Li	4Sg	7Cp
17	16Sc	0Cp	9Cp	22Aq	25Pi	12Ta	19Ge	12Le	5Li	12Sc	29Sg	2Aq
19	10Sg	24Cp	2Aq	17Pi	20Ar	10Ge	18Cn	12Vi	4Sc	9Sg	24Cp	25Aq
21	4Cp	18Aq	26Aq	12Ar	18Ta	10Cn	19Le	12Li	1Sg	4Cp	18Aq	19Pi
23	27Cp	12Pi	21Pi	9Ta	16Ge	10Le	19Vi	9Sc	26Sg	28Cp	11Pi	13Ar
25	21Aq	7Ar	17Ar	7Ge	15Cn	9Vi	17Li	5Sg	20Cp	22Aq	6Ar	9Ta
27	15Pi	3Ta	13Ta	5Cn	14Le	7Li	13Sc	29Sg	13Aq	16Pi	1Ta	6Ge
29	10Ar		11Ge	4Le	13Vi	3Sc	8Sg	23Cp	7Pi	10Ar	28Ta	4Cn
31	6Ta		8Cn		10Li		2Cp	17Aq		6Ta		4Le

1975

	Jan	Feb	Mar	Apr	May	Jun	Jul	Aug	Sep	Oct	Nov	Dec
1	19Le	12Li	21Li	11Sg	14Cp	29Aq	0Ar	15Ta	2Cn	9Le	2Li	11Sc
3	18Vi	10Sc	19Sc	6Cp	9Aq	23Pi	24Ar	10Ge	0Le	8Vi	2Sc	9Sg
5	16Li	6Sg	15Sg	1Aq	3Pi	17Ar	19Ta	7Cn	0Vi	9Li	1Sg	7Cp
7	13Sc	1Cp	10Cp	24Aq	26Pi	11Ta	16Ge	6Le	0Li	9Sc	29Sg	3Aq
9	9Sg	25Cp	4Aq	18Pi	21Ar	7Ge	13Cn	6Vi	0Sc	7Sg	25Cp	28Aq
11	4Cp	19Aq	28Aq	12Ar	16Ta	4Cn	12Le	6Li	29Sc	4Cp	20Aq	22Pi
13	28Cp	12Pi	21Pi	7Ta	12Ge	3Le	12Vi	5Sc	25Sg	29Cp	14Pi	16Ar
15	22Aq	6Ar	15Ar	2Ge	8Cn	1Vi	11Li	2Sg	20Cp	24Aq	8Ar	10Ta
17	16Pi	0Ta	10Ta	28Ge	6Le	0Li	8Sc	28Sg	15Aq	17Pi	2Ta	5Ge
19	9Ar	25Ta	5Ge	25Cn	4Vi	28Li	5Sg	23Cp	9Pi	11Ar	26Ta	1Cn
21	4Ta	22Ge	1Cn	24Le	3Li	25Sc	1Cp	18Aq	2Ar	5Ta	22Ge	28Cn
23	0Ge	20Cn	29Cn	23Vi	2Sc	22Sg	26Cp	12Pi	26Ar	0Ge	18Cn	26Le
25	28Ge	20Le	29Le	22Li	0Sg	18Cp	21Aq	5Ar	20Ta	25Ge	15Le	24Vi
27	27Cn	21Vi	29Vi	21Sc	26Sg	13Aq	15Pi	29Ar	15Ge	21Cn	13Vi	22Li
29	27Le		29Li	19Sg	22Cp	7Pi	9Ar	23Ta	11Cn	18Le	12Li	20Sc
31	28Vi		27Sc		17Aq		3Ta	19Ge		17Vi		18Sg

1976

	Jan	Feb	Mar	Apr	May	Jun	Jul	Aug	Sep	Oct	Nov	Dec
1	2Cp	19Aq	19Pi	25Ar	27Ta	14Cn	21Le	13Li	6Sg	14Cp	3Pi	6Ar
3	28Cp	14Pi	4Ar	18Ta	22Ge	10Le	18Vi	11Sc	4Cp	10Aq	27Pi	0Ta
5	24Aq	8Ar	28Ar	12Ge	17Cn	7Vi	16Li	9Sg	0Aq	6Pi	21Ar	23Ta
7	18Pi	1Ta	22Ta	7Cn	13Le	5Li	15Sc	7Cp	26Aq	0Ar	15Ta	17Ge
9	12Ar	25Ta	16Ge	4Le	11Vi	4Sc	13Sg	4Aq	21Pi	24Ar	8Ge	12Cn
11	5Ta	20Ge	11Cn	2Vi	10Li	4Sg	11Cp	0Pi	15Ar	18Ta	2Cn	7Le
13	0Ge	17Cn	9Le	1Li	10Sc	3Cp	9Aq	25Pi	9Ta	11Ge	27Cn	3Vi
15	26Ge	15Le	8Vi	2Sc	10Sg	0Aq	4Pi	19Ar	3Ge	5Cn	23Le	0Li
17	23Cn	15Vi	9Li	2Sg	9Cp	26Aq	29Pi	13Ta	27Ge	1Le	20Vi	28Li
19	21Le	15Li	9Sc	0Cp	6Aq	21Pi	23Ar	7Ge	22Cn	28Le	19Li	28Sc
21	20Vi	14Sc	7Sg	27Cp	1Pi	15Ar	17Ta	1Cn	19Le	26Vi	19Sc	28Sg
23	19Li	11Sg	5Cp	22Aq	25Pi	9Ta	11Ge	28Cn	18Vi	26Li	20Sg	27Cp
25	17Sc	8Cp	0Aq	16Pi	19Ar	3Ge	25Le	25Le	18Li	26Sc	19Cp	24Aq
27	14Sg	3Aq	25Aq	10Ar	12Ta	28Ge	24Vi	24Vi	18Sc	26Sg	16Aq	20Pi
29	11Cp	28Aq	19Pi	4Ta	6Ge	24Cn	23Li	23Li	17Sg	24Cp	12Pi	14Ar
31	7Aq		13Ar		1Cn		22Sc	22Sc		20Aq		8Ta

1977

	Jan	Feb	Mar	Apr	May	Jun	Jul	Aug	Sep	Oct	Nov	Dec
1	20Ta	4Cn	12Cn	29Le	5Li	28Sc	7Cp	29Aq	17Ar	19Ta	3Cn	6Le
3	14Ge	29Cn	7Le	27Vi	4Sc	28Sg	6Aq	26Pi	11Ta	13Ge	27Cn	0Vi
5	8Cn	26Le	5Vi	26Li	5Sg	28Cp	4Pi	21Ar	5Ge	7Cn	21Le	25Vi
7	4Le	23Vi	3Li	25Sc	4Cp	26Aq	1Ar	15Ta	29Ge	1Le	17Vi	23Li
9	0Vi	21Li	2Sc	25Sg	3Aq	22Pi	25Ar	9Ge	23Cn	26Le	15Li	22Sc
11	27Vi	19Sc	0Sg	23Cp	0Pi	17Ar	19Ta	3Cn	18Le	23Vi	14Sc	22Sg
13	24Li	18Sg	29Sg	20Aq	25Pi	10Ta	13Ge	27Cn	15Vi	21Li	14Sg	23Cp
15	23Sc	16Cp	26Cp	16Pi	20Ar	4Ge	7Cn	23Le	12Li	20Sc	14Cp	22Aq
17	22Sg	13Aq	23Aq	10Ar	13Ta	28Ge	1Le	19Vi	10Sc	19Sg	12Aq	19Pi
19	21Cp	10Pi	19Pi	4Ta	7Ge	22Cn	26Le	16Li	9Sg	18Cp	9Pi	15Ar
21	19Aq	6Ar	14Ar	28Ta	1Cn	17Le	22Vi	14Sc	7Cp	16Aq	5Ar	9Ta
23	15Pi	0Ta	8Ta	22Ge	25Cn	12Vi	19Li	12Sg	5Aq	12Pi	0Ta	3Ge
25	10Ar	24Ta	2Ge	16Cn	20Le	9Li	17Sc	11Cp	3Pi	8Ar	24Ta	27Ge
27	4Ta	17Ge	25Ge	11Le	16Vi	7Sc	16Sg	9Aq	29Pi	3Ta	18Ge	21Cn
29	28Ta		20Cn	7Vi	13Li	6Sg	15Cp	7Pi	25Ar	27Ta	12Cn	15Le
31	22Ge		15Le		13Sc		15Aq	4Ar		21Ge		9Vi

1978

	Jan	Feb	Mar	Apr	May	Jun	Jul	Aug	Sep	Oct	Nov	Dec
1	22Vi	11Sc	22Sc	15Cp	24Aq	15Ar	20Ta	5Cn	19Le	22Vi	10Sc	17Sg
3	18Li	10Sg	20Sg	14Aq	22Pi	10Ta	14Ge	28Cn	13Vi	18Li	8Sg	16Cp
5	16Sc	9Cp	19Cp	11Pi	18Ar	5Ge	8Cn	22Le	8Li	14Sc	6Cp	15Aq
7	15Sg	9Aq	18Aq	9Ar	13Ta	29Ge	1Le	16Vi	4Sc	12Sg	5Aq	14Pi
9	15Cp	8Pi	16Pi	5Ta	8Ge	23Cn	25Le	11Li	1Sg	10Cp	3Pi	11Ar
11	16Aq	6Ar	14Ar	0Ge	2Cn	16Le	19Vi	7Sc	29Sg	8Aq	1Ar	7Ta
13	14Pi	2Ta	9Ta	24Ge	26Cn	10Vi	14Li	4Sg	28Cp	6Pi	28Ar	3Ge
15	11Ar	26Ta	4Ge	18Cn	20Le	5Li	11Sc	3Cp	27Aq	5Ar	24Ta	28Ge
17	6Ta	20Ge	28Ge	12Le	14Vi	2Sc	9Sg	3Aq	26Pi	2Ta	19Ge	22Cn
19	0Ge	14Cn	22Cn	6Vi	10Li	1Sg	9Cp	3Pi	24Ar	28Ta	14Cn	15Le
21	24Ge	8Le	16Le	2Li	8Sc	1Cp	10Aq	2Ar	21Ta	23Ge	7Le	9Vi
23	17Cn	3Vi	11Vi	0Sc	7Sg	1Aq	10Pi	29Ar	16Ge	18Cn	1Vi	3Li
25	12Le	28Vi	7Li	28Sc	7Cp	1Pi	8Ar	25Ta	10Cn	11Le	25Vi	29Li
27	6Vi	25Li	5Sc	27Sg	7Aq	28Pi	4Ta	20Ge	3Le	5Vi	21Li	26Sc
29	2Li		3Sg	26Cp	5Pi	25Ar	29Ta	13Cn	27Le	0Li	18Sc	25Sg
31	28Li		1Cp		2Ar		23Ge	7Le		26Li		25Cp

1979

	Jan	Feb	Mar	Apr	May	Jun	Jul	Aug	Sep	Oct	Nov	Dec
1	10Aq	3Ar	11Ar	1Ge	4Cn	18Le	20Vi	5Sc	23Sg	0Aq	23Pi	2Ta
3	10Pi	1Ta	9Ta	26Ge	29Cn	12Vi	14Li	1Sg	21Cp	29Aq	23Ar	0Ge
5	8Ar	27Ta	5Ge	21Cn	22Le	6Li	9Sc	28Sg	21Aq	29Pi	22Ta	27Ge
7	4Ta	21Ge	0Cn	14Le	16Vi	1Sc	6Sg	27Cp	21Pi	29Ar	19Ge	23Cn
9	0Ge	15Cn	24Cn	8Vi	10Li	28Sc	4Cp	28Aq	21Ar	28Ta	15Cn	18Le
11	24Ge	9Le	18Le	2Li	6Sc	26Sg	4Aq	28Pi	19Ta	25Ge	10Le	12Vi
13	18Cn	3Vi	12Vi	27Li	3Sg	25Cp	4Pi	26Ar	16Ge	20Cn	4Vi	5Li
15	12Le	27Vi	6Li	23Sc	0Cp	24Aq	2Ar	24Ta	11Cn	14Le	27Vi	29Li
17	6Vi	21Li	1Sc	20Sg	29Cp	22Pi	0Ta	19Ge	5Le	7Vi	22Li	25Sc
19	0Li	16Sc	26Sc	18Cp	27Aq	20Ar	27Ta	14Cn	29Le	1Li	17Sc	22Sg
21	24Li	13Sg	23Sg	16Aq	25Pi	17Ta	22Ge	8Le	22Vi	25Li	13Sg	19Cp
23	20Sc	12Cp	21Cp	15Pi	23Ar	13Ge	17Cn	2Vi	16Li	20Sc	10Cp	18Aq
25	18Sg	11Aq	20Aq	13Ar	20Ta	8Cn	11Le	25Vi	11Sc	16Sg	7Aq	16Pi
27	18Cp	12Pi	20Pi	11Ta	17Ge	3Le	5Vi	19Li	6Sg	13Cp	5Pi	14Ar
29	18Aq		19Ar	8Ge	12Cn	26Le	28Vi	14Sc	2Cp	10Aq	3Ar	12Ta
31	18Pi		17Ta		6Le		22Li	9Sg		9Pi		9Ge

1980

	Jan	Feb	Mar	Apr	May	Jun	Jul	Aug	Sep	Oct	Nov	Dec
1	23Ge	10Le	1Vi	15Li	18Sc	5Cp	12Aq	5Ar	28Ta	6Cn	23Le	26Vi
3	19Cn	4Vi	24Vi	9Sc	13Sg	2Aq	10Pi	4Ta	26Ge	2Le	17Vi	20Li
5	14Le	28Vi	18Li	3Sg	9Cp	29Aq	9Ar	2Ge	22Cn	26Le	11Li	13Sc
7	8Vi	21Li	12Sc	29Sg	5Aq	27Pi	7Ta	29Ge	17Le	20Vi	5Sc	8Sg
9	1Li	15Sc	6Sg	25Cp	3Pi	26Ar	5Ge	25Cn	11Vi	14Li	29Sc	3Cp
11	25Li	11Sg	2Cp	23Aq	1Ar	25Ta	2Cn	20Le	5Li	8Sc	23Sg	28Cp
13	20Sc	7Cp	0Aq	22Pi	1Ta	23Ge	29Cn	15Vi	29Li	2Sg	18Cp	24Aq
15	16Sg	6Aq	29Aq	22Ar	1Ge	21Cn	24Le	9Li	23Sc	26Sg	14Aq	22Pi
17	14Cp	6Pi	29Pi	22Ta	29Ge	16Le	19Vi	2Sc	17Sg	21Cp	11Pi	20Ar
19	13Aq	6Ar	29Ar	21Ge	26Cn	11Vi	12Li	26Sc	13Cp	18Aq	10Ar	19Ta
21	12Pi	5Ta	28Ta	17Cn	21Le	4Li	6Sc	21Sg	10Aq	17Pi	10Ta	19Ge
23	11Ar	3Ge	26Ge	12Le	15Vi	28Li	1Sg	18Cp	8Pi	17Ar	10Ge	17Cn
25	9Ta	29Ge	21Cn	6Vi	8Li	23Sc	26Sg	16Aq	9Ar	17Ta	9Cn	14Le
27	6Ge	24Cn	16Le	0Li	2Sc	18Sg	23Cp	15Pi	9Ta	17Ge	6Le	10Vi
29	2Cn	19Le	9Vi	24Li	27Sc	15Cp	22Aq	15Ar	8Ge	15Cn	2Vi	4Li
31	27Cn		3Li		22Sg		21Pi	14Ta		11Le		20Li

1981

	Jan	Feb	Mar	Apr	May	Jun	Jul	Aug	Sep	Oct	Nov	Dec
1	10Sc	24Sg	2Cp	19Aq	25Pi	19Ta	28Ge	19Le	6Li	9Sc	23Sg	26Cp
3	4Sg	20Cp	27Cp	17Pi	25Ar	19Ge	27Cn	15Vi	1Sc	3Sg	17Cp	20Aq
5	29Sg	17Aq	25Aq	17Ar	26Ta	19Cn	24Le	11Li	25Sc	27Sg	11Aq	16Pi
7	24Cp	15Pi	23Pi	17Ta	26Ge	16Le	20Vi	5Sc	19Sg	21Cp	7Pi	14Ar
9	21Aq	13Ar	23Ar	17Ge	24Cn	12Vi	15Li	29Sc	13Cp	16Aq	5Ar	13Ta
11	19Pi	12Ta	22Ta	15Cn	21Le	7Li	9Sc	23Sg	8Aq	13Pi	5Ta	13Ge
13	17Ar	10Ge	21Ge	11Le	16Vi	1Sc	3Sg	17Cp	5Pi	12Ar	5Ge	13Cn
15	15Ta	8Cn	18Cn	6Vi	10Li	24Sc	27Sg	13Aq	3Ar	12Ta	5Cn	13Le
17	14Ge	4Le	14Le	1Li	4Sc	18Sg	22Cp	10Pi	2Ta	11Ge	4Le	10Vi
19	12Cn	0Vi	9Vi	25Li	27Sc	13Cp	17Aq	8Ar	1Ge	10Cn	1Vi	5Li
21	9Le	25Vi	4Li	19Sc	21Sg	8Aq	14Pi	6Ta	0Cn	8Le	26Vi	0Sc
23	5Vi	20Li	28Li	12Sg	16Cp	3Pi	11Ar	5Ge	27Cn	4Vi	21Li	24Sc
25	0Li	13Sc	22Sc	6Cp	11Aq	0Ar	9Ta	3Cn	24Le	29Vi	15Sc	17Sg
27	24Li	7Sg	15Sg	1Aq	7Pi	29Ar	8Ge	1Le	20Vi	24Li	8Sg	11Cp
29	17Sc		10Cp	27Aq	4Ar	28Ta	7Cn	28Le	15Li	18Sc	2Cp	5Aq
31	12Sg		5Aq		4Ta		5Le	24Vi		11Sg		0Pi

1982

	Jan	Feb	Mar	Apr	May	Jun	Jul	Aug	Sep	Oct	Nov	Dec
1	13Pi	4Ta	14Ta	8Cn	16Le	6Li	10Sc	25Sg	9Aq	12Pi	1Ta	8Ge
3	9Ar	2Ge	13Ge	5Le	13Vi	1Sc	4Sg	18Cp	4Pi	8Ar	29Ta	8Cn
5	7Ta	1Cn	11Cn	3Vi	9Li	25Sc	28Sg	12Aq	29Pi	6Ta	28Ge	7Le
7	6Ge	0Le	9Le	29Vi	4Sc	19Sg	22Cp	7Pi	26Ar	4Ge	27Cn	6Vi
9	6Cn	28Le	7Vi	25Li	28Sc	13Cp	15Aq	3Ar	23Ta	2Cn	25Le	3Li
11	6Le	26Vi	4Li	20Sc	22Sg	6Aq	10Pi	29Ar	21Ge	0Le	22Vi	29Li
13	4Vi	22Li	29Li	14Sg	16Cp	1Pi	6Ar	26Ta	19Cn	28Le	19Li	24Sc
15	1Li	16Sc	24Sc	8Cp	10Aq	26Pi	2Ta	25Ge	18Le	26Vi	15Sc	18Sg
17	26Li	10Sg	18Sg	1Aq	4Pi	23Ar	1Ge	24Cn	17Vi	23Li	9Sg	12Cp
19	20Sc	4Cp	11Cp	26Aq	1Ar	22Ta	0Cn	24Le	14Li	19Sc	3Cp	5Aq
21	14Sg	28Cp	6Aq	22Pi	29Ar	22Ge	0Le	22Vi	11Sc	13Sg	27Cp	29Aq
23	8Cp	23Aq	1Pi	20Ar	28Ta	22Cn	0Vi	20Li	5Sg	7Cp	21Aq	23Pi
25	2Aq	19Pi	28Pi	20Ta	28Ge	21Le	28Vi	15Sc	29Sg	1Aq	15Pi	19Ar
27	27Aq	16Ar	26Ar	19Ge	28Cn	19Vi	24Li	9Sg	23Cp	25Aq	11Ar	16Ta
29	23Pi		25Ta	18Cn	26Le	15Li	19Sc	3Cp	17Aq	20Pi	9Ta	16Ge
31	20Ar		24Ge		23Vi		13Sg	27Cp		17Ar		16Cn

1983

	Jan	Feb	Mar	Apr	May	Jun	Jul	Aug	Sep	Oct	Nov	Dec
1	1Le	24Vi	2Li	21Sc	24Sg	8Aq	10Pi	26Ar	14Ge	22Cn	15Vi	24Li
3	1Vi	21Li	0Sc	16Sg	18Cp	2Pi	4Ar	21Ta	12Cn	21Le	14Li	21Sc
5	29Vi	17Sc	26Sc	10Cp	12Aq	26Pi	29Ar	19Ge	11Le	20Vi	12Sc	18Sg
7	26Li	12Sg	20Sg	4Aq	6Pi	21Ar	26Ta	18Cn	12Vi	20Li	9Sg	13Cp
9	21Sc	6Cp	14Cp	28Aq	0Ar	18Ta	25Ge	18Le	12Li	18Sc	5Cp	7Aq
11	15Sg	29Cp	8Aq	22Pi	26Ar	16Ge	25Cn	19Vi	10Sc	15Sg	29Cp	1Pi
13	9Cp	23Aq	2Pi	18Ar	24Ta	16Cn	25Le	18Li	6Sg	9Cp	23Aq	25Pi
15	2Aq	17Pi	26Pi	15Ta	22Ge	15Le	24Vi	15Sc	1Cp	3Aq	17Pi	19Ar
17	26Aq	12Ar	22Ar	12Ge	21Cn	14Vi	22Li	10Sg	25Cp	27Aq	12Ar	15Ta
19	20Pi	8Ta	18Ta	10Cn	19Le	12Li	18Sc	5Cp	19Aq	21Pi	7Ta	12Ge
21	15Ar	5Ge	15Ge	8Le	17Vi	8Sc	13Sg	28Cp	13Pi	16Ar	4Ge	10Cn
23	11Ta	3Cn	13Cn	6Vi	15Li	4Sg	7Cp	22Aq	7Ar	11Ta	1Cn	9Le
25	9Ge	2Le	12Le	5Li	11Sc	28Sg	1Aq	16Pi	2Ta	8Ge	29Cn	9Vi
27	9Cn	2Vi	11Vi	2Sc	7Sg	23Cp	25Aq	10Ar	28Ta	5Cn	28Le	7Li
29	9Le		10Li	29Sc	2Cp	16Aq	19Pi	5Ta	24Ge	3Le	26Vi	4Sc
31	9Vi		7Sc		26Cp		13Ar	1Ge		1Vi		1Sg

1984

	Jan	Feb	Mar	Apr	May	Jun	Jul	Aug	Sep	Oct	Nov	Dec
1	14Sg	0Aq	21Aq	5Ar	9Ta	26Ge	3Le	27Vi	20Sc	27Sg	13Aq	16Pi
3	9Cp	24Aq	15Pi	0Ta	4Ge	24Cn	2Vi	26Li	17Sg	22Cp	8Pi	10Ar
5	3Aq	18Pi	8Ar	24Ta	0Cn	22Le	1Li	24Sc	13Cp	17Aq	1Ar	3Ta
7	27Aq	11Ar	2Ta	20Ge	27Cn	20Vi	29Li	20Sg	8Aq	11Pi	25Ar	28Ta
9	21Pi	6Ta	27Ta	16Cn	25Le	18Li	27Sc	16Cp	2Pi	5Ar	19Ta	23Ge
11	15Ar	1Ge	23Ge	14Le	24Vi	17Sc	23Sg	11Aq	26Pi	28Ar	14Ge	19Cn
13	10Ta	28Ge	20Cn	14Vi	23Li	14Sg	19Cp	5Pi	19Ar	22Ta	9Cn	16Le
15	6Ge	26Cn	20Le	14Li	21Sc	11Cp	14Aq	29Pi	13Ta	17Ge	6Le	14Vi
17	4Cn	27Le	20Vi	13Sc	19Sg	6Aq	8Pi	22Ar	8Ge	12Cn	4Vi	13Li
19	3Le	27Vi	20Li	11Sg	15Cp	0Pi	2Ar	16Ta	3Cn	9Le	2Li	11Sc
21	4Vi	27Li	19Sc	7Cp	10Aq	24Pi	26Ar	11Ge	0Le	8Vi	2Sc	10Sg
23	3Li	24Sc	16Sg	2Aq	4Pi	18Ar	20Ta	8Cn	29Le	8Li	1Sg	7Cp
25	1Sc	20Sg	12Cp	26Aq	28Pi	13Ta	16Ge	6Le	0Li	8Sc	29Sg	4Aq
27	28Sc	15Cp	6Aq	20Pi	22Ar	8Ge	14Cn	6Vi	0Sc	7Sg	26Cp	29Aq
29	23Sg	9Aq	0Pi	14Ar	17Ta	5Cn	13Le	6Li	29Sc	5Cp	22Aq	24Pi
31	18Cp		23Pi		13Ge		12Vi	6Sc		1Aq		17Ar

1985

	Jan	Feb	Mar	Apr	May	Jun	Jul	Aug	Sep	Oct	Nov	Dec
1	29Ar	13Ge	21Ge	9Le	16Vi	10Sc	19Sg	9Aq	27Pi	29Ar	13Ge	17Cn
3	23Ta	9Cn	17Cn	8Vi	16Li	10Sg	17Cp	6Pi	21Ar	23Ta	7Cn	12Le
5	18Ge	7Le	15Le	8Li	16Sc	9Cp	14Aq	1Ar	15Ta	16Ge	2Le	8Vi
7	15Cn	6Vi	15Vi	8Sc	16Sg	6Aq	10Pi	25Ar	8Ge	11Cn	28Le	5Li
9	13Le	6Li	15Li	8Sg	15Cp	2Pi	5Ar	18Ta	3Cn	6Le	26Vi	4Sc
11	11Vi	4Sc	14Sc	6Cp	11Aq	27Pi	29Ar	12Ge	28Cn	3Vi	25Li	4Sg
13	9Li	2Sg	13Sg	2Aq	6Pi	21Ar	22Ta	7Cn	25Le	2Li	26Sc	4Cp
15	8Sc	29Sg	9Cp	27Aq	0Ar	14Ta	17Ge	3Le	24Vi	3Sc	26Sg	3Aq
17	5Sg	25Cp	5Aq	21Pi	24Ar	8Ge	12Cn	1Vi	24Li	3Sg	25Cp	0Pi
19	3Cp	21Aq	0Pi	15Ar	18Ta	3Cn	8Le	0Li	23Sc	2Cp	22Aq	26Pi
21	29Cp	16Pi	24Pi	9Ta	12Ge	29Cn	6Vi	28Li	22Sg	29Cp	17Pi	20Ar
23	25Aq	10Ar	18Ar	2Ge	6Cn	25Le	4Li	27Sc	19Cp	25Aq	11Ar	13Ta
25	19Pi	3Ta	12Ta	27Ge	2Le	23Vi	2Sc	25Sg	15Aq	20Pi	5Ta	7Ge
27	13Ar	27Ta	5Ge	22Cn	28Le	21Li	0Sg	22Cp	11Pi	14Ar	28Ta	1Cn
29	7Ta		0Cn	18Le	26Vi	20Sc	28Sg	18Aq	5Ar	8Ta	22Ge	26Cn
31	1Ge		26Cn		25Li		26Cp	14Pi		1Ge		22Le

1986

	Jan	Feb	Mar	Apr	May	Jun	Jul	Aug	Sep	Oct	Nov	Dec
1	5Vi	26Li	7Sc	0Cp	8Aq	27Pi	1Ta	15Ge	29Cn	2Vi	21Li	28Sc
3	1Li	24Sc	5Sg	28Cp	5Pi	22Ar	24Ta	8Cn	24Le	29Vi	20Sc	29Sg
5	29Li	22Sg	3Cp	25Aq	0Ar	15Ta	18Ge	3Le	20Vi	27Li	20Sg	29Cp
7	28Sc	21Cp	1Aq	20Pi	24Ar	9Ge	12Cn	28Le	17Li	25Sc	19Cp	27Aq
9	27Sg	19Aq	28Aq	15Ar	18Ta	3Cn	6Le	24Vi	15Sc	24Sg	17Aq	24Pi
11	26Cp	16Pi	24Pi	10Ta	12Ge	27Cn	1Vi	21Li	13Sg	23Cp	14Pi	20Ar
13	25Aq	11Ar	19Ar	4Ge	6Cn	21Le	27Vi	18Sc	12Cp	20Aq	10Ar	14Ta
15	21Pi	6Ta	14Ta	27Ge	0Le	17Vi	24Li	17Sg	10Aq	17Pi	5Ta	8Ge
17	16Ar	29Ta	7Ge	21Cn	25Le	14Li	22Sc	16Cp	8Pi	13Ar	29Ta	2Cn
19	10Ta	23Ge	1Cn	16Le	21Vi	12Sc	21Sg	15Aq	5Ar	9Ta	23Ge	26Cn
21	3Ge	18Cn	25Cn	13Vi	19Li	12Sg	21Cp	13Pi	0Ta	3Ge	17Cn	20Le
23	27Ge	13Le	21Le	11Li	19Sc	13Cp	21Aq	10Ar	25Ta	27Ge	11Le	14Vi
25	22Cn	10Vi	19Vi	11Sc	19Sg	12Aq	18Pi	5Ta	19Ge	20Cn	5Vi	10Li
27	18Le	8Li	17Li	11Sg	19Cp	10Pi	14Ar	29Ta	13Cn	15Le	1Li	7Sc
29	15Vi		17Sc	10Cp	18Aq	6Ar	9Ta	23Ge	7Le	10Vi	29Li	6Sg
31	12Li		16Sg		14Pi		3Ge	17Cn		7Li		7Cp

1987

	Jan	Feb	Mar	Apr	May	Jun	Jul	Aug	Sep	Oct	Nov	Dec
1	22Cp	14Pi	22Pi	10Ta	14Ge	28Cn	0Vi	16Li	6Sg	14Cp	8Pi	16Ar
3	22Aq	12Ar	20Ar	6Ge	8Cn	22Le	24Vi	12Sc	4Cp	13Aq	5Ar	12Ta
5	20Pi	7Ta	15Ta	0Cn	1Le	16Vi	20Li	10Sg	3Aq	12Pi	3Ta	8Ge
7	16Ar	2Ge	10Ge	24Cn	25Le	11Li	16Sc	9Cp	3Pi	10Ar	29Ta	3Cn
9	11Ta	26Ge	4Cn	18Le	20Vi	8Sc	15Sg	9Aq	2Ar	8Ta	25Ge	27Cn
11	5Ge	19Cn	28Cn	12Vi	16Li	7Sg	16Cp	9Pi	0Ta	4Ge	19Cn	21Le
13	29Ge	13Le	22Le	8Li	14Sc	7Cp	16Aq	8Ar	26Ta	29Ge	13Le	15Vi
15	23Cn	8Vi	17Vi	5Sc	13Sg	7Aq	15Pi	5Ta	21Ge	23Cn	7Vi	9Li
17	17Le	3Li	13Li	4Sg	13Cp	6Pi	13Ar	1Ge	15Cn	17Le	1Li	5Sc
19	11Vi	29Li	10Sc	2Cp	12Aq	3Ar	9Ta	25Ge	9Le	11Vi	27Li	2Sg
21	6Li	27Sc	7Sg	1Aq	10Pi	20Ar	4Ge	19Cn	3Vi	6Li	24Sc	1Cp
23	3Sc	25Sg	6Cp	29Aq	6Ar	24Ta	28Ge	12Le	27Vi	2Sc	23Sg	1Aq
25	0Sg	24Cp	4Aq	26Pi	2Ta	19Ge	22Cn	6Vi	23Li	29Sc	22Cp	1Pi
27	0Cp	23Aq	3Pi	23Ar	27Ta	13Cn	15Le	1Li	19Sc	27Sg	20Aq	29Pi
29	0Aq		1Ar	19Ta	22Ge	6Le	9Vi	26Li	16Sg	25Cp	18Pi	26Ar
31	0Pi		27Ar		16Cn		4Li	22Sc		23Aq		22Ta

1988

	Jan	Feb	Mar	Apr	May	Jun	Jul	Aug	Sep	Oct	Nov	Dec
1	5Ge	21Cn	11Le	25Vi	29Li	17Sg	25Cp	19Pi	11Ta	17Ge	4Le	5Vi
3	29Ge	14Le	5Vi	20Li	25Sc	15Cp	24Aq	18Ar	8Ge	13Cn	28Le	29Vi
5	24Cn	8Vi	29Vi	15Sc	22Sg	14Aq	23Pi	15Ta	4Cn	7Le	21Vi	23Li
7	17Le	2Li	23Li	11Sg	19Cp	12Pi	21Ar	12Ge	28Cn	1Vi	15Li	18Sc
9	11Vi	26Li	18Sc	8Cp	17Aq	11Ar	18Ta	7Cn	22Le	25Vi	9Sc	14Sg
11	5Li	21Sc	14Sg	6Aq	16Pi	8Ta	15Ge	1Le	16Vi	18Li	5Sg	11Cp
13	0Sc	19Sg	12Cp	5Pi	14Ar	5Ge	10Cn	25Le	9Li	13Sc	1Cp	9Aq
15	26Sc	17Cp	11Aq	5Ar	12Ta	1Cn	4Le	19Vi	3Sc	8Sg	28Cp	7Pi
17	24Sg	18Aq	11Pi	3Ta	9Ge	26Cn	28Le	12Li	28Sc	4Cp	26Aq	5Ar
19	24Cp	18Pi	11Ar	1Ge	5Cn	20Le	22Vi	7Sc	24Sg	1Aq	24Pi	3Ta
21	25Aq	17Ar	9Ta	27Ge	0Le	14Vi	16Li	2Sg	21Cp	0Pi	23Ar	1Ge
23	24Pi	15Ta	6Ge	22Cn	24Le	8Li	10Sc	28Sg	20Aq	29Pi	22Ta	28Ge
25	22Ar	11Ge	2Cn	16Le	18Vi	2Sc	6Sg	27Cp	20Pi	29Ar	20Ge	24Cn
27	19Ta	5Cn	26Cn	10Vi	12Li	28Sc	4Cp	27Aq	21Ar	28Ta	16Cn	19Le
29	14Ge	29Cn	20Le	4Li	7Sc	26Sg	4Aq	27Pi	20Ta	25Ge	11Le	13Vi
31	8Cn		13Vi		3Sg		4Pi	27Ar		21Cn		7Li

1989

	Jan	Feb	Mar	Apr	May	Jun	Jul	Aug	Sep	Oct	Nov	Dec
1	19Li	3Sg	12Sg	0Aq	8Pi	1Ta	10Ge	0Le	17Vi	19Li	4Sg	8Cp
3	13Sc	0Cp	8Cp	29Aq	7Ar	1Ge	8Cn	26Le	11Li	13Sc	28Sg	3Aq
5	9Sg	28Cp	6Aq	28Pi	7Ta	29Ge	5Le	20Vi	4Sc	7Sg	23Cp	29Aq
7	6Cp	27Aq	5Pi	29Ar	7Ge	27Cn	0Vi	14Li	28Sc	1Cp	19Aq	26Pi
9	4Aq	27Pi	5Ar	29Ta	5Cn	22Le	24Vi	8Sc	23Sg	27Cp	17Pi	25Ar
11	3Pi	26Ar	5Ta	27Ge	1Le	16Vi	18Li	2Sg	18Cp	24Aq	16Ar	25Ta
13	2Ar	24Ta	4Ge	23Cn	26Le	10Li	12Sc	27Sg	16Aq	23Pi	17Ta	25Ge
15	0Ta	21Ge	1Cn	18Le	20Vi	4Sc	7Sg	24Cp	15Pi	23Ar	17Ge	23Cn
17	27Ta	17Cn	26Cn	12Vi	14Li	28Sc	2Cp	22Aq	15Ar	24Ta	15Cn	20Le
19	24Ge	12Le	21Le	5Li	8Sc	24Sg	29Cp	21Pi	15Ta	23Ge	12Le	15Vi
21	20Cn	6Vi	15Vi	29Li	2Sg	20Cp	27Aq	20Ar	14Ge	20Cn	7Vi	10Li
23	15Le	29Vi	8Li	23Sc	27Sg	17Aq	26Pi	19Ta	11Cn	16Le	1Li	3Sc
25	9Vi	23Li	2Sc	18Sg	23Cp	15Pi	24Ar	17Ge	7Le	10Vi	25Li	27Sc
27	3Li	17Sc	26Sc	13Cp	20Aq	13Ar	22Ta	14Cn	1Vi	4Li	19Sc	22Sg
29	27Li		21Sg	10Aq	18Pi	12Ta	20Ge	9Le	25Vi	28Li	13Sg	17Cp
31	21Sc		17Cp		17Ar		17Cn	4Vi		22Sc		13Aq

1990

	Jan	Feb	Mar	Apr	May	Jun	Jul	Aug	Sep	Oct	Nov	Dec
1	26Aq	18Ar	28Ar	22Ge	29Cn	17Vi	21Li	4Sg	19Cp	22Aq	11Ar	19Ta
3	23Pi	16Ta	27Ta	20Cn	26Le	12Li	14Sc	28Sg	14Aq	19Pi	11Ta	20Ge
5	21Ar	15Ge	25Ge	16Le	21Vi	6Sc	8Sg	23Cp	11Pi	18Ar	11Ge	20Cn
7	20Ta	13Cn	23Cn	11Vi	15Li	0Sg	2Cp	19Aq	9Ar	17Ta	11Cn	18Le
9	19Ge	10Le	19Le	6Li	9Sc	23Sg	27Cp	15Pi	7Ta	17Ge	9Le	15Vi
11	17Cn	6Vi	14Vi	0Sc	3Sg	18Cp	22Aq	13Ar	6Ge	15Cn	6Vi	10Li
13	15Le	1Li	9Li	24Sc	26Sg	12Aq	18Pi	11Ta	4Cn	12Le	1Li	5Sc
15	11Vi	25Li	3Sc	17Sg	21Cp	8Pi	16Ar	9Ge	2Le	9Vi	26Li	29Sc
17	5Li	19Sc	27Sc	11Cp	15Aq	5Ar	14Ta	8Cn	29Le	4Li	20Sc	22Sg
19	29Li	13Sg	21Sg	6Aq	12Pi	4Ta	13Ge	6Le	25Vi	29Li	14Sg	16Cp
21	23Sc	8Cp	15Cp	3Pi	10Ar	4Ge	12Cn	3Vi	20Li	23Sc	7Cp	10Aq
23	17Sg	3Aq	11Aq	1Ar	10Ta	4Cn	11Le	29Vi	15Sc	17Sg	1Aq	5Pi
25	12Cp	1Pi	9Pi	1Ta	10Ge	3Le	8Vi	24Li	8Sg	10Cp	26Aq	1Ar
27	9Aq	29Pi	8Ar	2Ge	10Cn	0Vi	4Li	19Sc	2Cp	4Aq	22Pi	28Ar
29	6Pi		8Ta	2Cn	8Le	26Vi	29Li	12Sg	26Cp	0Pi	19Ar	27Ta
31	4Ar		8Ge		5Vi		23Sc	6Cp		27Pi		28Ge

1991

	Jan	Feb	Mar	Apr	May	Jun	Jul	Aug	Sep	Oct	Nov	Dec
1	13Cn	4Vi	12Vi	1Sc	4Sg	18Cp	20Aq	7Ar	28Ta	7Cn	0Vi	7Li
3	12Le	2Li	9Li	25Sc	28Sg	12Aq	15Pi	4Ta	26Ge	5Le	27Vi	3Sc
5	10Vi	27Li	5Sc	19Sg	21Cp	6Pi	11Ar	1Ge	25Cn	3Vi	21Li	29Sc
7	7Li	22Sc	0Sg	13Cp	15Aq	1Ar	8Ta	0Cn	24Le	1Li	20Sc	23Sg
9	2Sc	16Sg	23Sg	7Aq	10Pi	29Ar	6Ge	0Le	23Vi	28Li	15Sg	17Cp
11	26Sc	9Cp	17Cp	2Pi	7Ar	28Ta	6Cn	0Vi	20Li	24Sc	9Cp	11Aq
13	19Sg	3Aq	12Aq	28Pi	5Ta	28Ge	7Le	28Vi	16Sc	19Sg	2Aq	4Pi
15	13Cp	28Aq	7Pi	26Ar	4Ge	28Cn	6Vi	25Li	11Sg	13Cp	26Aq	29Pi
17	7Aq	24Pi	4Ar	25Ta	4Cn	27Le	4Li	21Sc	5Cp	6Aq	21Pi	25Ar
19	2Pi	21Ar	1Ta	25Ge	3Le	25Vi	0Sc	15Sg	29Cp	1Pi	17Ar	23Ta
21	28Pi	19Ta	0Ge	23Cn	1Vi	20Li	24Sc	9Cp	23Aq	26Pi	15Ta	22Ge
23	24Ar	17Ge	28Ge	21Le	28Vi	15Sc	18Sg	2Aq	18Pi	23Ar	14Ge	22Cn
25	22Ta	16Cn	26Cn	18Vi	23Li	9Sg	12Cp	26Aq	14Ar	21Ta	13Cn	22Le
27	21Ge	14Le	24Le	14Li	18Sc	3Cp	6Aq	22Pi	11Ta	19Ge	12Le	21Vi
29	21Cn		21Vi	9Sc	12Sg	27Cp	0Pi	17Ar	9Ge	18Cn	10Vi	18Li
31	20Le		18Li		6Cp		25Pi	14Ta		16Le		13Sc

1992

	Jan	Feb	Mar	Apr	May	Jun	Jul	Aug	Sep	Oct	Nov	Dec
1	26Sc	11Cp	1Aq	16Pi	19Ar	8Ge	16Cn	10Vi	2Sc	7Sg	23Cp	25Aq
3	20Sg	4Aq	25Aq	11Ar	16Ta	7Cn	16Le	9Li	29Sc	3Cp	17Aq	19Pi
5	14Cp	28Aq	19Pi	6Ta	13Ge	6Le	15Vi	7Sc	24Sg	27Cp	11Pi	13Ar
7	7Aq	22Pi	14Ar	3Ge	11Cn	5Vi	13Li	3Sg	19Cp	21Aq	5Ar	8Ta
9	1Pi	17Ar	10Ta	0Cn	9Le	3Li	10Sc	27Sg	12Aq	15Pi	0Ta	4Ge
11	25Pi	13Ta	6Ge	28Cn	8Vi	0Sc	6Sg	22Cp	6Pi	9Ar	26Ta	2Cn
13	20Ar	10Ge	4Cn	27Le	6Li	26Sc	0Cp	15Aq	0Ar	4Ta	23Ge	0Le
15	17Ta	8Cn	2Le	26Vi	3Sc	21Sg	25Cp	9Pi	24Ar	29Ta	20Cn	29Le
17	15Ge	8Le	2Vi	24Li	0Sg	16Cp	18Aq	3Ar	20Ta	26Ge	18Le	27Vi
19	15Cn	8Vi	1Li	21Sc	25Sg	10Aq	12Pi	27Ar	16Ge	23Cn	16Vi	25Li
21	15Le	8Li	0Sc	17Sg	20Cp	3Pi	6Ar	23Ta	13Cn	21Le	15Li	22Sc
23	15Vi	6Sc	27Sc	12Cp	13Aq	27Pi	1Ta	19Ge	11Le	21Vi	13Sc	19Sg
25	14Li	1Sg	22Sg	6Aq	7Pi	22Ar	27Ta	18Cn	11Vi	20Li	10Sg	14Cp
27	10Sc	26Sg	16Cp	29Aq	2Ar	19Ta	25Ge	18Le	11Li	18Sc	6Cp	9Aq
29	5Sg	19Cp	9Aq	24Pi	27Ar	16Ge	24Cn	18Vi	10Sc	15Sg	1Aq	3Pi
31	29Sg		3Pi		24Ta		24Le	18Li		11Cp		26Pi

1993

	Jan	Feb	Mar	Apr	May	Jun	Jul	Aug	Sep	Oct	Nov	Dec
1	8Ar	23Ta	2Ge	21Cn	29Le	23Li	2Sg	21Cp	7Pi	10Ar	24Ta	28Ge
3	3Ta	20Ge	28Ge	20Le	29Vi	22Sc	29Sg	16Aq	1Ar	3Ta	19Ge	24Cn
5	29Ta	18Cn	26Cn	19Vi	28Li	20Sg	25Cp	10Pi	24Ar	27Ta	14Cn	21Le
7	26Ge	18Le	26Le	20Li	27Sc	16Cp	20Aq	4Ar	18Ta	22Ge	11Le	19Vi
9	25Cn	18Vi	26Vi	19Sc	25Sg	12Aq	14Pi	28Ar	13Ge	17Cn	8Vi	17Li
11	24Le	18Li	27Li	17Sg	21Cp	6Pi	8Ar	22Ta	8Cn	15Le	8Li	16Sc
13	24Vi	16Sc	25Sc	13Cp	16Aq	0Ar	2Ta	17Ge	6Le	14Vi	8Sc	15Sg
15	22Li	12Sg	22Sg	8Aq	10Pi	24Ar	26Ta	14Cn	6Vi	14Li	7Sg	13Cp
17	19Sc	8Cp	17Cp	2Pi	4Ar	18Ta	22Ge	12Le	6Li	15Sc	6Cp	10Aq
19	15Sg	2Aq	11Aq	25Pi	28Ar	14Ge	20Cn	12Vi	6Sc	14Sg	2Aq	5Pi
21	11Cp	26Aq	5Pi	19Ar	23Ta	11Cn	18Le	12Li	5Sg	11Cp	27Aq	29Pi
23	5Aq	20Pi	29Pi	14Ta	18Ge	9Le	18Vi	11Sc	2Cp	6Aq	21Pi	23Ar
25	29Aq	13Ar	22Ar	9Ge	15Cn	7Vi	17Li	9Sg	27Cp	1Pi	15Ar	17Ta
27	23Pi	7Ta	17Ta	5Cn	12Le	6Li	15Sc	5Cp	22Aq	25Pi	9Ta	12Ge
29	17Ar		12Ge	1Le	10Vi	4Sc	12Sg	0Aq	16Pi	18Ar	3Ge	7Cn
31	11Ta		8Cn		9Li		8Cp	25Aq		12Ta		4Le

1994

	Jan	Feb	Mar	Apr	May	Jun	Jul	Aug	Sep	Oct	Nov	Dec
1	18Le	11Li	20Li	13Sg	20Cp	8Pi	11Ar	24Ta	8Cn	12Le	2Li	10Sc
3	16Vi	9Sc	20Sc	11Cp	17Aq	2Ar	4Ta	18Ge	4Le	10Vi	2Sc	10Sg
5	14Li	7Sg	17Sg	7Aq	11Pi	26Ar	28Ta	13Cn	0Li	9Sc	2Cp	10Cp
7	12Sc	4Cp	14Cp	2Pi	5Ar	20Ta	22Ge	9Le	0Vi	9Sc	2Cp	9Aq
9	10Sg	0Aq	10Aq	26Pi	29Ar	14Ge	17Cn	7Vi	29Li	8Sg	0Aq	6Pi
11	8Cp	26Aq	5Pi	20Ar	23Ta	8Cn	13Le	5Li	28Sc	7Cp	27Aq	1Ar
13	5Aq	21Pi	0Ar	14Ta	17Ge	4Le	10Vi	3Sc	26Sg	4Aq	22Pi	25Ar
15	1Pi	15Ar	23Ar	8Ge	11Cn	0Vi	8Li	1Sg	24Cp	0Pi	16Ar	19Ta
17	25Pi	9Ta	17Ta	2Cn	7Le	27Vi	6Sc	29Sg	20Aq	25Pi	10Ta	12Ge
19	19Ar	2Ge	11Ge	27Cn	3Vi	26Li	5Sg	27Cp	16Pi	19Ar	4Ge	6Cn
21	13Ta	27Ge	5Cn	24Le	1Li	25Sc	3Cp	24Aq	11Ar	13Ta	27Ge	1Le
23	7Ge	23Cn	1Le	22Vi	1Sc	24Sg	1Aq	20Pi	5Ta	7Ge	22Cn	26Le
25	2Cn	21Le	29Le	22Li	1Sg	23Cp	28Aq	14Ar	28Ta	0Cn	16Le	23Vi
27	29Cn	21Vi	29Vi	23Sc	1Cp	20Aq	24Pi	8Ta	22Ge	25Cn	13Vi	20Li
29	27Le		29Li	22Sg	29Cp	16Pi	18Ar	2Ge	16Cn	20Le	10Li	19Sc
31	26Vi		29Sc		25Aq		12Ta	26Ge		18Vi		18Sg

1995

	Jan	Feb	Mar	Apr	May	Jun	Jul	Aug	Sep	Oct	Nov	Dec
1	3Cp	25Aq	3Pi	21Ar	24Ta	8Cn	11Le	29Vi	20Sc	29Sg	22Aq	29Pi
3	3Aq	22Pi	0Ar	15Ta	17Ge	2Le	6Vi	25Li	18Sg	27Cp	19Pi	24Ar
5	1Pi	17Ar	25Ar	9Ge	11Cn	26Le	2Li	23Sc	16Cp	25Aq	15Ar	19Ta
7	27Pi	11Ta	19Ta	3Cn	5Le	22Vi	29Li	22Sg	15Aq	22Pi	10Ta	13Ge
9	22Ar	5Ge	13Ge	27Cn	0Vi	19Li	27Sc	21Cp	13Pi	19Ar	5Ge	7Cn
11	15Ta	29Ge	7Cn	22Le	25Vi	18Sc	27Sg	21Aq	10Ar	14Ta	29Ge	1Ar
13	9Ge	23Cn	1Le	19Vi	25Li	19Sg	27Cp	19Pi	6Ta	8Ge	22Cn	25Le
15	3Cn	19Le	27Le	17Li	25Sc	19Cp	27Aq	16Ar	1Ge	2Cn	16Le	19Vi
17	28Cn	16Vi	25Vi	17Sc	25Sg	18Aq	24Pi	11Ta	24Ge	26Cn	11Vi	15Li
19	23Le	13Li	13Li	16Sg	25Cp	16Pi	20Ar	5Ge	18Cn	21Le	6Sc	12Sc
21	20Vi	11Sc	22Sc	15Cp	23Aq	11Ar	14Ta	28Ge	13Le	16Vi	5Sg	12Sg
23	17Li	9Sg	20Sg	13Aq	19 Pi	6Ta	8Ge	22Cn	8Vi	13Li	5Sg	13Cp
25	14Sc	7Cp	18Cp	9Pi	14Ar	1Ge	2Le	15Li	11Sc	5Li	5Cp	13Aq
27	13Sg	6Aq	16Aq	5Ar	9Ta	23Ge	26Cn	12Vi	2Sc	11Sg	4Aq	12Pi
29	12Cp		13Pi	0Ta	2Ge	17Cn	21Le	9Li	0Sg	10Cp	2Pi	9Ar
31	11Aq		8Ar		26Ge		16Vi	6Sc		8Aq		4Ta

1996

	Jan	Feb	Mar	Apr	May	Jun	Jul	Aug	Sep	Oct	Nov	Dec
1	16Ta	1Cn	21Cn	6vi	9Li	28Sc	7Cp	1Pi	22Ar	27Ta	13Cn	15Le
3	10Ge	25Cn	15Le	1Li	5Sg	28Cp	7Pi	28Ar	19Ta	23Ge	1Vi	2Li
5	4Cn	19Le	10Vi	27Li	5Sg	28Cp	7Pi	28Ar	15Ge	17Cn	1Vi	2Li
7	28Cn	13Vi	5Li	25Sc	3Cp	27Aq	5Ar	23Ta	9Cn	11Le	25Vi	28Li
9	22Le	8Li	1Sc	23Sg	2Aq	25Pi	1Ta	18Ge	3Le	5Vi	24Li	24Sc
11	16Vi	4Sc	28Sc	21Cp	0Pi	21Ar	26Ta	12Cn	26Le	29Vi	16Sc	23Sg
13	11Li	1Sg	26Sg	20Aq	28Pi	17Ta	21Ge	6Le	20Vi	24Li	14Sg	22Cp
15	8Sc	0Cp	25Cp	18Pi	24Ar	12Ge	15Cn	29Le	15Li	26Aq	12Cp	21Aq
17	6Sg	0Aq	24Aq	15Ar	20Ta	6Cn	9Le	23Vi	11Sc	18Sg	11Aq	20Pi
19	6Cp	29Aq	22Pi	11Ta	15Ge	0Le	2Vi	18Li	7Sg	15Cp	9Pi	17Ar
21	6Aq	28Pi	20Ar	7Ge	9Cn	24Le	26Vi	15Sc	5Cp	14Aq	7Ar	14Ta
23	6Pi	26Ar	16Ta	1Cn	3Le	17Vi	21Li	10Sg	3Aq	12Pi	4Ta	9Ge
25	4Ar	21Ta	11Ge	25Cn	27Le	12Li	17Sc	9Cp	3Pi	11Ar	0Ge	5Cn
27	0Ta	16Ge	5Cn	19Le	21Vi	15Sg	15Sg	9Aq	2Ar	9Ta	26Ge	29Cn
29	25Ta	9Cn	29Cn	13Vi	17Li	7Sg	15Cp	9Pi	0Ta	5Ge	21Cn	23Le
31	19Ge		23Le		14Sc		16Aq	8Ar		1Cn		16Vi

1997

	Jan	Feb	Mar	Apr	May	Jun	Jul	Aug	Sep	Oct	Nov	Dec
1	28Vi	14Sc	23Sc	13Cp	22Aq	15Ar	23Ta	12Cn	27Le	0Li	15Sc	19Sg
3	23Li	10Sg	19Sg	11Aq	21Pi	13Ta	20Ge	6Le	21Vi	24Li	10Sg	16Cp
5	18Sc	9Cp	17Cp	11Pi	19Ar	10Ge	15Cn	0Vi	15Li	18Sc	6Cp	13Aq
7	16Sg	9Aq	17Aq	10Ar	18Ta	6Cn	10Le	24Vi	8Sc	13Sg	3Aq	11Pi
9	16Cp	9Pi	17Pi	9Ta	15Ge	2Le	4Vi	18Li	3Sg	9Cp	0Pi	9Ar
11	16Aq	9Ar	17Ar	7Ge	11Cn	26Le	27Vi	12Sc	29Sg	6Aq	29Pi	8Ta
13	16Pi	7Ta	16Ta	3Cn	6Le	19Vi	21Li	7Sg	27Cp	5Pi	28Ar	6Ge
15	14Ar	3Ge	12Ge	29Cn	0Vi	13Li	16Sc	4Cp	26Aq	5Ar	28Ta	4Cn
17	11Ta	28Ge	7Cn	22Le	23Vi	8Sc	12Sg	3Aq	27Pi	5Ta	26Ge	0Le
19	6Ge	23Cn	1Le	15Vi	17Li	4Sg	10Cp	3Pi	27Ar	4Ge	22Cn	25Le
21	1Cn	16Le	25Le	9Li	13Sc	2Cp	10Aq	2Ar	26Ta	1Cn	17Le	19Vi
23	26Cn	10Vi	19Vi	4Sc	9Sg	1Aq	9Pi	2Ta	23Ge	27Cn	11Vi	13Li
25	19Le	4Li	13Li	0Sg	7Cp	29Aq	8Ar	0Ge	18Cn	21Le	5Li	7Sc
27	13Vi	28Li	7Sc	26Sg	5Aq	28Pi	6Ta	26Ge	12Vi	15Vi	29Li	2Sg
29	7Li		3Sg	24Cp	3Pi	26Ar	3Ge	21Cn	6Vi	8Li	23Sc	28Sg
31	1Sc		29Sg		1Ar		29Ge	15Le		2Sc		25Cp

1998

	Jan	Feb	Mar	Apr	May	Jun	Jul	Aug	Sep	Oct	Nov	Dec
1	9Aq	2Ar	12Ar	5Ge	11Cn	28Le	0Li	14Sc	28Sg	2Aq	23Pi	1Ta
3	8Pi	1Ta	11Ta	2Cn	7Le	22Vi	24Li	8Sg	24Cp	0Pi	22Ar	1Ge
5	6Ar	29Ta	9Ge	28Cn	2Vi	16Li	18Sc	3Cp	22Aq	29Pi	21Ta	19Ge
7	4Ta	26Ge	6Cn	23Le	25Vi	9Sc	12Sg	0Aq	21Pi	0Ta	23Ge	0Le
9	2Ge	22Cn	1Le	17Vi	19Li	4Sg	8Cp	28Aq	21Ar	0Ge	21Cn	26Le
11	29Ge	17Le	26Le	10Li	13Sc	29Sg	5Aq	26Pi	20Ta	28Ge	18Le	21Vi
13	25Cn	11Vi	20Vi	4Sc	7Sg	25Cp	2Pi	25Ar	18Ge	25Cn	12Vi	15Li
15	21Le	5Li	13Li	28Sc	2Cp	22Aq	0Ar	24Ta	15Cn	21Le	6Li	9Sc
17	15Vi	28Li	7Sc	23Sg	28Cp	19Pi	29Ar	22Ge	11Le	15Vi	0Sc	3Sg
19	8Li	5Ar	1Sg	18Cp	25Aq	17Ar	27Ta	19Cn	6Vi	9Li	24Sc	27Sg
21	2Sc	17Sg	26Sg	15Aq	23Pi	17Ta	25Ge	15Le	1Li	3Sc	18Sg	22Cp
23	27Sc	14Cp	22Cp	13Pi	22Ar	15Ge	22Cn	10Vi	24Li	27Sc	12Cp	18Aq
25	22Sg	12Aq	20Aq	13Ar	22Ta	14Cn	19Le	4Li	18Sc	21Sg	8Aq	14Pi
27	20Cp	12Pi	20Pi	13Ta	20Ge	10Le	14Vi	28Li	12Sg	15Cp	4Pi	11Ar
29	18Aq		20Ar	13Ge	19Cn	6Vi	8Li	22Sc	7Cp	11Aq	2Ar	10Ta
31	18Pi		20Ta		15Le		2Sc	16Sg		8Pi		10Ge

1999

	Jan	Feb	Mar	Apr	May	Jun	Jul	Aug	Sep	Oct	Nov	Dec
1	24Ge	15Le	24Le	11Li	14Sc	28Sg	2Aq	20Pi	12Ta	21Ge	14Le	20Vi
3	23Cn	12Vi	20Vi	5Sc	8Sg	23Cp	27Aq	17Ar	11Ge	20Cn	10Vi	15Vi
5	21Le	7Li	15Li	29Sc	1Cp	17Aq	23Pi	15Ta	9Cn	17Le	6Li	10Sc
7	17Vi	1Sc	9Sc	23Sg	26Cp	13Pi	20Ar	14Ge	7Le	13Vi	1Sc	4Sg
9	11Li	25Sc	3Sg	17Cp	21Aq	10Ar	19Ta	13Cn	4Vi	9Li	25Sc	27Sg
11	5Sc	19Sg	27Sg	12Aq	17Pi	10Ta	19Ge	11Le	0Li	4Sc	19Sg	21Cp
13	29Sc	14Cp	22Cp	9Pi	15Ar	10Ge	18Cn	9Vi	25Li	28Sc	13Cp	15Aq
15	23Sg	9Aq	17Aq	8Ar	16Ta	10Cn	17Le	5Li	20Sc	22Sg	6Aq	10Pi
17	18Cp	7Pi	15Pi	8Ta	17Ge	9Le	14Vi	0Sc	14Sg	16Cp	1Pi	6Ar
19	14Aq	5Ar	14Ar	8Ge	16Cn	6Vi	10Li	24Sc	8Cp	10Aq	27Pi	4Ta
21	11Pi	3Ta	14Ta	7Cn	14Le	1Li	4Sc	18Sg	2Aq	6Pi	26Ar	4Ge
23	9Ar	2Ge	13Ge	4Le	10Vi	26Li	28Sc	12Cp	28Aq	3Ar	26Ta	4Cn
25	7Ta	0Cn	11Cn	1Vi	5Li	20Sc	22Sg	7Aq	25Pi	2Ta	26Ge	4Le
27	5Ge	27Cn	8Le	26Vi	0Sc	14Sg	16Cp	3Pi	24Ar	2Ge	26Cn	3Vi
29	4Cn		3Vi	20Li	23Sc	7Cp	11Aq	0Ar	23Ta	2Cn	24Le	29Vi
31	2Le		29Vi		17Sg		7Pi	28Ar		0Le		25Li

2000

	Jan	Feb	Mar	Apr	May	Jun	Jul	Aug	Sep	Oct	Nov	Dec
1	7Sc	21Sg	11Cp	25Aq	29Pi	19Ta	28Ge	21Le	13Li	17Sc	2Cp	4Aq
3	1Sg	15Cp	5Aq	21Pi	27Ar	19Ge	28Cn	20Vi	9Sc	13Sg	26Cp	28Aq
5	24Sg	9Aq	0Pi	18Ar	26Ta	19Cn	28Le	18Li	5Sg	7Cp	20Aq	22Pi
7	18Cp	4Pi	26Pi	16Ta	25Ge	18Le	26Vi	14Sc	29Sg	0Aq	14Pi	18Ar
9	12Aq	29Pi	23Ar	15Ge	24Cn	16Vi	22Li	8Sg	22Cp	24Aq	10Ar	15Ta
11	7Pi	26Ar	20Ta	14Cn	22Le	13Li	17Sc	2Cp	19Pi	7Ta	14Ge	
13	2Ar	23Ta	18Ge	12Le	19Vi	8Sc	11Sg	26Cp	11Pi	15Ar	5Ge	13Cn
15	29Ar	22Ge	17Cn	9Vi	16Li	2Sg	5Cp	20Aq	6Ar	12Ta	4Cn	13Le
17	27Ta	21Cn	15Le	6Li	11Sc	26Sg	29Cp	3Le	10Ge	3Le	3Le	12Vi
19	27Ge	20Le	13Vi	2Sc	6Sg	20Cp	23Aq	9Ar	29Ta	8Cn	1Vi	9Li
21	27Cn	18Vi	10Li	27Sc	29Sg	14Aq	17Pi	5Ta	27Ge	6Le	29Vi	5Sc
23	26Le	15Li	6Sc	21Sg	23Cp	8Pi	12Ar	2Ge	25Cn	4Vi	25Li	0Sg
25	24Vi	11Sc	1Sg	15Cp	17Aq	3Ar	9Ta	1Cn	24Le	2Li	21Sc	25Sg
27	21Li	5Sg	25Sg	9Aq	11Pi	29Ar	7Ge	0Le	23Vi	29Li	16Sg	19Cp
29	15Sc	29Sg	19Cp	3Pi	7Ar	28Ta	6Cn	0Vi	21Li	25Sc	11Cp	13Aq
31	9Sg		13Aq		5Ta		6Le	29Vi		20Sg		6Pi

INDEX

Illustration credits

All illustrations Fabbri Publications except the following:
Kevin Jones Associates: 6(m), 8, 9, 10, 11, 12, 13, 14, 15, 16/17, 18, 27 (both), 28 (all), 29, 37(m), 42 (br), 43(b), 61(t), 63, 69, 72, 75, 76(b), 77(both), 83(b), 85, 87(tl), 91, 92(r), 93, 94, 99(b), 100, 101, 102, 109(both), 117, 118, 124, 125, 131(b), 132, 133, 134, 140, 141, 148, 149, 153(b), 156, 157, 162, 163, 164, 176, 178, 182, 184, 188, 190, 194, 196, 199, 201, 206, 209, 211, 212, 218, 220, 224, 226, 230, 235, 236, 238, 241, 243.
Michael Fuller: 32(t), 37(t), 37(b), 38(both), 39(all), 40(all), 41(both), 42(t), 43(t), 44, 45(both), 46(t), 47(both), 49, 51, 55(r), 56(l), 58(r), 59, 61(b), 62, 68, 76(t), 83(t), 92(tl), 99(t), 107, 115, 123, 131(t), 139, 147, 155.
Wilson Design Associates: 36.

Picture Credits

Corbis UK Ltd: 58, 73(l), 105(l), 137(r), 161(l); John Heseltine 22; David Lees 23; Francis G. Mayer 24, 113(r); The State Russian Museum 25; The Corcoran Gallery of Art 26; Gail Mooney 30; Gianni Dagli Orti 31, 42(bl), 56; National Gallery Collection 32, 65(both); Roger Ressmeyer/1989/NASA 33; Macduff Everton 46; Roger Wood 54, 55, 60; Historical Picture Archive 64; Bettmann/UPI 73(r), 145(r), 161(r); Bettmann 81(both), 89(both), 97, 113(l), 121(both), 129(l), 137(l), 145(l), 153, 245; Bettmann/Reuter 97(r); Austrian Archives 105(r); Leonard de Selba 129(r).